*W*oolf *S*tudies *A*nnual

Volume 12, 2006

PACE UNIVERSITY PRESS • NEW YORK

Pace University Press
41 Park Row, Rm. 1510
New York, NY 10038

Printed in the United States of America

ISSN 1080-9317
ISBN 0-944473-75-X (pbk: alk.ppr.)

Member

Council of Editors of Learned Journals

™ paper used in this publication meets the minimum requirements of American National Standard for Information Sciences–Permanence of Paper for Printed Library Materials,
ANSI Z39.48–1984

Many thanks to readers for volume 12: Judith Allen (U of Pennyslvania), Jessica Berman (U of Maryland Baltimore County), Pamela Caughie (Loyola U Chicago), Pat Cramer (U Conn Stamford), Ann Gibaldi Campbell (Woodlands Academy, IL), Penny Farfan (U of Calgary), Sally Greene (Independent Scholar), Jesse Matz (Kenyon C), Eleanor McNees (U of Denver), Diana Royer (Miami U, OH), Sally Ruddick (New School U, Emerita), Bonnie Kime Scott (San Diego SU), Alice Stavely (Stanford U).

Woolf Studies Annual is indexed in the *American Humanities Index*, *ABELL* and the *MLA Bibliography*.

Burnhams,
Naphill,
Nr. H. Wycombe,
Bucks.
October 15th, 193

Dear Miss Virginia Woolf,

May I tell you how grateful I am to you for "The Waves". I have been reading your work since I was at school and it has always helped me to have an unmuddled attitude to life, to see the vividness and importance of every minute, the significance of every action.

"The Waves" was a tremendous adventure. I have just read it a second time. So rarely, in prose, is anyone so keenly appreciative of individual words. It is like a symphony. Suddenly the English language is translated into fluid music, like Greek, so that a man who knew not a word of it, ~~and~~ could listen to it and realise its force and beauty and exquisiteness.

I feel compelled to write to you, because I do feel believe in gratitude, and even from a very young and unimportant person it must give you a warm feeling to know you are so valued.

Yours very sincerely,
Elizabeth Close (aged 20.)

P.S. I shall never forget the sight of Susan's little screwed handkerchief lying, with her tears knotted in it.

Contents

Woolf
Studies
Annual

Volume 12, 2006

REVIEWS

Abbreviations

AHH	*A Haunted House*
AROO	*A Room of One's Own*
BP	*Books and Portraits*
BTA	*Between the Acts*
CDB	*The Captain's Death Bed and Other Essays*
CE	*Collected Essays (4 vols.)*
CR1	*The Common Reader*
CR2	*The Common Reader, Second Series*
CSF	*The Complete Shorter Fiction*
D	*The Diary of Virginia Woolf (5 vols.)*
DM	*The Death of the Moth and Other Essays*
E	*The Essays of Virginia Woolf (6 Vols.)*
F	*Flush*
FR	*Freshwater*
GR	*Granite & Rainbow: Essays*
JR	*Jacob's Room*
L	*The Letters of Virginia Woolf (6 Vols.)*
M	*The Moment and Other Essays*
MEL	*Melymbrosia*
MOB	*Moments of Being*
MT	*Monday or Tuesday*
MD	*Mrs. Dalloway*
ND	*Night and Day*
O	*Orlando*
PA	*A Passionate Apprentice*
RF	*Roger Fry: A Biography*
TG	*Three Guineas*
TTL	*To the Lighthouse*
TW	*The Waves*
TY	*The Years*
VO	*The Voyage Out*

"You see you kind of belong to us, and what you do matters enormously": Letters from Readers to Virginia Woolf

Beth Rigel Daugherty

Writing to Virginia Woolf about *Three Guineas* from Springfield, MA in 1938, Agnes K. Potter says her comments are from "the point of view of this ordinary reader" (Snaith, "*Three Guineas* Letters" 97). Q. D. Leavis, however, would have us believe that Woolf did not *have* ordinary readers; *Three Guineas* "is a conversation between [Woolf] and her friends" (272). Woolf's careful and honest description of her class position leads to Leavis's assumption that all Woolf's readers must be of Woolf's own class. Anna Snaith's edition of the letters written to Woolf after the publication of *Three Guineas* proves that such a narrow construction of Woolf's readership is not accurate.[1] Similarly, Melba Cuddy-Keane's investigations of the readers "spotting" *The Common Reader* (*Virginia Woolf* 110-14) and of individual readers like John Farrelly ("From Fan-Mail" 3-32) succeed in "break[ing] down categories that have identified high culture with high class" and show that definitions of Woolf's readership must include respect for "both the intellectual impulse and the intellectual accomplishment of non-privileged, non-specialist readers" ("Imbricated" 5).

Following Q. D. Leavis's lead, however, Jonathan Rose recently argues that Woolf's essay "Middlebrow" calls for cultural triage and asserts that modernists made literature difficult to make the common reader "illiterate once again" and to preserve "a body of culture as the exclusive property of a coterie" (394). He does caution, though, that "no two individual reading histories [are] alike," that generalizations about readers, though not "completely groundless," neglect the "more complicated and ambiguous" use of literacy, and that "[t]he only workable method is to consult the readers themselves" (367).

Exactly.

[1] See her discussion in "Wide Circles: The *Three Guineas* Letters," *Woolf Studies Annual* 6 (2000): 1-12 and her discussions of Woolf's reading public throughout *Virginia Woolf: Public and Private Negotiations*, but particularly in Chapter 5, "Respondents to *Three Guineas*," 113-29.

As Anna Snaith and Melba Cuddy-Keane discovered, one of the best ways to consult readers themselves is through their letters to Woolf.[2] Because, as Helen Waddell points out when she encloses someone else's letter about *The Waves* in her own note to Woolf, "in spite of all that has already been said in print, there is something in the manuscript word and in the circumstances of the writing that makes it valuable" (Letter 78). I discovered the same thing in the summer of 2001. At a session called "Archives in the Age of Mechanical Reproduction" during the Eleventh Annual Conference on Virginia Woolf at the University of Bangor in Wales, Bet Inglis, the retired Assistant Librarian in the Manuscripts Section at the University of Sussex, talked about the treasures in the Monks House Papers and casually mentioned that someone should take a look at the correspondence between Virginia Woolf and Elizabeth Bowen housed there. When I got to the Sussex archives the next week, planning to spend the entire summer on the drafts of early reviews written by Virginia Stephen, I thought I might take an afternoon to follow up on her suggestion. That digression quickly became an obsession, an archive-junkie race through the correspondence *to* Virginia Woolf located in Letters III of the Monks House Papers (SxMs 18). But what intrigued me, what I became addicted to, were not the letters from Elizabeth Bowen, engaging as they are. No, although the known correspondents in the author-named files in Letters III certainly claimed some of my attention, what I could not stop reading and transcribing that crazed summer were the letters in a box tantalizingly called Correspondence of Various Persons re: Books, Articles.[3] Woolf's readers came alive as I read their letters, and I could not turn my back on them. "[G]iving a voice . . . to the silent reader" (Carr), this collection of letters grows out of and builds on the fine work of Snaith, Cuddy-Keane, and Oldfield, increases the number of actual (as opposed to imagined) readers Woolf

[2] See also Sybil Oldfield's edition of the condolence letters written to Leonard Woolf and Vanessa Bell in *Afterwords: Letters on the Death of Virginia Woolf.* The essays in *Reading Acts: U. S. Readers' Interactions with Literature, 1800-1950*, edited by Barbara Ryan and Amy M. Thomas, model various ways to track down, examine, and interpret readers. See also Janice Radway, *A Feeling for Books: The Book-of-the-Month Club, Literary Taste, and Middle-Class Desire*, Cecilia Konchar Farr, *Reading Oprah: How Oprah's Book Club Changed the Way America Reads*, Joan Shelley Rubin, *The Making of Middlebrow Culture*, and Elizabeth Long, *Book Clubs: Women and the Uses of Reading in Everyday Life*.

[3] Someone still needs to examine the correspondence between Virginia Woolf and Elizabeth Bowen! Indeed, many small sets of correspondence could be constructed by combining the letters to Woolf housed at various archives with Woolf's published and unpublished letters, and many articles could grow out of such pairings. Merry M. Pawlowski provides a model for such a set of correspondence in *Woolf Studies Annual* 8 ("The Virginia Woolf and Vera Douie Letters" 3-62).

scholars can consult, and moves Woolf studies, particularly studies of her reception, another step closer to a full record of letters written to Virginia Woolf about her work and thus to a more accurate view of the "far wider circle" Woolf hoped to reach (*L*6 420).[4]

The 137 letters included here come from 121 correspondents who respond to particular books by Woolf or who shed light on Woolf's reputation during her lifetime. Thus, these letters are not a discrete set of correspondence like the *Three Guineas* letters, the letters between Vera Douie and Virginia Woolf, or the condolence letters. Rather, they range from 1915 to 1941, from *The Voyage Out* to *Roger Fry*, from ordinary readers to an emissary for the Prime Minister, from neighbors in Sussex to strangers from other countries, from friends to officials. Readers may notice some puzzling gaps, though. One can surmise why so few letters about Woolf's early works might have survived, but it is harder to understand why so few letters about her bestseller *The Years* seem to have survived. Yet the box filled with folders of letters about *To the Lighthouse*, *Orlando*, *A Room of One's Own*, *The Waves*, *Three Guineas*, and *Roger Fry* contains no folder for *The Years*.

[4] Although this collection sprawls in size and subject matter, it is, in fact, limited; see "Location and filing of letters" below. A full record of readers' letters about Woolf's work will require a great deal more detecting and transcribing and collecting. How many more letters to Woolf may be tucked away in other archives or repositories, for example? (To mention just one possible lead, Woolf mentions sending Margaret Llewelyn Davies a letter she had received from Mrs. Burman about *Life As We Have Known It* [*L*4 392]—might that letter be in the Llewelyn Davies Papers at Girton? Or in another archive that contains Davies manuscripts?) In addition, space concerns prevented my including *all* the letters in the Monks House Papers that could be perceived as letters from readers about Woolf's works. Siegfried Sassoon's note about *Jacob's Room* and Enid Jones's letter about reading *Orlando* are just two examples of the many letters not published here. Also, as Sybil Oldfield's work in *Afterwords* makes clear, letters to Leonard Woolf about Virginia Woolf's work during and after her life must be part of Woolf reception studies. The Leonard Woolf Archive at Sussex (SxMs13), besides housing the condolence letters collected by Sybil Oldfield, contains letters in the known correspondents files such as one written in 1961 by Heidi von Born describing the transformation she underwent when she read Woolf in Sweden at age 16 (III Correspondence), correspondence in IID4 (Personal Life; Virginia; Letters articles & books about VW's writing) that includes letters from people wanting to write a biography; and letters in IID17i (Personal Life; Virginia; Miscellaneous materials relating to Virginia Woolf; Posthumous fan mail addressed to LW) that come from students, admirers, and a working class reader. In addition, many of the letters to Leonard Woolf in the Hogarth Press archive at the University of Reading discuss enthusiasm for reading or teaching Woolf and announce plans for theses, dissertations, books, and articles. These letters, along with some of those in the Leonard Woolf Archive at Sussex, may revise our opinions that Woolf's reputation plummeted after her death or that her feminism was unnoticed between the 1940s and the 1970s.

Consulting Woolf's readers makes a much more complex picture of Woolf's readership and of the relationship between Woolf and her readers emerge. For example, Rachel Dyce Sharp, communicating her dislike of the public school scenes in *Roger Fry* and justifying her decision to complain directly to the biography's author, writes to Woolf, "Because if the public doesn't express itself who's to blame? You see you kind of belong to us, and what you do matters enormously." Sharp may be a nurserywoman absorbed with getting tomatoes ready for the market, but she also reads, is aware of the entire body of Woolf's work, and wants Woolf to go on writing: "your use of words is like water in a thirsty land" (Letter 130). She bears out Cuddy-Keane's observation that middle-class and working-class readers often welcomed, embraced, and perhaps transformed high culture ("Imbricated" 5). Rather than assume Woolf is working to preserve culture as a coterie's exclusive property, Rachel Dyce Sharp claims Woolf as *readers'* property, as *her* property, at least "kind of." That ambivalence captures the uneasy border occupied by a reader during reading, the border between ownership and being owned; Woolf both does and does not belong to readers. By using the word "belong," Sharp calls up a complex blend of ownership, longing, allegiance, comfort, and intimacy. Furthermore, Woolf *matters*. What she *does*, what she *writes*, has significance, meaning, and influence.

These readers *care* about what Woolf writes. That's why they write to her, of course. And in doing so, they reveal why they care, what they care about, and something about their own circumstances. Woolf scholars may want to consult individual correspondents, as Melba Cuddy-Keane did John Farrelly, but what do these letter writers, when consulted as a group of readers, tell us about themselves and their relationship with Woolf and her work? Located in history rather than ideology or theory, the actual readers in these letters 1) describe their relationship with Woolf in a vocabulary of intimacy and knowledge; 2) illustrate conventions of writing fan mail that demand apology for the relationship being assumed; 3) assert that Woolf's readership is wider and more diverse than commonly thought; 4) reflect Woolf's encouragement of youth; 5) demonstrate an enthusiastic United States response that predates the scholarship of the 1970s; and 6) demand that we re-think our construction of Woolf's audience.

Woolf's readers often use inclusive vocabulary, claiming a relationship of intimacy, knowledge, friendship. Without preliminaries, for example, Isabel Forbes Milton testifies to an ongoing relationship: "For years in Minnesota, in Illinois, I have been writing you letters in my mind" (Letter 93). Wanda Fraiken Neff notes that *A Room of One's Own* seems "so intimately written for me alone," but then recognizes that her friends and her husband's women students all say the same thing (Letter 45). Hoping she has not bored Woolf, Elizabeth Cox Wright explains that she has become like an articulate friend who is hard to escape

(Letter 44); Virginia Tooker wishes she knew Woolf but then realizes "I do know you" (Letter 15); Richard Greenleaf mentions his "intense love of every word" of her fiction (Letter 144); and John Farrelly becomes "very fond of the person I . . . constructed from your writing" (Letter 132; "From Fan-Mail" 21). As Margaret Laurie writes, "It is like coming home to read your books, but a home brightened and made infinitely exciting" (Letter 99).

Woolf's readers express gratitude for what they receive from her–health (Letters 18 and 31), "an unmuddled attitude toward life" (Letter 84), a moment when "one sees and feels everything much more clearly" (Letter 48), the removal of scales from eyes and wax from ears (Letter 120). Wanting to meet her in person, Isabel Forbes Milton settles for looking forward to the next book, knowing "I shall meet you fully there" (Letter 150). Correspondents sometimes confess that their response to Woolf is more powerful than what they feel for other authors (Letter 62). Grace Wilson, almost 20 years after her note to Woolf thanking her for the beauty and truth of *The Waves* (Letter 72), notes in her diary that she has just read "'Inward Companion' – Walter de la Mare. I was so much moved by this that I wrote him a note. I have only done this once before – to Virginia Woolf" (Ketterer). Woolf draws readers together, creating friends (Letter 93) and opportunities for understanding–"knowing you a little helped [my half-brother and me] to know each other better" (Letter 82). And at least one reader believes Woolf encourages a genuine give and take in the writer/reader conversation. E. Clark writes,

> You are not of those [. . .] scribes, who for all their good writing make it clear that their word is law. "I know all about this. You don't. You must take my word for it. Take it or leave it." You have always, it seemed to me, had a game with your reader, have played—& fair. [. . .] Conversation is like a game of tennis—there are 2 sides to the game—& each must keep its end up. (Letter 24).

On January 17, 1915, with *The Voyage Out* a couple of months away from publication, Virginia Woolf wrote to Thomas Hardy: "I have long wished to tell you how profoundly grateful I am to you for your poems and novels, but naturally it seemed an impertinence to do so." Marked by a shy approach, tentative language ("I felt that I might perhaps be allowed to thank you"), praise (she notes "the magnificent work which you have already done, and are still to do"), sense of debt, and decision "to satisfy a very old desire" (*L*2 58), the young writer's fan letter to the great author might have been the model for the correspondents collected here. Associating letters to authors with fan mail and associating fan mail with celebrity, fanaticism (the stem word for "fan"), and Americans (Letters 34 and 115), correspondents apologize for their intrusion, fear insincerity and sentimentality, do not want to bore or insult, pluck up courage, explain how rarely they write such letters, and consistently use the word "impertinent" to describe their endeavors. Writing letters that embody intimacy between reader and writer, the letter writers fear they have gone outside the bounds of propriety by assuming such intimacy exists. Wanting to express their desire, they also do not want to be associated with those who make such desires blatantly known. They have a horror of sounding like a "housemaid writing to Greta Garbo" (Letter 62). Writing a fan letter thus crosses class boundaries, risks foolishness, assumes equality; it feels forbidden, dangerous, selfish, and such a transgression requires apology. It is a matter of great relief, even celebration, then, when the author replies and thus forgives, even abets, the trespass. Woolf excitedly writes Janet Case, "Just got this letter from Thomas Hardy!" and asks Miss Case to keep the letter for her (*L*2 59), and John Farrelly is "unreasonably elated" when he receives a letter from Woolf, turning "the envelope round and round in my hand, noting the return adress [sic], the post-mark, the time the letter was mailed" and studying her handwriting as though it were a love letter (Letter 132; "From Fan-Mail" 21).

Based on the evidence provided by these readers, Woolf's common reader was neither a figment of her "exquisite" imagination nor a card-carrying elite; ordinary readers read and understood Woolf *as* she was published, long before anyone explained her to them. Certainly Woolf's modernism was not "beyond" popular authors, the working classes, or the uneducated. When Harriette Campbell writes to praise *The Waves*, she says she is "writing as one of the public who picks up a novel to be entertained. I am quite sure you wanted to reach people like myself and will be glad that you have succeeded" (Letter 73). E. G. J. Eastwood says she is "a woman living in 'one of those streets somewhere south of the river'," has a "very faint" hope of a scholarship to Oxford, and wants to write some day (Letter 50), and Miss E. J. Poignard says she is a "humble admirer of [Woolf's] talent" (Letter 46). Gladys Burlton earns a comfortable income, but is too tired to concentrate on writing at the end of the day (Letter 39), whereas M. P. Thomasset wants to write, but is "without £500 a year, without travel, without a room to herself and nothing of all that you say is essential to a writer!" (Letter 49). Anna B. Carolan, responding to "Women Must Weep" in the *Atlantic Monthly*, includes herself in the uneducated, those she hopes Woolf can reach and tell how to "help make the world a safe place to live in" (Letter 104).

Approximately 2/3 of the correspondents are women, 1/3 men; approximately 3/4 are English or European and 1/4 American or Canadian. Several other categories of readers emerge: writers (who can be further subdivided into established and nascent or would-be, well-known and unknown, serious and popular); academics; students; reviewers; common, ordinary, or "non-specialist" readers, what Gladys Burlton calls "ordinarily intelligent people" (Letter 39). Of these categories, the two largest, by my very unscientific count, are common readers (30) and writers (26). But these categories are porous; the readers themselves complicate any attempt to pigeonhole them. John U. Nef (Letter 90), W. G. Weedon (Letter 71) and Richard Braithwaite (Letter 77), for example, although professionals, are far outside their academic fields of economics, mathematics and oriental languages, and philosophy of science when they read Woolf, so should they be counted as common readers as well? And Frank Hallam Lyell, though he would become an academic, writes to Woolf when he is 20, long before he enters that category (Letter 64).

In addition to the numbers and kinds of readers in this collection, Virginia Woolf's fan mail surely represents many more people who were reading her with understanding and pleasure. Not only must we consider how often we ourselves have been moved by books but *not* written to the authors, not only must we consider how very nearly John Farrelly's first letter to Virginia Woolf was not sent (Letter 132 referring to Letter 125; "From Fan-Mail" 20-23), but we must also consider the testimony within the letters themselves. Wanda Fraiken Neff's observation that her reaction to Woolf is similar to those of her friends and her husband's women students (Letter 45), Emphie Case's enclosure of a letter to Janet Case that talks about Woolf's books (Letter 105), and Sebastian Sprott's comment that there "must be many people like me" (Letter 120) all point beyond the correspondent to a larger and more diverse readership. In addition, based on the evidence of a draft reply to a Herr Fisher tucked away in the manuscript portion of the Monks House Papers, the fan mail to Woolf we *have* may represent only a fraction of the fan mail she *received*. (The absence of more *Years* letters suggests the same thing.) In her draft reply, Woolf thanks Herr Fisher and his friends for reading her books (MHP B.2.e., ms 55). But there's no listing of a letter from Herr Fisher to Virginia Woolf in either the Monks House Papers or the Berg Collection, suggesting that Woolf did not keep (or someone else did not keep) all the fan mail she received.

I also suspect that Woolf answered most of the letters written to her, although not all the letters in this collection have published replies to them. The memory of her mother writing letters every evening (*MOB* 38), her upper middle class upbringing, and the presence of this draft to Herr Fisher all point to that conclusion. But since a letter from Woolf to Herr Fisher isn't in *The Letters of Virginia Woolf*, we must assume that her reply was not revised or not sent, was sent but destroyed during the war or thrown out when Herr Fisher died, or was sent and still resides in a basement or attic somewhere. P. H. Wallis says in his condolence letter to Leonard Woolf (*A* 169-70) that he received a reply to his earlier letter (Letter 26), but we do not have it. In other words, even when we do not have a reply, it may not be accurate to assume Woolf did not write one. Tracking down such stray letters may become yet another facet of Woolf reception studies.

This collection of correspondents shows that young people were attracted to Woolf's work throughout her career. Several correspondents give their age or mention their youth (Letters 13, 50, 64, 84, 88, 89, 93, 125), whereas others we now know were young at the time (such as Elizabeth Jenkins in Letter 38, Dorothy Livesay in Letter 54, Eudora Welty in Letter 66, and W. Denham Sutcliffe in Letter 114). They appreciate her advice "to see the vividness and importance of every minute, the significance of every action" (Letter 84), her ability to "[illuminate] our capacity to ourselves" (Letter 42), her nudges toward other writers (Letter 125; "From Fan-Mail" 20), and her encouragement of their minds. Margaret Laurie writes to say, for example, that Woolf's books are helping her "to keep from running quite to seed during the intellectually lean years . . . when my baby, my house, and my garden leave me so little time for the other world" (Letter 99).

One young correspondent thanks Woolf for the criticism of her manuscript (Letter 108). Margaret E. Thomas writes from Girton to thank her for capturing "the subtle atmosphere of discouragement which prevents so many intelligent women from ever plunging wholeheartedly into artistic work" (Letter 34) and then later asks Woolf about publishing an edition of Girton poets (Letter 55). Several young women who would later become well-known writers write to Woolf: Elizabeth Coles (Taylor) (Letter 84), Elizabeth Jenkins (Letter 38), Antonia White, who says she used a photograph of Woolf clipped from *Vogue* to comfort her while she wrote "advertisements for corsets and disinfectants and baking powder" (Letter 62), Dorothy Livesay, who writes to thank Woolf for *A Room of One's Own* because she thinks reading it has helped her father understand why she must "struggle" to "escape from . . . the family circle" (Letter 54), and Eudora Welty, who looks forward to more novels like *To the Lighthouse* that "will stun me speechless" (Letter 66). But other young writers, ones who did not become so famous, take heart from Woolf as well. Beatrice Brown writes that *A Room of One's Own* has made it easier for her, a beginner, to write, "with a clearer head & fewer unhelpful misgivings" (Letter 42), Maboth Moseley says Woolf's work "has influenced me greatly" (Letter 13), and Richard Greenleaf believes that whatever he creates, "a large part [will] be a direct heritage from Virginia Woolf" (Letter 144).

These letter writers also show that the United States reception of her work was strong and enthusiastic from the beginning, so much so that Lyn Newman, a friend who was living in Princeton at the time, writes to encourage Leonard and Virginia to begin 1938 by coming to America: "Virginia, you would get a tremendous welcome, you are much read and appreciated" (Letter 101). Many of the longest fan letters are from the United States, and these letters seem characterized by the correspondents' willingness to jump right into a conversation with Woolf. Alvah B. Flood from Montana writes, "I reckon I had as well follow the crowd in making the first word of what I am about to say to you 'Dear'." He then proceeds to discuss his interpretation, though he is "not a scholar of literature," of "The New Dress" as it appeared in *Forum*, and notes that most of us are afflicted with Mabel's inability to defy convention: "we wilt when our fellows hiss rather than . . . say 'Go to it, old man'" (Letter 11). Elizabeth Cox Wright describes her situation as a wife, mother, and student of English history who has "a nagging feeling that if I were a man my study of 15th century humanism would some day amount to something; as it is I go through periods of nervousness about it which sap whatever ability I may have" (Letter 44). Motier Harris Fisher writes two fascinating and detailed letters about the lives of girls and women in the U.S. (Letters 115 and 116); with a few topical changes, her letters could have been written just last week. Isabel Forbes Milton takes the day off from teaching 150 students in Bronxville, New York to "[smoke and drink] tea in the morning sun and [follow] the beautifully weighted sentences of Virginia Woolf," noting Woolf's awareness of "not only . . . the dilemmas of consciousness in this age but of the larger economic & social questions" and wondering "if your English public prizes you as much as we Americans do?" (Letter 93). Marion Holden Bemis confides in Woolf her desire to write, describing how she has "always made phrases, written them on scattered sheets, or watched them wing through the ceiling as I lay in bed of a morning" and has spent "years of scribbling on scraps" (Letter 82); in doing so, she may have provided Woolf with some of Isa's mannerisms in *Between the Acts*. Eudora Welty writes with the confidence of a 22-year-old who would become a great writer–her praise of *To the Lighthouse* in 1931 is a lovely back story for the 1981 foreword she wrote for Harcourt's edition of the novel, and her criticism of *The Waves* is wonderful in its audaciousness and clarity (Letter 66).

Finally, and perhaps most important, these letters to Virginia Woolf show us how real readers can complicate and enrich reception studies. The measure of an author's readership and impact goes beyond numbers of books sold or even numbers of times a book is checked out of a library. How do we learn about and count the "clever Oxford woman" who wrote to Anne E. Smith about her pleasure in reading "Mr. Bennett and Mrs. Brown" (Letter 10)? What about the evidence of Mrs. K. B. Williamson writing to her sister, *not* to Virginia Woolf, about *The Waves* and the "feeling that overwhelms one in a new and powerful work of imagination" (Letter 78a)? What about Montague Bull's statement that he "so enjoyed 'The Lighthouse'" that he "posted away six copies" (Letter 18)? What about Virginia Tooker's comment that "I read 5 pages or so [of *To the Lighthouse*] then I read it again to Caroline—then we go to Dora's with it under the arm and we read those 5 pages again and if Marguerite comes in at the end as she did last night, we read aloud together what precedes the 5 pages" (Letter 15)? Or Edith Freedom Smith's missive from Pennsylvania, that says "You may be interested to know that a friend and I are having a Virginia Woolf winter!" (Letter 43)? What about Motier Harris Fisher's comment that "small groups of women in various parts of the United States have read your 'Three Guineas'" (Letter 115)? We cannot ignore these "amateur" readers, their borrowing and lending habits, their reading practices, their reviews for small newspapers and newsletters, their book clubs. We must take into account the way books travel from hand to hand, letters travel from house to house, and word travels from mouth to mouth.

To construct a more complex common reader for Woolf and for modernism in the 21st century, then, we must look to the readers themselves, recovering letters, listening to stories, finding descendants and diaries and details. To assess Woolf's reputation in the 1920s and 1930s and beyond, we must counterpose the construction of readers occurring at the time in works such as Q. D. Leavis's *Fiction and the Reading Public* with someone like James A. Mackereth who writes the following to Woolf about his response to *A Room of One's Own*: "What a happy marriage there is between your manner and your spirit. And how warm and persuasive are your words & phrases in the truth of that happiness. We love more than art when we write like that" (Letter 47).[5] To capture the living feel of modernism as it was being created and being read, to remove it from abstraction and hierarchies and the language of exclusion, we must posit a "tangled mesh of readers" for the "tangled mesh of modernists" we now know about (Scott 10). Because these letters from readers reveal that Virginia Woolf's books *are*, after all, conversations between her and her friends. It's just that her friends are more numerous and more varied than we had imagined.

[5] See Todd Avery and Patrick Brantlinger, in "Reading and Modernism," Allison Pease, in "Readers with Bodies," Catherine Turner, in *Marketing Modernism Between the Two World Wars*, and Robert Scholes, in "Exploring the Great Divide" for a few of the studies that have begun to complicate our understanding of modernism.

Works Cited

Avery, Todd and Patrick Brantlinger. "Reading and Modernism: 'Mind Hungers' Common and Uncommon." *A Concise Companion to Modernism.* Ed. David Bradshaw. Oxford: Blackwell, 2003. 243-61.

Carr, Katy. "Miss E J Poignard." E-mail communication to author. 11 August 2004.

Cuddy-Keane, Melba. "From Fan-Mail to Readers' Letters: Locating John Farrelly." *Woolf Studies Annual* 11 (2005): 3-32.

—. "Imbricated Voices: Modernism's Historical Readers." Paper presented at the Modernist Studies Association Conference, 9 October 1999.

—. *Virginia Woolf, the Intellectual, & the Public Sphere.* Cambridge: Cambridge UP, 2003.

Farr, Cecilia Konchar. *Reading Oprah: How Oprah's Book Club Changed the Way America Reads.* Albany: SUNY Press, 2005.

Ketterer, David. "Grace Wilson." E-mail communication to author. 2 September 2005.

Leavis, Q. D. "Caterpillars of the Commonwealth Unite!" *Scrutiny* 7 (September 1938): 203-14. Rpt. *Virginia Woolf: Critical Assessments.* Vol. II. Ed. Eleanor McNees. Mountfield, East Sussex: Helm, 1994. 272-81.

—. *Fiction and the Reading Public.* 1932. London: Chatto & Windus, 1996.

Long, Elizabeth. *Book Clubs: Women and the Uses of Reading in Everyday Life.* Chicago: U of Chicago P, 2003.

Oldfield, Sybil, ed. *Afterwords: Letters on the Death of Virginia Woolf.* New Brunswick, NJ: Rutgers UP, 2005.

Pawlowski, Merry M. "The Virginia Woolf and Vera Douie Letters: Woolf's Connections to the Women's Service Library." *Woolf Studies Annual* 8 (2002): 3-62.

Pease, Allison. "Readers with Bodies: Modernist Criticism's Bridge Across the Cultural Divide." *Modernism/Modernity* 7.1 (2000): 77-97.

Radway, Janice. *A Feeling for Books: The Book-of-the-Month Club, Literary Taste, and Middle-Class Desire.* Chapel Hill: U of North Carolina P, 1997.

Rose, Jonathan. *The Intellectual Life of the British Working Classes.* New Haven: Yale UP, 2001.

Rubin, Joan Shelley. *The Making of Middlebrow Culture.* Chapel Hill: U of North Carolina P, 1992.

Ryan, Barbara and Amy M. Thomas, eds. *Reading Acts: U. S. Readers' Interactions with Literature, 1800-1950.* Knoxville, TN: U of Tennessee P, 2002.

Scholes, Robert. "Exploring the Great Divide: High and Low, Left and Right." *Narrative* 11 (2003): 245-69.

Scott, Bonnie Kime, ed. *The Gender of Modernism*. Bloomington: Indiana UP, 1990.

Snaith, Anna. *Virginia Woolf: Public and Private Negotiations*. New York: St. Martin's, 2000.

—. "Wide Circles: The *Three Guineas* Letters." *Woolf Studies Annual* 6 (2000): 1-12.

—, ed. "*Three Guineas* Letters." *Woolf Studies Annual* 6 (2000): 17-168.

Turner, Catherine. *Marketing Modernism Between the Two World Wars*. Amherst: U of Massachusetts P, 2003.

Woolf, Leonard. Correspondence of Leonard Woolf. Letters III. Leonard Woolf Archive. SxMs13. University of Sussex Library.

—. Personal Life; Virginia; Letters articles & books about VW's writing. IID4. Leonard Woolf Archive. SxMs13. University of Sussex Library.

—. Personal Life; Virginia; Miscellaneous materials relating to Virginia Woolf; Posthumous fan mail addressed to LW. IID17.i. Leonard Woolf Archive. SxMs13. University of Sussex Library.

Woolf, Virginia. Correspondence of Various Persons re: Books, Articles. Monks House Papers. SxMs18. University of Sussex Library.

—. Correspondence of Virginia Woolf. Letters III. Monks House Papers. SxMs18. University of Sussex Library.

—. *The Letters of Virginia Woolf.* Eds. Nigel Nicolson and Joanne Trautmann. 6 vols. New York: HBJ, 1975-80.

—. Manuscripts B: Literary. Monks House Papers. SxMs18. University of Sussex Library.

—. *Moments of Being*. Ed. Jeanne Schulkind. San Diego: HBJ, 1985.

Location and filing of letters

The Monks House Papers collection is divided into letters and manuscripts, with the letters then being further divided into three parts: Letters I, Correspondence between Leonard and Virginia Woolf, Letters II, Correspondence of Leonard Woolf, and Letters III, Correspondence of Virginia Woolf. Letters III consists of 10 boxes, numbered 69-78, of letters written *to* Virginia Woolf. The first nine boxes are filled with alphabetically arranged folders, one folder to each known correspondent—the letters from Elizabeth Bowen, for example, are located in Box 70, Bosanquet–Cecil. The last box, Box 78, Correspondence of Various Persons re: Books, Articles, is divided into two main parts, "Letters from readers about VW's Books" and "Letters from agents, editors, publishers, etc." The "Letters from readers about VW's Books" are sorted into the following folders: Letters about specific books; Letters about *Orlando*; Letters about *Roger Fry*; Letters about *A Room of One's Own*; Letters about *Three Guineas*; Letters about *To the Lighthouse*; Letters about *The Waves*. The "Letters from agents, editors, publishers, etc." are divided into the following folders: Chambrun/Harpers concerning "The Duchess and the Jeweller"; Donald Brace; Letters about articles; Correspondence about publications; and three folders of fan mail labeled Letters about various books, Fan mail, and Miscellaneous fan mail. The labels and distinctions do not always seem accurate or consistent, but for the most part, they serve a useful organizational function. Two hundred and eighteen letters are filed in the Correspondence of Various Persons box, with 58 of those devoted to *Three Guineas* and 160 spread through the other folders.

As Anna Snaith has pointed out, Anne Olivier Bell, not Woolf, sorted the letters into those from known and unknown correspondents, and some anomalies result (*WSA* 6: 3); in fact, some correspondents appear in both locations. Thus, I have followed Snaith's lead and not maintained the distinction between "known" and "unknown" in the collection below. Each letter's specific location is provided in italics at the end of it. If two names are given, such as *Stephen-Turner*, the correspondent's folder can be found in alphabetical order within that particular known correspondent box. If two phrases are given, such as *Letters from agents, editors, publishers, etc., Correspondence about publications*, the first phrase refers to one of the two main divisions within the Various Persons box, and the second phrase refers to the actual folder the letter is in.

Thirty of the 137 letters collected here are located in the known correspondents' boxes, and they were included to ensure representation of all of Woolf's major works (except for *Night and Day*) and to add a common reader to the collection, Elizabeth Read. The remaining 107 letters are located in the Correspondence of Various Persons box. Thus, 53 letters in the Correspondence of Various Persons box have been omitted here, including 26 letters about "The

Duchess and the Jeweller" and 27 letters from editors or publishers. Although these 53 letters are interesting, they deal more with practical concerns than with the relationship between Woolf and her readers; some, such as the letter dated November 24, 1937 from Denys Kilham Roberts asking Woolf to join a selection committee at Penguin to choose the world's greatest books or the letter dated October 26, 1938 from Gerald Hopkins at Oxford University Press asking Woolf to consider allowing some of her titles to become part of the World's Classics series, do suggest something about her stature in the late 30s. The 58 letters about *Three Guineas* in the Correspondence of Various Persons box have already been published in Anna Snaith's edition, *WSA* 6 (2000): 1-168.

Transcription of letters

I have transcribed the letters exactly as they are, letting stand all errors, except for the common use of hyphens as end stops, which I have changed to periods, and except for the letter from G. Lowes Dickinson (see footnote to letter 61). Because working with many different correspondents and their handwriting creates even more chance for error, I would appreciate learning about alternative readings, corrections, or additions for the transcriptions below. Embossed or printed letterheads appear in small caps, and I have noted whether letters are typed or handwritten and where enclosures are mentioned in the letter but have not survived. Letters marked with an asterisk refer to transcriptions (rather than original letters) held by the University of Sussex. Brief descriptions are provided for the two letters from John Farrelly, Jr., which were published in their entirety in Melba Cuddy-Keane's "From Fan-Mail to Readers' Letters: Locating John Farrelly," *WSA* 11 (2005): 3-32.

I have arranged the letters chronologically, interweaving letters from the different folders in the Various Persons box and letters from known correspondents. All letters in this collection have a date, with brackets indicating a surmise based on context or external evidence. Letters with fully known dates (all parts of the date supplied by the correspondent) and letters with partially known dates (with some parts of the date supplied by the correspondent and other parts supplied by a librarian or by me) have been organized in chronological order based on the entire date. Letters with no date provided by the correspondent appear with a year in brackets and after the chronologically arranged letters for that year. I have noted when correspondents have other letters within this collection or in the collections edited by Anna Snaith and Sybil Oldfield.

Editorial markings

The editorial markings I have used are as follows:

[   ] = illegible
[example?] = uncertain reading
[example] = editorial comment
<example> = correspondent's insertion
~~example~~ = correspondent's cancellation
{example} = correspondent's square brackets

Abbreviations

In addition to the standard abbreviations for Woolf's works, I have used the following abbreviations in footnotes:

A = *Afterwords*, ed. Sybil Oldfield
WSA 6 = "The *Three Guineas* Letters," ed. Anna Snaith

Acknowledgments

As I worked on this project, I was often reminded of W. S. Lewis's comment to Woolf about his work on the footnotes for the Walpole correspondence: "This much I know, the satisfaction one gets from answering one of these minute questions is prodigious, out of all proportion to the importance of the thing discovered" (Letter 113). To the many people and reference works who contributed to my "prodigious" satisfaction over the last few years, thank you!

I cannot thank Dorothy Sheridan, Joy Eldridge, and Fiona Courage enough for making my work in the Monks House Papers in the Sussex Library Special Collections rooms a joy for two summers; your cheerful searches, supportive answers to numerous questions, and delightful conversations made the time fly by. Thanks, also, to Bet Inglis for answering questions even in her retirement. Other staff members in Special Collections, Judy Pickering, Lucy Pearson, and Helen Monk, helped with photocopies and procedural questions, Karen Watson took care of the scanning of the letter for the frontispiece, and Sandra Koa-Wing and Vicky Payne checked my transcriptions once I was back in the States. Institute of Development Studies at Sussex and Kathy and Paul Myles in Lewes offered shelter and hospitality, and Doris King, Julia Briggs, Anna Snaith, Stuart Clarke, and Marion Dell provided wonderful meals and good conversation. Other sojourners in the archives were delightful lunchtime companions, including Elizabeth Shih, Merry Pawlowski, Alex Zwerdling, and Mary Lou Emery.

Other archivists, curators, and librarians in the UK and US have searched collections, forwarded requests to copyright holders, combed reference works for biographical information, suggested leads, and discussed Woolf with me. Thank you, one and all: Adrian Reginald Allan, University of Liverpool; Elaine Ardia,

Bates College; Michael Bott and Verity Andrews, University of Reading; Ellen Cordes, Yale University; Robin Darwall-Smith, Magdalen College, University College, Oxford University; Nancy Edwards, British Library; Jonathan Harrison, St. John's College, Cambridge University; Brian Hubner, University of Manitoba; Peter Jones and Patricia McGuire, King's College, Cambridge University; Karen Kukil, Smith College; Carol Marshall, Kenyon College; Nancy R. Miller, University of Pennsylvania; Leslie A. Morris and William P. Stoneman, Harvard University; Christine Nelson, The Morgan Library; Jonathan Pepler, Cheshire County; Kate Perry, Girton College, Cambridge University; Jacque Roethler and Sidney F. Huttner, University of Iowa; Andy Sawyer, University of Liverpool; William G. Simpson, John Rylands University Library of Manchester; Nicky Sugar, Royal Holloway, University of London; Anne Thomson, Newnham College, Cambridge University; Susan Odell Walker and Margaret Powell, The Lewis Walpole Library, Yale University; and Jocelyn K. Wilk, Columbia University.

Otterbein College supported this project in many ways. Patti Frick, Vice President for Academic Affairs, the sabbatical program, the Humanities Advisory Committee, the Faculty Development Committee, and the White Fund were all instrumental in funding my research travel to England. Patti Rothermich, Reference Librarian, and Allen Reichert, Electronic Access Librarian, helped me search for and find Interlibrary Loan materials, arcane facts, and hundreds of references, along with the usual books and periodicals. No matter how obscure my questions or how tenuous my reasons for asking, they gladly went on the hunt. The English Department and its Chair, Alison Prindle, encouraged my work by giving me formal and informal venues for talking about it and by supporting all my grant proposals, and Rebecca Bowman, dear friend and colleague, listened cheerfully to my many "detective stories," and Shirley Sandridge, student research assistant extraordinaire, tracked down current zip codes for old U.S. addresses and did some preliminary searches for correspondents early in the project. Aaron Thompson, Instructional Technology, saw to it that my computer and email remained up and running.

Many Woolfian colleagues deserve my gratitude and more: Pierre-Eric Villeneuve, for his delight in and expertise about Woolf's letters; Melba Cuddy-Keane, for her clear focus on real readers, her ability to track down their stories, and her generous pointers at the beginning of this project; Diane Gillespie, for her unstinting support over the years and her meticulous work on *Roger Fry*; Anna Snaith, for her edition of the *Three Guineas* letters, a model for us all; Sibyl Oldfield, for her determination to publish the condolence letters and her kindness in sharing names of letter writers and addresses of copyright holders with me before the publication of *Afterwords*; Stuart Clarke, for his encyclopedic knowledge and willingness to research both the sublime and the mundane; Stephen Barkway, for his knowledge of the Easdales; Vara Neverow, for her friendship; Naomi Black, for her knowledge of feminist movements; S. P. Rosenbaum, for his knowledge of the Girton archives; Marilyn Smith, for the right book at the right time; Helen Southworth, for the translations *into* French that helped me correspond with current copyright holders and for the translations *from* the French that grace this edition; and Mark Hussey, for his support of this project and all things Woolfian. In addition, this project is deeply indebted to the footnotes provided by Anne Olivier Bell in *The Diary of Virginia Woolf* and by Joanne Trautmann and Nigel Nicolson in *The Letters of Virginia Woolf*.

Undertaking such a project was immensely eased by the existence of the Internet. The WATCH file (Writers, Artists, and Their Copyright Holders), cooperatively organized and operated by the University of Reading and the Harry Ransom Humanities Research Center at the University of Texas at Austin, provides copyright information and advice along with the names and addresses of copyright holders in its files; google.com turns up the darndest things, including addresses, biographical information, and genealogical sites; biographical databases provide dates and footnote material; and the sites for the Royal Mail and United States Postal Service give shots in the dark a chance of landing somewhere!

In addition, I want to thank Candace Barnes for an address; Katy Carr, Sprowston Heritage, for her memories of reading Woolf; Charles A. Culman for a genealogical web site; Jack Finefrock, Bookstore Manager, Kenyon College, for forwarding materials to the Sutcliffe family; Richard Ford for a referral; David Ketterer, biographer of John Wyndham, for permission to quote from Grace Wilson's unpublished diary; Kathy Kovalick for a Quaker genealogical search; David Laibman, Editor of *Science and Society*, for his research on my behalf; Walter Benn Michaels, Michael Anania, and Douglas Bicknese of the University of Illinois at Chicago, for answers to queries; David Sutton, the University of Reading, for cheerfully answering copyright questions; Barbara Will, Dartmouth College, for information about Bernard Faÿ; and Helen Wright, Alumni Officer at Girton, Cambridge University, for her interest and referrals.

But my deepest and most heartfelt gratitude goes to the many relatives, descendants, friends, neighbors, literary executors, and occupants who freely gave their assistance to an academic who arrived in their mailboxes out of the blue. I was overwhelmed by people's willingness to take the time to answer my questions. Kind strangers diligently searched for information about previous apartment or house owners; obligingly delivered my query letter to those who could best answer it; warmly shared anecdotes and biographical facts and books; generously gave permission for publication; and gently let me know when I had reached a dead end. Thank you for your conversations via post, fax, phone, and email; I wish I could have used all your stories: Marie-Louise Adams, Dobrile Arezina, Ann Bean, Samantha Becnel, Bernard W. Berkowitz, K. Bishop, Rosanna Bruno, Belinda Bullard, Lucy Carter, Annabel Cole, Lee Coles, Elinor Cooper, Hannah Crowdy, Kirbie Crowe, A. N. G. Duckworth-Chad, Sister Phillipa Edwards, Vincent Faÿ, Ian Fowler, Cathy Fox, Tory Gray, Margaret Harris, Joanna Hylton, Joanna Kingham, A. K. S. Lambton, Frances Lawrence, Jonathan Lear, David Mayor, David Morley, Evelyn S. Nef, William and Edward Newman, Henry Oakeley, Charles Osborne, Mary Weedon Pollock, Fred Ponsonby, Lorna Pugh, S. Reis, Simon Rendall, Alan Ritchie, Diana Rothenstein, Miriam Rothschild, Leslie D. Fisher Rush, John Saunders, John Stachiewicz, Jay Stewart, John and Jenny Sutcliffe, Sarah Sutcliffe, Maya Tcholakova, Mary Trevelyan, and Linda Yahn.

Finally, to Joanna Kingham, who allowed her mother's letter to be reproduced for the frontispiece, especial thanks, and to Gary, whose email correspondence during the summer of 2001 was an especial delight, thank you.

Published Materials

I am grateful to R. R. Bowker LLC for their permission to reprint the letter from F. B. Adams Jr., which originally appeared in Lola L. Szladits, "The Art and Craft of Collecting Manuscripts," *Book Collecting: A Modern Guide*, ed. Jean Peters (NY and London: R. R. Bowker Company, 1977): 74-75.

Unpublished materials

I am grateful to Dorothy Sheridan, Head of Special Collections in the Library at the University of Sussex, for the Library's permission, as owner of the original and transcribed letters appearing in this edition, to publish. I am also deeply indebted to the following individuals and institutions, as copyright holders, for granting me permission to print hitherto unpublished letters: Permissions Department, Harcourt for Donald C. Brace; King's College Library, Cambridge University for Richard Braithwaite; David Morley for Harriette Campbell; David Higham Associates for David Cecil; A. K. S. Lambton for Eleanor (Nelly) Cecil; Joanna Kingham for Elizabeth Coles; Annabel Cole for Pamela Diamand; A. N. G. Duckworth-Chad for George Duckworth; Vincent Faÿ for Bernard Faÿ; Annabel Cole for Agnes Fry and Isabel Fry; E. M. Chilver for Sally Graves; Leslie D. Fisher Rush for Motier Harris Fisher; Henry Oakeley for John Hayward; David Higham Associates for Richard Hughes; Elizabeth Jenkins for Elizabeth Jenkins; Simon Rendall for Ann McKnight Kauffer; Charles Osborne for Alice Lehmann; Yale Committee on Literary Property for W. S. Lewis; Jay Stewart for Dorothy Livesay; *The Yale Review* for Helen McAfee; The

University of Liverpool for Arnold McNair; Victoria Gray and David Mayor for Beatrice (Bobo) Mayor; John Saunders, Valerie Eliot, and Margaret Ellis for Hope Mirrlees; The University of Manchester for Walter Moberly; Charles Morgan for J. P. Morgan; Evelyn S. Nef for John U. Nef; Edward I. Newman for Lyn Newman; Fred Ponsonby for Arthur Ponsonby; Alan Ritchie for Alice Ritchie; Lucy Carter and Diana Rothenstein for William Rothenstein; Miriam Rothschild for Victor Rothschild; The National Trust for Sebastian Sprott; Royal Holloway, University of London for Caroline F. E. Spurgeon; Margaret Harris for Christina Stead; John Sutcliffe for W. Denham Sutcliffe; Margaret Bullard for Margaret E. Thomas; Mary Trevelyan for Elizabeth Trevelyan; Philippa Edwards for Helen Waddell; Mary W. Pollock for W. G. Weedon; Russell & Volkening, Inc. for Eudora Welty; Curtis Brown Literary Agency for Antonia White.

I have made every reasonable effort to trace and contact copyright holders prior to publication, but in some cases, it has been impossible to do so. I would be glad to rectify any omissions at the earliest opportunity, so any further information about copyright holders should be sent to me or to the publisher.

Chronological Index of Letters from Readers

1. Eleanor Cecil — April 22, 1915 (to Leonard Woolf)
2. Sylvia Lynd — October 27, 1922
3. Hope Mirrlees — December 12, 1922
4. Beatrice Mayor — July 3, 1925
5. E. S. P. Haynes — July 3, [1925]
6. Olive Heseltine — [Summer 1925]
7. Blair Niles — September 16, 1925
8. Bernard Faÿ — [November?] 12, [1925]
9. Eily Darwin — [1925]
10. Anne E. Smith — April 4, 1927
11. Alvah B. Flood — May 2, 1927
12. Aubrey Herbert — May 2, [1927]
13. Maboth Moseley — May 9, 1927
14. Aubrey Herbert — May 11, [1927]
15. Virginia Tooker — May 20, 1927
16. George Duckworth — May 28, 1927
17. [Potter?] Lucky — May 30, 1927
18. Montague Bull — June 16, 1927
19. Bernard Faÿ — June 18, 1927
20. Anne E. Smith — June 19, 1927
21. Mary W. Findlater — October 17, 1927
22. Donald C. Brace — July 3, 1928
23. Alice Ritchie — July 31, 1928
24. E. Clark — October 23, 1928
25. Helen McAfee — October 23, 1928
26. P. H. Wallis — October 28, [1928]
27. Bea Howe — [October/November] 6, [1928]
28. Emerald Cunard — [early November 1928]
29. Henry S. Canby — November 7, 1928
30. Elena Richmond — November 9, 1928
31. Anonymous — November 13, 1928
32. F. Pollock — December 4, 1928
33. Berta Ruck — December 22, 1928
34. Margaret E. Thomas — October 28, 1929
35. M. G. Ostle — October 28, 1929
36. Theodora Bosanquet — November 6, 1929
37. Caroline F. E. Spurgeon — November 7, 1929
38. Elizabeth Jenkins — November 22, 1929
39. Gladys Burlton — December 2, 1929

40. Lois Jarred — December 4, 1929
41. Eleanor D. Hill — December 30, 1929
42. Beatrice Brown — [1929]
43. Edith Freelove Smith — [late 1929/early 1930]
44. Elizabeth Cox Wright — January 12, 1930
45. Wanda Fraiken Neff — January 12, 1930
46. E. J. Poignard — January 19, 1930
47. James A. Mackereth — January 22, 1930
48. Erika Wilbuch — January 27, 1930
49. M. P. Thomasset — January 31, 1930
50. E. G. J. Eastwood — February 7, 1930
51. Max Judge — February 10, 1930
52. Emily S. Judge — February 19, 1930
53. Emily S. Judge — March 16, 1930
54. Dorothy Livesay — April 1, 1930
55. Margaret E. Thomas — May 24, 1930
56. John Hayward — October 12, 1931
57. Hilda Finnemore — October 13, 1931
58. Milla Tcholakova — October 15, 1931
59. George Duckworth — October 16, 1931
60. John Hampson Simpson — October 21, 1931
61. G. Lowes Dickinson — October 23, [1931]
62. Antonia White — October 24, 1931
63. Faith Henderson — October 27, 1931
64. Frank Hallam Lyell — November 20, 1931
65. Doris B. Borst — November 23, 1931
66. Eudora Welty — November 23, 1931
67. Fernande Hélie — November 26, 1931
68. Ogden W. Heath — November 27, 1931
69. Richard Hughes — November 27, [1931]
70. Joan Easdale — December 5, 1931
71. W. G. Weedon — December 5, 1931
72. Grace Wilson — December 15, 1931
73. Harriette R. Campbell — December 17, 1931
74. Gladys E. Easdale — [1931]
75. Anonymous — [1931]
76. M. I. Rowell — January 8, 1932
77. Richard Braithwaite — January 9, 1932
78. Helen Waddell — February 16, 1932
    78a. Mrs. K. B. Williamson — January 4, 1932 (enclosure)

79. L. C. Rose — February 17, 1932
80. Elizabeth Read — June 23, 1932
81. Elizabeth Read — August 14, [1932]
82. Marion Holden Bemis — September 6, 1932
83. Sophy Sanger — October 4, 1932
84. Elizabeth Coles — October 15, 1932
85. Victor Rothschild — [1932]
86. Walter H. Moberly — March 22, 1933
87. Walter H. Moberly — March 29, 1933
88. F. B. Adams, Jr. — April 3, [1933]
89. Richard Greenleaf — June 26, 1933
90. John U. Nef — August 20, 1933
91. Elizabeth Read — September 5, [1933]
92. Harriet Gaylord — November 14, [1933]
93. Isabel Forbes Milton — February 6, 1935
94. H. G. Vincent for the Prime Minister - May 15, 1935
95. Camille Mayran — December 2, 1935
96. Sally Graves — [post-1935]
97. Christina Stead — December 15, 1936
98. R. Nash — July 22, 1937
99. Margaret Laurie — August 19, 1937
100. Hudson Strode — November 12, [1937]
101. Lyn Newman — December 22, 1937
102. Sally Graves — [1937]
103. Mrs. Lillian A. Bray — April 28, 1938
104. Anna B. Carolan — May 25, 1938
105. E. S. Case — July 10, 1938
106. Donald Brace — August 23, 1938
107. Phyllis Moir — October 29, 1938
108. Ann McKnight Kauffer — February 9, 1939
109. Arnold D. McNair — March 1, 1939
110. Arnold D. McNair — March 3, 1939
111. Tangye Lean — March 3, [1939]
112. Simone Rohr — March 19, 1939
113. W. S. Lewis — April 19, 1939
114. W. Denham Sutcliffe — [November 1939]
115. Motier Harris Fisher — May 14, 1940
116. Motier Harris Fisher — July 12, 1940
117. Alice Lehmann — July 18, 1940
118. Pamela Diamand — July 21, [1940]

119. William Rothenstein — August 11, 1940
120. Sebastian Sprott — August 11, [1940]
121. G. Davis — August 19, [1940]
122. George Williamson — August 31, 1940
123. David Cecil — [late August/early September 1940]
124. Elizabeth Trevelyan — September 1, [1940]
125. John Farrelly, Jr. — September 4, 1940
126. Arthur Ponsonby — September 8, 1940
127. Agnes Fry — September 23, 1940
128. Lord Bicester — October 1, 1940
    128a. Jack Morgan — September 12, 1940 (enclosure)
129. Isabel Fry — October 11, 1940
130. Rachel Dyce Sharp — October 26, 1940
131. Mary Gordon — November 4, 1940
132. John Farrelly, Jr. — January 18, 1941
133. S. K. Ratcliffe — January 24, 1941
134. Rachel Dyce Sharp — March 9, 1941
135. Rachel Dyce Sharp — March 12, 1941

1
Handwritten; to Leonard Woolf
April 22, 1915

LAMBTON CASTLE,
PENCE HOUSES.
April 22.15

Dear Mr Woolf

One of the few things I have enjoyed lately has been Virginia's book which I sent for as soon as it came out & read with the greatest delight. I would have liked to tell her how much I enjoyed it but I hear she is ill & does not want to be bothered with letters. I am so very sorry she isn't well & I hope she soon will be again & able to enjoy her success. The book is so amazingly fresh & [salt?] it is as good as going to sea – and there are particular things in it which only one in a million can do as they ought to be done. I couldn't have told her how much pleasure it had given me but I would have liked to try. I was amused at getting a letter from the trenches – from a very young guardsman – asking if I had read a new novel called 'The Voyage out' which he had found very entertaining – especially I gathered from its description of political conversation which he no doubt finds pleasantly reminiscent of his elderly uncles. They lead the most painfully boring life I gather (I mean the young men out there – elderly uncles naturally do everywhere) so Virginia deserves a war medal for cheering them up apart from everything else. I do so hope she will be strong again soon – Perhaps someday you will give her my love.

yours sincerely
Eleanor Cecil

I ought to add that I owe you a debt of pleasure too for your book which I read in Paris last autumn & especially for a description of two sisters in it.

Bosanquet-Cecil

Lady Eleanor Cecil (1868-1956), Nelly, was a great friend of Woolf's, worked with her on the "The Book on the Table" series for the *Cornhill* in 1908, was married to Lord Robert Cecil (a peace activist), and later expressed enthusiasm for *Three Guineas* (*WSA* 6: 35). Her postscript refers to Leonard's *The Wise Virgins* (1914).

See also her letters to Leonard Woolf and Vanessa Bell in *A* 9-11, 180-81.

2
Handwritten
October 27, 1922

5 Seaview Terrace, St. Ives, Cornwall.
~~32, Queen's Gate, S.W.7.~~
~~Telephone Western 3175.~~

27 - 10- '22.

Dear Mrs Woolf, We were horrified to see in the "Daily News" today your book reviewed between Silas Hocking & God knows whom. Had my husband not been away you would have been treated as a serious artist – whether with hostility or with admiration – certainly not like this. Do please accept our apologies. We are very sorry (& cross) that they should be necessary.

Yours ever sincerely
Sylvia Lynd

Letters from readers, Letters about specific books

Sylvia Dryhurst Lynd (1888-1952) was the wife of Robert Lynd (1879-1949), who was the literary editor of *The Daily News*. She wrote poetry (*Collected Poems*, 1945), short stories (*The Mulberry Bush and Other Stories*, 1925, rpt. 1970), and novels (*The Chorus*, 1915 and *The Swallow Dive*, 1921) and was the literary editor of the *News Chronicle* for many years. Lewis Bettany reviewed *Jacob's Room* on October 27, 1922, along with Arnold Bennett's *Lillian*, Joseph Hocking's *Prodigal*, and Gladys St. John-Loe's *Dust of the Dawn*.

3
Handwritten
December 12, 1922

~~STATION SHELFORD, G.E.R.~~
~~TELEGRAMS &~~
~~28 SHELDFORD.~~
~~TELEPHONE~~

4 rue de Chevreuse
Paris VIme

Dec. 12. 1922

~~Mount Blow,~~
~~Great Shelford,~~
~~Cambridge.~~

My dear Virginia –

I simply must write to you about *Jacob's Room*. I have admired all your writings enormously but never has any of them swept me off my feet as this ~~have~~ has. To be honest, the beginning (Mrs Flanders & the children & the sea-side) so bored me with its ceaseless flickering of minute observation that I decided I couldn't read it. Then yesterday I began again (right in Trinity) & read on & on, my amazement & admiration growing with every page. I suppose the "libido" of writing has always been a morbid craving to swallow the round green world & all its contents like a pill & to possess it, & I believe you are the first person that has been able to glut that appetite – it is a book which must give *complete* satisfaction to writer & reader alike.

Then, as well, in it you solve for the first time the dilemma of modern literature, by colonising the shadowy New World *imperially* so that it falls into line with & forms an organic whole with the old world of tradition.

It is astonishing how certain pages are *exactly* like Matisse – the same seductive virtuosity, the tip of pen or brush the antenna through which one feels the world – & then other pages are infinitely greater than Matisse, as great writing *must* be.

I am going to begin, these next few days, rewriting my own book, but yours has put me horribly out of conceit with it. However, I think it is in my favour to be able to admire it as wildly as I do.

Yrs.
Hope Mirrlees

MacCarthy-Murry

Hope Mirrlees (1887-1978) was perhaps working on *The Counterplot*, a novel she published in 1924. Hogarth Press had published her long poem *Paris* in 1919. Her other works include *Madeleine, One of Love's Jansenists* (1919), *Lud-in-the Mist* (1926), a fantasy, and *A Fly in Amber: Being an Extravagant Biography of the Romantic Antiquary Sir Robert Bruce Cotton* (1962).

See her letter to Leonard Woolf in *A* 76.

4
Handwritten
July 3, 1925

Dutchlands
Great Missenden
Bucks

July 3rd 1925

Dear Virginia,

I have just finished reading "Mrs. Dalloway". I feel it is absurd to write to you, as of course you know what a wonderful book it is, but I simply must let you know how thrilled I have been by it. I think it is much the greatest modern book. I have never known anything like it – its intoxicating beauty, page after page of pure poetry, and its depth of feeling about people, such detail yet such exaltation, so restrained yet like a torrent pouring from beginning to end – but I must stop this!

Only I have been so absolutely carried away by it – intoxicated, thats the only word. Yet on every page I felt whole worlds of thought being opened out. I wanted to stop, but I couldn't, it was like being swept along. I thought "Jacob's Room" great. But I thought it was something that couldn't be done again, and certainly not done better. But this!

But I feel I shall bore you with my praise. But it's the truth, and much more. I felt I wanted to read on for months and months. It was magic. But clearly I must stop. There's no need to answer. Yours Beatrice Mayor

Letters from readers, Letters about specific books

Beatrice Mayor (1885-1971), Bobo, was staying in a cottage at Great Missenden while her children were at Isabel Fry's experimental farm school at Mayortorne. Along with plays such as *Thirty Minutes in a Street* (1926) and *Little Earthquake* (1939), Beatrice Mayor wrote poetry, works for children, and a novel, *The Stream* (1933). She was the niece of Beatrice Webb and married Robert (Robin) John Grote Mayor (1869-1947), Fellow of King's College, Cambridge, in 1912.

See her letter to Vanessa Bell in *A* 193-94.

5
Handwritten
July 3, [1925]

3rd July

Dear Mrs. Woolf

I have been reading "The Common Reader" with keen pleasure & if you have not sent a copy to GK's Weekly I shd much enjoy writing about it. If you suffer from any anti-Popish or other prejudice against the paper please do not trouble further; otherwise a copy sent to me c/o GK's Weekly 21 Essex St WC2 wd do the trick.

I so seldom like any book nowadays that I rarely volunteer to write about one & I cannot read your novels or anyone else's nowadays; but your essays really captivate me & there is a delicious flavour of Leslie Stephen in them.

I entirely agree with your praise of Max Beerbohm; but perhaps he has told you as he told me what an effort writing is for him as compared with drawing. Please excuse pencil; my pen is used up in signing cheques & business letters & the pencil writes more steadily.

Yours sincerely
ESP Haynes

Farrell-Lubbock

Edmund Sidney Pollock Haynes (1877-1949) wrote books about law (*The Decline of Liberty in England*, 1916), divorce, religious persecution, and women (including a pamphlet entitled *Much Ado About Women* in 1927). *GK's Weekly* (financed by G. K. Chesterton) began in 1925 and became *The Weekly Review* in 1936. Woolf must have sent a copy of *The Common Reader*, because Haynes' review appeared in *GK's Weekly* a month later (15 August 1925: 501).

6
Handwritten
[Summer 1925]

LITTLE LOVETT'S END
HEMEL HEMPSTEAD,
HERTS.

My dear Virginia

The Daily News authorises me to offer you a very humble apology both for their delay in noticing The Common Reader, & for giving it to an inferior reviewer. The reason is that Sylvia Lynd who wished to review it herself has been intermittently ill since Easter – She kept it, hoping for a lucid interval in which to do it justice, but after an operation which she has had just lately passed it reluctantly on to me – I neednt say with what delight I read it, and how I wish I could have had an opportunity of expressing my [sincere?] admiration for Mrs. Dalloway. The appearance of two books by you has made it a wonderful summer!

Yours ever
Olive Heseltine.

Letters from readers, Letters about specific books

Olive Heseltine (1877-1950) reviewed *The Common Reader* in *The Daily News* on August 4, 1925. She published a history of conversation in *Conversation* (1927), a couple of novels under the pen-name of Jane Dashwood, and *Lost Content*, brief childhood reminiscences, in 1948. Her *Essays and Sketches* were published posthumously in 1961. Woolf's reply has been printed as letter 5 in "Covered with honey: five unpublished letters by Virginia Woolf" by Hermione Lee in *TLS*, 3 March 2000: 14. Lee notes that the reply must have been written some time between August and October. The five unpublished letters from Virginia Woolf to Olive Heseltine are in the Monks House Papers at Sussex.

7
Typed; signed
September 16, 1925

BLAIR NILES
144 EAST 36TH STREET
NEW YORK CITY

September 16th. 1925

Dear Virginia Woolf;

Mrs. Dalloway is as stimulating, as exciting, as life itself. I feel about it as you do about some great and personal experience. That, and The Common Reader, have been the high lights of the year for me.

And now may I ask if you will not be good enough to tell me the author of the quotation from the Russian which you so effectively use twice in the Common Reader? It occurs on pages 217 and 245. "You must make yourself akin to people. You must understand them, not with the head, for that is easy, but with the heart" etc.

I want to use it in a book I am doing — an interpretation of Haiti, where God knows it is time that someone tried to understand with the heart.

Faithfully,
Blair Niles

Letters from readers, Letters about specific books

Blair Niles was the pseudonym for Mary Blair Rice (1880-1959), whose most well-known book is *Strange Brother* (1931; rpt. 1975), a novel about gay life in Manhattan. She also helped found the Society of Women Geographers and wrote many travel books, including *Casual Wanderings in Ecuador* (1923), *Black Haiti* (1926), which does not seem to include the quotation she asks about here, and *Condemned to Devil's Island* (1928). The quotation is from "The Village Priest" by Elena Militsina in *The Village Priest, and Other Stories* by Elena Militsina and Mihail Saltikov and translated by Beatrix L. Tollemache, a book Woolf reviewed in "The Russian View" in the *TLS*, 19 December 1918 (*CR*1 256).

8
Handwritten
[November?] 12, [1925]

TELEGRAMS
THACKERAY WESTCENT LONDON
TELEPHONES MUSEUM 1230-1231

THACKERAY HOTEL
(OPPOSITE THE BRITISH MUSEUM)
GREAT RUSSELL STREET
LONDON W.C. 1

Thursday morning
[11?]. XII

Madame,
I am a Frenchman—as my English shows it—and in London only for a few days. I have a deep admiration for you – I really think "Mrs Dalloway" one of the three or four great books I ever read - and I should take it for a great privilege and honor and pleasure if I could see you before leaving London – (I am leaving Sunday morning).

This is a very "brusque" letter. Kindly excuse me. And please believe me

Yours respectfully,
Bernard Faÿ

P.S. My friend R. Mortimer told me I could write to you.

Letters from readers, Letters about specific books

Before World War II, Bernard Faÿ (1893-1979) was decorated for bravery in Belgium and at Verdun in World War I, was a professor of French Literature at the University of Clermont-Ferrand and then filled the Chair of American Civilization at the Collège de France, and was known for his biographies of Benjamin Franklin and F. D. Roosevelt. He became General Director of the French National Library in 1940. After World War II, he was sentenced to life imprisonment for collaborating with the enemy, in particular, directing initiatives against Free Masonry. As Janet Malcolm notes in *The New Yorker*, Faÿ also helped protect Gertrude Stein during the Occupation (2 June 2003: 57-81). He escaped from the Hôpital d'Angiers on September 30, 1951, taught at the University of Freiburg in Switzerland, and was pardoned by Minister of Justice François Mitterand in 1957, when he was allowed to return to France. Barbara Will, Professor of English, Dartmouth College, is writing a book, tentatively titled "Unlikely Collaboration: Gertrude Stein, Bernard Faÿ, and the Vichy Dilemma," about the subtle complexities of the relationship between Stein and Faÿ and between modernism and fascism.

Although "11 XII" would normally be read as 11 December, December 11 was not a Thursday in 1925, and November 12 was. See letter 19 as well.

9
Handwritten
[1925]

TEL. KEN. 557.

5, ONSLOW SQUARE, S.W.

Dear Virginia – You are a wonder & I love you! – I wish I could tell you what your book has meant to me. I've been ill - a [feeling?] of [ ] – but Mrs. Dalloway has provided the most enchanting escape from the depressions of illness & looking forward to an operation – What a strange woman you are – what a mixture – poet – painter – magician – cockney – your touch so light subtle & secure – it takes ones breath away – & of course I cant really appreciate your genius to the full not being a literary cove!

– Thank you ever so much for writing Mrs. Dalloway. Can you write another ? Do please soon – While I try to write [here?] & try to find out how you produced the magic of London – & kept the threads of the story so exquisitely balanced – (if you can balance a thread!)—I'm utterly done in & [confused?] – I cant see how it is done only that there is not a word out of place. – but in spite of the radiant bubble like quality of the book – there is a deep horror in it. which I suppose enhances the beauty – for much of the suicide story is full of beauty, too.

You'll laugh at (– hang – my pen has given out.) this gushing letter – but remember I'm Irish – I have had the greatest delight in your book though I cant put it into words.

Yours ever Eily Darwin.

Letters from readers, Letters about specific books

Eily (Elinor) Mary Monsell Darwin (d. 1954), wood-engraving artist, was married to

Charles Darwin's grandson and Gwen Darwin Raverat's brother, Bernard Darwin, a *Times* golf correspondent. He wrote and she illustrated several children's books, among them *The Tale of Mr. Tootleoo* (1926) and *Oboli, Boboli, and Little Joboli* (1938).

10
Handwritten
April 4, 1927

TELEPHONE
No. 745

BATTLEDOWN HOUSE,
CHELTENHAM.

4. 4. 27.

My dear Mrs Virginia Woolf,

Ever since your extremely nice friend, Miss Snowden, came to see us I have been wishing to tell you what pleasure her little visit gave us, my health has been so uncertain and has prevented my doing almost any writing & I hope you will forgive the delay, also, that you will excuse this effort, my hand is unsteady. My husband has always been interested in art & he found Miss Snowden very congenial, & we hope she will come again; it was so kind of you to think of it. I suppose you are not likely, yourself, to come to Cheltenham?

This afternoon in looking over letters (I am, just now, confined to my room) I came across this – from a clever Oxford woman – "Thank you ever so much for 'Mr. Bennett and Mrs. Brown.' It is delicious, & quite new to us. I had to start reading it at once & couldn't stop till I finished it." I am really not happy in sending you this shabby little note & wish it were better written.

I wonder, might I send my love to you?

Yours sincerely,
Anne E. Smith

Sackville-Stapledon (Snowden folder)

In a letter dated April 20, 1927, Margery Snowden describes the elderly Mrs. Alexandre

Smith as a "great admirer" of Woolf. Margery's visit to the home on Battledown Hill led her to believe that Mr. Smith bought pictures, china, and enamels for collectors, and she describes seeing the couple in an old-fashioned landau with horses and coachman coming right down the center of a High Street crowded with cars. See letter 20 as well.

11
Typed
May 2, 1927

Dear Mrs. Woolf: -

I reckon I had as well follow with the crowd, in making the first word of what I am about to say to you, "Dear"; still I, often feel a sesne of its unfitness—something of protest, and wonder why some one fertile in conceptions has not improved on it, or evolved something that might be used in the alternative on choice, to give a little of variety. There is a need it seems to me, that being fulfilled, would be refreshing. Not every one addressed in letters is "dear" to the addressor. Well, may be I quibble; my sense of dissatisfaction mayhap is a mere finicism, if I make it known what I mean.

Virginia Woolf, novelist: not often have I heard of her. Somewhere, by someone—both forgotten—only the impression remaining that the commentator's opinion challenged deference, which mentioned a novel of your writing—Sunday and Monday, if the title is recalled rightly as being of out standing merit among books appearing about that time, which I could not fix with more of approach to definiteness than the rest.

Thereafter there was a latent want to read something written by the woman, who challenged such an estimate. It came in the May issue of the Forum, through The New Dress.

I have read it twice and went in a ways on a third venture, halting enroute to undertake what I am at. It was an undertaking of labor rather than entrancement. Not food for babes nor the superficial is it: no no. After repeating "NO" through scatter-wit, I had to leave the machine, and what I was going to say escaped me.

I am not a scholar in literature: that I realize; although I may have had the notion not avowed often, due to a certain sensitiveness to the opinion of my fellows, and the quality of hypocrisy called modesty, that I have something of critical insight. One may comment and take the chance of what is said not rising to the dignity of "criticism". Having done with digression for the moment and again taking up "The New Dress", must say and that ungrudgingly, that it has substantive fiber-virility-originality-an individuality of its own; so it appears to me; which estimate may do you credit overmuch. Some one of scholarship in literature might detect imitation in its flavor-inspiration at second-hand.

What you are driving at all the time, I have not determined. This may be due to defect of perception on my part. I have difficulty with some of your sentences - a trouble you may have with some appearing here.

Mabel as I diagnose her mental poise wanted to have an individuality of her own - to be able to stand alone and in defiance of convention; but lacked stamina to put it across when in contact with those she would disregard. Under the stress of a feeling of ridicule or derision which sensed was felt if having no other expression than the exasperating smile that goads so much, all that independence of what "they would say" evanesced like the morning mist. Defiance of convention was an at-home mental attitude with Mabel; face-up with it, she wilted—was the veriest moral poltroon. But after all are not most of us so afflicted? We take on more of the heroic, when the ordeal to be faced is at a distance; more especially is this true, when our fellows hiss rather than when than say "Go to it, old man".

I will likely read T.N.D. again: enough additional can be had from it to pay, I suspect.

I have wanted to do this, but a deterrent to the getting at it, was a feeling of not having the matter well enough in-hand to undertake it. It has been done in time when I have waiting to be called away to a~~nother~~ duty. That still waits. But I am through with this all but a going to make corrections and revise phraseology here and there. Alvah B. Flood, Camas Mont., U.S.A. 5/2/27.

Mrs. Virginia Woolf, somewhere in England

Letters from agents, editors, publishers, etc., Miscellaneous fan mail

12
Handwritten
May 2 [1927]

OXFORD UNIVERSITY ENGLISH CLUB.

May 2nd University College

Oxford.

Dear Mrs Woolf.

I ought long ago to have replied to your letter but was compelled to await the meeting of my Committee which took place this afternoon.

I am extremely grateful to you for promising to come down on the 18th of May. Perhaps you would be kind enough to let me know soon what the title of your paper will be.

Shall you be staying with Mr. Fisher at New College or shall we arrange something for you.

Yours sincerely,
Aubrey Herbert,
Secretary.

Letters from agents, editors, publishers, etc., Letters about articles

---

Aubrey Herbert (1905-1981) was also President of the Oxford Union, a university-wide debating society, in 1928. See letter 14 as well. Evidently Woolf had refused Mr. Herbert's first invitation to come speak to the English Club; see her letter dated March 1, 1927 as printed in *Virginia Woolf Miscellany* 53 (spring 2000): 2.

13
Handwritten
May 2 [1927]

KENSINGTON 1075.

19, QUEEN'S GATE TERRACE,
S.W.7.

9.v.27.

Dear Mrs Woolf,

May I express my appreciation of To the Lighthouse? To me the Ramsays are the outstanding personalities—one cannot use so bald a term as 'characters'—of the season. I am twenty years old and an aspirant to literature (my first novel is coming out shortly) and your work, in conjunction with that of Mr. Aldous Huxley, has influenced me tremendously. There is one point which I find difficult to explain, however. — In its relation to the modern novel isn't the plot similar ~~(& as useless)~~ to the relation of the appendix (& as useless) to the human body?

If I am unduly acquisitive please attribute it to my appreciation of your work.

Sincerely Yours,
Maboth Moseley. (Miss.)

Letters from readers, Letters about To the Lighthouse

Maboth Moseley (b. 1906) published three novels, beginning with *Cold Surge* in 1930, *This Lady Was a Gentleman* in 1931, and *God Created Them Apart* in 1932, plus *War Upon Women: A Topical Drama* in 1934, and *Irascible Genius*, a biography of Charles Babbage, computer pioneer, in 1964.

14
Handwritten
May 11, [1927]

OXFORD UNIVERSITY ENGLISH CLUB.
University College,
Oxford

May 11th

Dear Mrs. Woolf.

I am terribly sorry – but I took rooms at the Clarendon before I got your note. Do you object to that hotel, very much. The Committee would be much honoured if you will dine with them – & your friend too – before the meeting which will be at 8.30 in St Hughes College's CR.

If so be you can dine with us, might I call for you at 7. pm. at the Clarendon & take you over to dinner.

I think that is all. We are so looking forward to Wednesday.

Yours very sincerely
Aubrey Herbert
Secretary

Letters from agents, editors, publishers, etc., Letters about articles

---

See letter 12 for biographical information. A letter from Woolf dated May 9, 1927, published in *Virginia Woolf Miscellany* 53 (Spring 2000): 2, led to this reply from Herbert.

15
Handwritten
May 20, 1927

Dear Mrs Woolf

I would like to know you. You have given me one of the most exciting adventures of my life – adventure in awareness. Though I may be one of the insignificant persons living off the Brompton road, it gives me courage to move my own tree farther to the middle of my picture. A really creative experience, reading your "To the Lighthouse". I write to you before I have finished it—I shall never finish it – it is part of the "eternal present". I read 5 pages or so then I read it again to Caroline – then we go to Dora's with it under the arm and we read those 5 pages again and if Marguerite comes in at the end as she did last night, we read aloud together what precedes the 5 pages and the 5 pages.

The people have not been created or even chosen to serve the purposes of the book—they live and function completely as people. During the dinner, one is aware of Mr Ramsay, of the children, all the time ones attention focusses where you would have it focus, just as it does at ones own family table.

The level of consciousness in that book! What one ~~does~~ absorbs with ones eyes—the dish of fruit, matching color with color, shape with shape—while ones mind is occupied in one place, ones feelings another, ones body a third—

I should like to know how you developed this tool you have that ferrets out the most secret processes of thought and feeling. That Mrs Ramsay should "suspect a thorn in this tangle and disengaging it find it to be this" "She listened: it sounded as if the hall door were open, the bedroom doors open –" "She used the branches of the elm tree to stabilize her position" – "Pure hearted heroic man! But simultaneously she remembered that he objected to dogs on chairs"—all too exciting that you should know that is the way one thinks! – and the business of Q to R to Z – superb of course.

I should like to know you—and I do know you—

Virginia Tooker

Carmel by the Sea
California
Box 483
May 20th 1927

Letters from readers, Letters about To the Lighthouse

A Virginia Tooker is listed as one of the authors of a cartoon map done of Berkeley in

1927-28, "This is the map of Berkeley town: its streets go winding up & down, an oak-covered campus wears for a crown with people & places of renown." It includes portraits of Bishop George Berkeley and Henry Durant.

16
Handwritten
May 28, 1927

17, Park Street, W.1.
tel. grosvenor 1023.

28 May.27.

My dear old Goat,

Just a line to say that I am in the middle of the 'Lighthouse'. It is a masterpiece & leaves me brimful of the music of your words. I have not dared to look to the end & am fearful that it may not end happily as I want it to do for you seem to me to be sitting at some great organ & playing a Bach fugue ~~for~~ of your own composition. I just wonder & listen & watch & seem myself to be some handmaid waiting at table. Im going in & out of the various rooms or watching them all at meals – some of them in some of their moods I know – Leslie, Walter Headlam, & the Woolly one – others I don't. Anyhow you are a genius & it is a work of genius & no one has ever written anything like it not even yourself, before, & you have never reached anything like the same perfection of expression. But, as I say, I have only read half & I dread that it may not end happily, working up to some great major chord as it ought to do or as I think it might & long for it to do. Anyhow you at last spell analyse with an 's' which redeems at last your reputation as a Greek scholar.

Infernal sciatica has laid me low again, for the last fortnight I have been mainly bedridden, swathed in thermogen & heaped about with hot water bottles: but I am to get up for luncheon today & as the capture of a 'long-chained streptococcus' has been officially established from a series of what the dentist calls 'extractions,' though it let loose a flood of poison which has been the cause of this attack, still it is hoped that the breed is being eliminated by degrees & that I may be a whole man before the grave finally claims me for its own, in place of the palsied hobbler that I have been for months past.

So fare thee well & if you have a box of Morisons life pills by you, send them along & I will take them in due course.

Your affect old Bar
G. H. D.

Clifford-Eliot

George Duckworth (1868-1934), the eldest of Herbert and Julia Duckworth's three children, was Virginia Woolf's half-brother. After a career as a civil servant, he was knighted in 1927. See also letter 59.

17
Handwritten
May 30, 1927

CLERKENWELL 7085.

19C, PERCY CIRCUS,
W.C. 1.
May 30th, 1927.

Dear Mrs Woolf,

I should have written to you at once to thank you for returning the stories and particularly for your criticism. I missed the opportunity however before you left and then thought that in Italy you would prefer to dispense with a reminder of King's X, however slight.

I am very happy at the moment in "To the Lighthouse." Unfortunately I read the reviews first.

I hope you will be able to visit me soon would you suggest the day? Also I hope I may come to see the Hogarth Press in action if that is not asking to great a favour.

I am:
yours sincerely,
[Potter?] Lucky

Letters from agents, editors, publishers, etc., Letters about various books

18
Handwritten
June 16, 1927

BEAUFOY HOUSE,
84, MAIDA VALE,
LONDON. W. 9.
16th June 1927

Mrs Virginia Woolf
Dear Madame

I hope you will pardon my trespassing on your time and especially as my request is such a big one. It is this will you please send me an autographed portrait of yourself?

Now as I ask so much of you please tell me if there is anything I can do for you and you will find me ready and delighted to serve you.

I take this opportunity to send you my many many thanks for the happiness and comfort I have derived from your writings. When recovering from a recent operation I passed many enjoyable hours re-reading your books. I am sure if you could peep in sick rooms and see the joy you give you would feel you have not written in vain. I so enjoyed "The Lighthouse" I posted away six copies including one to my dear brother who lives on the far away Chatham Islands

I hope you will write much more and have a long life full of happiness

Just one of your grateful readers
Montague Bull

Letters from readers, Letters about To the Lighthouse

The Chatham Islands are a group of 10 Pacific Islands east of New Zealand.

19
Handwritten (picture of Grand Canyon on stationery)
June 18, 1927

Du GRAND CANYON NATIONAL PARK ARIZONA.

EL TOVAR
FRED HARVEY.

le 18 VI. 27.

Madame,

Vous ne m'avez jamais vu, bien que j'aie cherché à vous voir l'autre année à Londres. Je vous ai écrit jadis pour vous dire combien j'admirais « Mrs Dalloway. » J'ai écrit un article sur ce grand livre, je l'ai publié—et la vie bruyante m'a poussé vers mille autres occupations. Ce printemps à N. Y je me suis trouvé à un Week End ennuyeux dans une chambre qui contenait « The Common Reader, » « Jacob's Room, » « To the Lighthouse. » Je les ai lus d'une traite, et j'ai pleuré comme un enfant de joie, de tristesse, d'admiration. Il me semble que vous êtes l'un des plus grands écrivains et l'une des plus exquises sensibilités qu'ait jamais connus la Littérature Anglaise. Je désire beaucoup vous connaître et écrire un « Grand » article sur votre œuvre. Je rentre en Europe (en France) en Août. Où pourrais je vous voir ? Avez vous la bonté de m'aider un peu ? Je vous assure que c'est du véritable amour que j'ai pour vos livres.

Veuillez agréer, je vous prie, Madame, l'expression de mes plus respectueux hommages.

Bernard Faÿ –

à New York. 27 West 44.
à Paris. 11 rue St Florentin. VIIIeme
Excusez cet absurde papier qui est une fatalité du lieu, et du moment –

[translation by Helen Southworth]
Madam,

We've never met, although I tried to see you a few years ago in London. I wrote to you once in order to tell you how much I admire Mrs Dalloway. I wrote an article on that great book, and published it—and hectic life has gotten me caught up in a thousand other projects. This spring in New York I found myself at a tiresome Weekend in a room which contained The Common Reader, Jacob's Room, To the Lighthouse. I read them all—in one go, and I wept like a child with joy, sadness and admiration. To my mind, you are among the great writers and one of the most exquisite sensibilities that English literature has ever known. I would very much like to get to know you and to write a "great" article on your work—I return to Europe (to France) in August. Where might I be able to see you? Are you willing to help me a little? I assure you that the love I have for your books is a true love.

Yours faithfully,
Bernard Faÿ –

in New York. 27 West 44.
in Paris 11 rue Saint Florentin VIIIth
Please excuse this absurd paper made necessary by the place and the moment

Letters from readers, Letters about To the Lighthouse

See letter 8 for biographical information.

20
Handwritten
June 19, 1927

TELEPHONE
No. 745

BATTLEDOWN HOUSE,
CHELTENHAM.

June 19.27.

My dear Mrs. Virginia Woolf, (This is presumption) I possess, & am reading "To the Lighthouse" & have just reached "Böeuf en Daube" & am so wonderstruck by the scene at the table it occurs to me to tell you how I love it. The trains of thought running through the minds of Lily Briscoe, & of Mrs. Ramsey so amazingly true, 'tis really a great 'mental uplift'(!) & you are a magician! At first I thought I should not be able, always, to follow Mrs. Ramsey but now I revere & enjoy. This does not, in the least, indicate that Helen Ambrose is less to me, certainly not. In Mrs. Ramsey (one <u>can't</u> say 'Mrs. R' of such a woman!) you have a mind 'worthy of your steel' & I thank you for bringing such to life. Have you read Mrs. Wharton's 'Twilight Sleep'? So clever, but not good enough matter for Edith Wharton. I do not quite know if I shd bother you with letters but knowing Mrs. Ramsey—think you will not be angry.

Affectionately yours
Anne E. Smith

How I wish we were having "Boeuf en Daube"!

Letters from readers, Letters about To the Lighthouse

See letter 10 for biographical description.

21
Handwritten
October 17, 1927

THE ROUNDEL GATE,
RYE,
17th Oct. 1927 SUSSEX.

Dear Mrs Woolf

You probably get only too many letters about your books—and we know well what a bother such letters are to answer!—but my sister & I always feel that the ones which ring true encourage a writer in spite of the trouble they entail.

So we want to tell you what a perfect thing we considered "To the Lighthouse" when we read it in Scotland a month ago. "Quite perfect" – to use a stupid phrase. It is so complete that it transcends its medium. You don't read it – you see it, feel it, realize it, and forget the printed page. Even the trophy of fruit on the dinner table with its pink shell, has perfume & substance—and the minds ~~that~~ creep through the empty house with their own sounds instead of words!

Mrs. Ramsay's death, I think, must come to every reader with a personal shock of regret.

We hope you will go forward now & feel braced up for further effort, & never be haunted by the Writer's Evil Genius—fear of the next book falling below the last! But you have fixed the target very high this time!

With great admiration, & thanks for the pleasure you have given us in "To the Lighthouse"—(I speak for my sister also)

Believe me

yours sincerely

Mary W. Findlater

Letters from readers, Letters about To the Lighthouse

Mary W. Findlater (1865-1963) and sister Jane Findlater (1866-1946) wrote popular novels, both together (*Crossriggs*, 1908; *Penny Moneypenny*, 1911, and *Beneath the Visiting Moon*, 1923) and separately, Mary publishing *Betty Musgrave*, 1899 and *The Rose of Joy*, 1903, among others, and Jane publishing *The Green Graves of Balgowrie*, 1896 and *The Story of a Mother*, 1902, among others. Woolf's reply, dated October 22, 1927, is published in Eileen MacKenzie's *The Findlater Sisters: Literature and Friendship* (1964), 116-17. She mentions meeting with "Mr Ashcroft & Miss Findlater, fervent admirers" on October 22 (*D*3 161).

22
Handwritten
July 3, 1928

383 MADISON AVENUE
NEW YORK

July 3, 1928

Dear Mrs. Woolf:

On finishing Orlando I feel I must tell you that no more satisfying and moving experience has come my way in a long time. The expectations raised by the first chapter are more than realized by the later ones. What an instrument the language becomes in your hand! And the clear beauty of the style is matched by the sharp delicacy of the fancy, and the extraordinary selection you have exercised in matters great and small over this vast scene.

Such a book is a challenge to a publisher. May a little of what inspired you descend on our unworthy heads!

Faithfully & gratefully yours
Donald C Brace

Letters from agents, editors, publishers, etc., Donald Brace

Donald Brace (1881-1955) and Alfred Harcourt, Columbia classmates, founded Harcourt Brace in 1919. They published John Maynard Keynes, Lytton Strachey, Sinclair Lewis, Carl Sandburg, and Katherine Anne Porter, among others, and Brace's trips to England led to contracts with many in the Bloomsbury Group.

Several letters from Donald Brace exist in the Monks House Papers, but this is the only handwritten one. See Woolf's reply, July 16, 1928, *L*3 513 (1910). Mark Hussey notes Selma Meyerowitz's assertion, based on her study of the Berg Collection correspondence between Leonard Woolf and Donald Brace, that "the American publisher took a personal interest in Woolf's work" (*Virginia Woolf A to Z* [NY: Facts on File, 1995], 41, referring to *VWM* 17: 7). Brace's correspondence with Woolf at Sussex bears this assertion out, as does his telegram after Woolf's death and Leonard Woolf's reply in *A* 52. See letter 106.

23
Handwritten
July 31, 1928

The Two Brewers Inn.
Shaftesbury
Dorset.

31.7.28.

Dear Mrs Woolf,

You once remarked that only ninnies wrote to you about your books – which is useful, because it relieves me of any self-consciousness now that I am doing it too. It seems to me it would be practically insincere to take Orlando down in silence – though anything like thanking, on the other hand, would be too awful & impertinent, & not what one wants to do anyway. But every now & then, but not with any other living writer, it does seem necessary to do something more than merely read (which is of course all that can be done reasonably). It is because there is nothing to discuss I think, no places to say here is good but there is better, it is so unusual to have to accept a whole book, & the experience produces such delight & despair that one makes a fool of oneself.

There is a man ~~at~~ who every year at Hendon gives an exhibition of flying; he gets the sky to himself for about a quarter of an hour, & it must all be a matter of style, because he is using the same medium as the hundreds of other perfectly competent pilots who perform before & after him, but he is right to a hair's breadth where the others are right to within half a yard.

Yours sincerely,
Alice Ritchie.

Letters from readers, Letters about Orlando

Alice Ritchie (1897-1941) was a part-time employee of Hogarth Press at this time, traveling with books. As Woolf notes in her reply, dated August 3, 1928, in *L6* 522 (1911a), Alice Ritchie was the first person besides herself and Leonard to read *Orlando*, so she asked Ritchie not to say anything to anyone until it was published (which occurred on October 2, 1928). In her diary entry for August 12th (*D3* 191), Woolf notes Alice's praise, but cannot accept it at face value, suspecting it is the result of a loan. Hogarth Press published Alice Ritchie's novel, *The Peacemakers*, in 1928 and *Occupied Territory* in 1930. Hogarth Press also published her posthumous children's book, *The Treasure of Li-Po*, with illustrations by Trekkie Ritchie Parsons, in 1948.

See her letter to Leonard Woolf in *A* 134-35.

24
Handwritten
October 23, 1928

WATER TOWER STUDIO
CHESTER.

23 X 28

Dear Madam,

Will you accept my congratulations, however puerile on "Orlando"? It certainly gives furiously to think, and one must out with (a bit of) it or burst. When one 'discovers' a pearl, one is apt to make oneself a general nuisance, crowing continuously like any barnyard chanticleer, even (you see) makes one fly (& flap flurriedly one's bedraggled wings) in the face of providence. If "Monday or Tuesday" was a comet, & that of no mean order, in our sky, if "Jacob's Room" was a lantern whose 1001 colours will always illume our night, Orlando is a fixed planet. I am no astronomer, but you will I think know what I mean. There is a <u>richness</u> of personality about it which of course would have been out of place in Jacob's room say. One wonders where you 'got the idea from.' This is a great deal of your charm as a writer. You are not of those mannish steady & stolidly, sometimes jolly Bank holiday, scribes, who for all their good writing make it clear that their word is law. "I know all about this. You don't. You <u>must</u> take my word for it. Take it or leave it." You have always, it seemed to me, had a game with your reader, have played – & fair. You may even on occasion have him, as they say, on a piece of string, & pull the leg. Conversation is like a game of tennis—there are 2 sides to the game—& each must keep its end up. Your writing always creates & suggests other images in the mind. To read your work is to indulge in the most stimulating intellectual exercise (this is not to say that you can't get our sympathies). Personally when I'm "fed" I always take you as one does the daily dozen. But I prose intolerably . . . . I wonder if I'm any better at verse. A sonnet of mine does a little express my feelings.

Innermost Asia & the furthest land
Lie rigidly mapped, & <u>Hic leaves</u>
<u>Sunt</u> to tame nomenclature gives place.
— Holiday mood royal mummies will unbind.
Life peters out to [astral?] [core?], to rind
Of ice, and pioneers in time & space

Epitomize the whole explorers' race,
Where all is known, & void.
                                        Remains the mind,
Uncharted jungle, with its beasts & beauties.
Red admirals by day, tigerish eyes by night
Illume its thickets. Yet nor Freud nor lover
Can pierce its tawny shades, its blinding light,
A tithe of all its prodigies & riches,
Never shall Human Sesame discover.

You can treasure the ages, & not forget the mind. You can throw a thousand beams into the mind, & because you are not puffed up continually enlighten, create, & recreate. Let me meet the "gentleman from America" & I will Tunney him to extinction!

Yours gratefully,
E. Clark.

Letters from readers, Letters about Orlando

Gene Tunney was the Heavyweight Boxing Champion from 1926-1928.

25
Handwritten
October 23, 1928

THE YALE REVIEW
A NATIONAL QUARTERLY

WILBUR CROSS
EDITOR
HELEN MCAFEE
MANAGING EDITOR
EDWARD BLISS REED
ASSISTANT EDITOR

YALE STATION
NEW HAVEN
CONNECTICUT

October 23 1928

Dear Mrs. Woolf,

Your letter offering to do just what I had asked you to do in one sent a few days ago—hold the "Evening at Dr. Burney's" in England until March when we could print it here—has just come to us. If "Life and Letters" wishes to publish it in its March number (or later), we shall be able to do the same and will do so with pleasure. And so we needn't press you for the manuscript immediately.

I hear "Orlando" being talked of wherever I go. May I say that I took it up with anxiety and put it down with exaltation? It is as noble and rich as Orlando's country seat, which I like to think of as Knole, remembering a happy day I spent there last June. I like to think of the whole record as an autobiography—of the sort I should have wished from you. Among the parts, I enjoyed especially, as a Near Eastener by adoption, the fabulous details of the Turkish interlude – a delightful reference to the old travellers. You have put us all once more in debt to the English language and the English mind, and I hope the reception of the book will add something, though it cannot add much, to the sense of accomplishment you must have had in writing it.

Very sincerely yours,
Helen McAfee

Letters from agents, editors, publishers, etc., Correspondence about publications

---

Helen McAfee (1884-1956) graduated from Smith College in 1903, did graduate work at

Yale University, and then taught at the American School for Girls in Constantinople before she became associated with *The Yale Review*, where she was managing editor from 1925 until 1949.

This letter was part of the negotiations about "Dr. Burney's Evening Party" for *The Yale Review*. See letters from Woolf dated September 23, 1928 (1925), October 7, 1928 (1937), and October 15, 1928 (1940) in *L*3 532, 544, 545. However, since cables from McAfee followed the first two letters, the one above may reply to the last letter from Woolf, dated October 15, or to another letter that has not survived, one more specific about the March date. See also *D*3 200.

26
Handwritten
October 28 [1928]

15 King Henry's Rd
N.W.3.

28th October

Dear Mrs Woolf,

I enclose a review of your remarkable book. Believe me, that I am very sensible of the honour of having been permitted to express my sense of its rich and whimsical contents. I am only too conscious that my 'prentice hand has failed to convey to the reader its unique quality. But if to write of it was the hardest of labours, to read it was an unalloyed joy. I have not ~~had~~ experienced such pleasure from any work of the imagination ~~since~~ in post-war days.

Faithfully yours
P.H. Wallis

Mrs Virginia Woolf
The Hogarth Press.
[enclosure missing]

Letters from readers, Letters about Orlando

According to the condolence letter Wallis sent to Leonard Woolf in 1941, he received a "gracious letter" in reply to the above (*A* 169-70), but Woolf's reply, the Wallis review of *Orlando*, and biographical information about P. H. Wallis have not been located.

27
Handwritten
[Octorber/November] 6, [1928]

6th

SLOANE 5880. 44, HANS MANSIONS,
KNIGHTSBRIDGE.

Dear Virginia,

I lunched with Clive yesterday & I was telling him that I had just finished Orlando & how I had thought of writing you a very little note because of all the pure pleasure you have given to me through it, only I refrained at the last moment. Because you are a Great Woman of English Letters & one is shy of saying anything that approaches the Art of the Great. But Clive persisted in saying you like little notes from admiring readers! And so, here it is.

For I go on struggling to form my very small [print?] letters & to read Orlando is almost to have bird's wings instead of literature, pinned down, really, transfixed, for one to read

May I just say how perfectly excited, amused, & carried away I was by your book. Thank you – I adore books.

Yours

Bea

Letters from readers, Letters about Orlando

Leonard Woolf identifies Bea as Beatrice Isabel Howe (b. 1898), who married Mark Lubbock in 1930. Bea had sent some stories to Woolf in 1926; see Woolf's letter rejecting the stories in *Charleston Magazine* issue 4 (winter/spring 1991/92): 6-7. See also Woolf's letter to Vanessa Bell, dated June 2, 1926, *L*3 271 (1644). Bea Howe was the author of *A Fairy Leapt Upon My Knee* (1927).

28
Handwritten
[early November 1928]

7, GROSVENOR SQUARE,
W. 1.

Dear Mrs Woolf

I will love to see you on Monday Nov. 5 – at 5 or 5:30 whichever suits you. I long to see you & tell you how much I love your Orlando. What a wonderful book & what style! You are the greatest of all English writers.

Yrs ever
Emerald Cunard

Letters from readers, Letters about Orlando

According to Woolf's diary, she had tea with Lady Cunard on November 7, 1928 (*D*3 200). Maud ('Emerald') Cunard (1872-1948) was a "patroness of the arts and celebrated hostess" (*D*3 202, n2). Rupert Hart-Davis edited a collection of letters written by George Moore to Lady Cunard, *Letters to Lady Cunard, 1895-1933* (1957).

29
Typed; signed
November 7, 1928

THE SATURDAY REVIEW
OF LITERATURE
25 WEST 45TH STREET, NEW YORK CITY

HENRY SEIDEL CANBY, Editor
AMY LOVEMAN, Associate Editor
WILLIAM ROSE BENÉT, Associate Editor
CHRISTOPHER MORLEY, Contributing Editor

November 7, 1928.

Mrs. Virginia Woolf,
52, Tavistock Square,
W.C.1,
London, England.

My dear Mrs. Woolf:

I am sending you a copy of "The Saturday Review," today, with the necessarily inadequate appreciation of mine of your "Orlando" – inadequate because you have put so much into that book which suggests comment that a really thoroughgoing study would have been so long as to be an impertinence. I got the greatest pleasure from "Orlando" and if I have misunderstood you, as I may very possibly have done, or said some foolish things please forgive me and believe that if I had felt that I could write ten thousand words one half as brilliant as your 60,000, I should have risked the impudence of letting so much annotation weight upon an admirable text.

I wish you would write some time for "The Saturday Review."

Very truly yours,
Henry S. Canby,
Editor-The Saturday Review.

MS
[enclosure missing]

Letters from readers, Letters about Orlando

Henry Seidel Canby (1878-1961) edited *The Saturday Review of Literature* from 1924-1936, taught at Yale University for more than 20 years, and acted as chairman of the Book-of-the-Month Club from 1926-1954. His review of *Orlando* was printed in *The Saturday Review of Literature* on 3 November 1928: 313, and is reprinted in Eleanor McNees, ed. *Virginia Woolf: Critical Assessments* (Mountfield: Helm, 1994) II: 416-21. Woolf had published "American Fiction" in the magazine on 1 August 1925: 1-3, but did not place anything else in it.

30
Handwritten
November 9, 1928

Nov:9/28 3, SUMNER PLACE, S.W.7.

Dear Virginia

Are you back from Burgundian adventures? & can we see you? or would you come to tea on Monday the 19th? In spite of being "carriage folk" we don't seem to get about Sussex as much as I hoped or I spend much of my time on the road to & from London, the dullest of all, instead of slipping over to Rodmell. Do try to make Monday possible as there seem to be so few days when Bruce & I are in together.

At the risk of being a bore, I want to tell you how immensely I enjoyed "Orlando". I had the fun of meeting her & found her as delightful as you made her & that is a great Compliment.

Yours ever
Elena Richmond

Letters from readers, Letters about Orlando

Elena Rathbone Richmond (1878-1964) had known the Stephen children in Kensington, and Thoby had admired her. A supporter of District Nursing, a pioneer in the registration of midwives, and the Queen's Institute representative on the Central Midwives Board from 1925-1951, she married Bruce Richmond, editor of *TLS*, in 1913.

31
Handwritten
November 13, 1928

A Nursing - Home
November 13th 28.

Dear Virginia Woolf,

I have no excuse for writing to you: but please accept this burst of gratitude.

I had a baby a few days ago. I spent a restless night of boredom and wretchedness. At 5 o'clock this morning in desperation I picked up a book my husband had brought me last evening—"Orlando"

I read until 8: and am a different creature.

What an exquisite book! I thank you on behalf of all sick persons for such stimulating and delightful reading.

From a sincerely grateful
convalescent

Letters from readers, Letters about Orlando

32
Handwritten
December 4, 1928

21 Hyde Park Place
W.2

Dec. 4 1928

Dear Virginia

Your brilliant fantasy 'Orlando' raises this puzzle among a lot of others—most likely intended—what are the proper limits of incredibility? – or perhaps rather

– why does the reader swallow the greater impossibilities and stick at smaller incongruities? —

Clearly you are free to play the devil with Greenwich time in a world where a man can turn into a woman – but to rub it in by mentioning thirty years – just that number – as his/her age at the critical point sets the reader a counting: Why, he must have been born about the time of the Civil War — and a page to Queen Elizabeth? — and what was Charles II about to send such a veteran old man on an embassy?

But I mean irrelevant little impossibilities — Cheroots in Constantinople temp. Charles II? They are of South-Indian or Philippine origin, unknown in Europe till c. 1725 < as that joyful book Hobson-Jobson shall fructify unto you> – and I don't believe Turks ever smoked them. One feels like exclaiming—now I know she's lying (for the whole thing rests on Lady ?'s recollection) (We are not told by what name she was called), nor her exact rank.

And scarlet trousers in Hyde Park – I never saw the like even in India where one sees most things of most colours. There is or was one Hussars regiment with red – not scarlet - trousers (The Cherubims per metatheism hope Sister Modesty be not looking over your shoulder) — Undress trousers of the Guard are blue-black with narrow red stripe for foot, broad for horse — As for policemen carrying a royal warrant even if it came through the Home Office—there she must be chaffing: and she has had experience enough of family business to know without my very learned friend Sayer's aid that no warrant or charter – nothing short of Act of Parliament—can make or alter a settlement. (The Truth! is rather that Her victory was in a judgment rendered with gusto by Westbury, or with pious searchings of heart by the pious Selborne wondering whether the facts or the law or both were bewitched—as of course they were)

The Moral a Brahman or Buddhist might draw is that it is not good to remember former lives except for the very wise and holy persons – the Buddha and a few others—who edify their disciples with episodes from them.

The country house is uncommonly like Knole but the situation (no doubt purposely) ambiguous, though the Old Kent Road rather gives it away.

Anyhow she can always say to any captious remarks that it was only her fun.

Yours sincerely
F. Pollock

Letters from readers, Letters about Orlando

Frederick Pollock (1845-1937) was a friend of Leslie Stephen's, collaborated with F. W. Maitland on *The History of English Law*, had a lengthy correspondence with Oliver

Wendell Holmes (published in 1941), and was Editor-in-Chief of *Law Reports* from 1895-1935; his work on contract and tort law is still consulted. Woolf mentions him in a letter to Saxon Sydney-Turner on May 31, 1925, *L3* 186 (1557).

33
Typed; signed [last line handwritten up side of page]
December 22, 1928

TEL.
WINDSOR 31.

MANOR COTTAGE.
CLEWER GREEN,
WINDSOR,
BERKS.

22nd December, 1928.

My dear Mrs. Virginia Woolf,

For some weeks now I have been intending to write to you; however, perhaps it may be just as well that I have waited until such time as there has abated what has no doubt been a spate of letters about your last book.

Will you ~~now~~ allow one whom you once buried (deeper than Caesar) now to praise it?

To praise is an impertinence – but Lord, how I did enjoy it. I even went to what you, as a writer, must confess was an extreme length in dealing with any book. I bought it – (and this after having read it in the Times Library.) Actions speak louder than words.

I also read it aloud to my husband. This was on the evening of the day when I had dragged him up for the first time into an aeroplane; with the result that the two things are inseparably connected in his mind. As he saw for the first time the countryside looking so different, so he also felt that it was from an aeroplane that he received this vivid, brilliant glimpse down onto English history. The Great Frost was marvelous but beaten, if I may say so, by the Great Damp a couple of centuries later. I hope you will not think all this is gratuitous, but will accept it as a small acknowledgement of great pleasure given to yours ever sincerely,

Berta RUCK

Letters from readers, Letters about Orlando

Berta Ruck (1878-1978), had been "buried" in *Jacob's Room.* See Bell, II, 91-92. Ruck was hugely popular, writing two novels a year for many years, for a total of almost 80. She married the writer Oliver Onions (later George Oliver) in 1909. Woolf's reply to this letter, dated December 25, 1928, is held in Manuscripts, Archives and Special Collections, New Holland Library, Washington State University. See Diane Gillespie, "Virginia Woolf and The Curious Case of Berta Ruck," *Woolf Studies Annual* 10 (2004): 109-38.

34
Handwritten
October 28, 1929

Girton College
Cambridge.

Oct 28th 1929.

Dear Mrs Woolf.

As I am the Secretary of the Odtaa Club at Girton & had the pleasure of hearing the paper you read to us, I am writing to thank you for sending a presentation copy of your book. I shall value it very much, chiefly because in it you have expressed far better than anyone else could, the subtle atmosphere of discouragement which prevents so many intelligent women from ever plunging wholeheartedly into artistic work. This sounds most prosaic as I have put it, but if I stop to think of elegant phraseology I shall never be able to express it at all. You can see that I come hot from reading your book, & feel so encouraged by it that I have dared to do what I have considered to be characteristic of American journalists—write to the author about it. You will I am sure receive plenty of congratulations from "those in authority" (to use a Cambridge phrase), and I don't expect this letter will be required to dispell any doubts you might have as to the reception your book will have; but I might as well write & tell you the effect it has had upon me personally. You noticed at once the sort of differences which exist in Cambridge between the men's & the women's Colleges, & there is no need to mention how strong is the disdain for women up here. As a matter of fact it doesn't upset me so much now as it used to, since I have quite a number of male friends & don't live in College any more, where the feeling of inferiority is intensified by the fact of everybody labouring under it. But at a Debate between Girton & King's yesterday, I was quite ashamed of myself for wincing under the cheap insults made against the female race in general & us in particular. The worst of this attitude to Girton is that it either depresses us extremely & takes away the spontaneity of our work, or else it makes us turn our thoughts to lighter things entirely,—such as looking after our figures & clothes & attractiveness—and so justify the superior young Dons in disparaging the quality of our brains. I have been sorely tempted, (& indeed have fallen, I'm afraid for long periods together,) to think only about such things, but all the time I have felt that it was 'An expense of spirit in a waste of shame' – So you can see that your book had the sort of effect on me that the Salvation Army claims to have on weak transgressors! Knowing myself I am sure that this sudden enthusiasm & freedom of spirit will fade sooner or later, but at the moment I am so much rejoicing in it that I thought I must write & thank you for bringing it about!

With very many thanks, & in the hope that you will write something else before long,

Yours very sincerely
Margaret E. Thomas.

Stephen-Turner

Margaret Thomas (1907-) married Sir Edward Bullard, the scientist, in 1931. She published three novels, *Wedlock's the Devil* (1951), *A Perch in Paradise* (1952), about Cambridge, and *Love Goes West* (1953), based on material from her husband's summer work at the Scripps Institution in the 1950s. Margaret, a student at Girton from 1926-1930, was one of the young women responsible for inviting Woolf to speak at Cambridge (*D*3 200-01, n4). Margaret Thomas was president of ODTAA (One Damn Thing After Another) in 1928 and Irene Bliss (later Spry) was secretary. Two unpublished letters from Virginia Woolf to Irene Bliss, dated January 29, 1928 and February [12?], 1928 are in the Girton archives (see S. P. Rosenbaum, ed. *Women & Fiction* [Oxford: Blackwell, 1992], xvii, and Naomi Black, *Virginia Woolf as Feminist* [Ithaca: Cornell UP, 2004], 110, 217, n26). See letter 55.

35
Handwritten
October 28, 1929

THE FROEBEL SOCIETY
AND JUNIOR SCHOOLS ASSOCIATION

Founded 1874. Incorporated 1891.
"CHILD LIFE" – Four times a year.
LENDING LIBRARY..
SCHOLASTIC AGENCY FOR TEACHERS
AND GOVERNESSES.
Hours 11 to 5 (Saturdays 11 to 1).
Library 11 to 6 (Saturdays 11 to 2).
Telephone: HOLBORN 7544
Secretary and Librarian –
Miss M. G. OSTLE,
N.F.U. Teacher's Cert. And Trainer's Diploma

4 BLOOMSBURY SQUARE
LONDON, W.C.1.

28
10
29.

Dear Madam:

From the sole of my shoes let me thank you for "A Room of One's Own." I read it in a Nursing Home & did not even remember the time to go to the theatre. The truth of the book lives & someday, let us hope, will be known. But only you have ever expressed it so convincingly.

Let me thank you again

Yours faithfully
M. G. Ostle

Letters from readers, Letters about A Room of One's Own

Mary Geraldine Ostle (b.1880) edited Evelyn Wilson's *The Notebooks of a Woman Alone* (1935), a project she says was "started" by *A Room of One's Own* when she writes to Woolf about *Three Guineas* (*WSA* 6: 18-19). The kindergarten movement spread through the establishment of Froebel Societies worldwide; the current International Froebel Society is housed in the School of Education Studies at Roehampton University.

36
Handwritten
November 6, 1929

38, CHEYNE WALK,
S.W.3
November 6 1929

Dear Mrs. Woolf

A natural timidity has kept me hesitating on the brink of writing to thank you for the delight of "A Room of One's Own" – for I don't know why your readers should suppose you want to know their opinions. But it has been a very great pleasure to me to hear a unanimous chorus going on everywhere and to see what a remarkable effect your wise and beautiful and immensely liberating book is having. We are buying it in dozens.

Yours sincerely
Theodora Bosanquet

Bosanquet-Cecil

Theodora Bosanquet (1881-1961) is best known as Henry James' amanuensis, and Hogarth Press published her *Henry James at Work* in 1924. But as Larry McMurtry points out in "Almost Forgotten Women" (*The New York Review of Books*, 7 November 2002: 51-52), she also wrote an excellent biography of Paul Valery (Hogarth Press, 1933). Her other works include a biography of Harriet Martineau (1927) and a novel with Clara Smith called *Spectators* (1916). She was Secretary of the International Federation of University Women between 1920-1935 and worked with Viscountess Rhondda as Literary Editor of *Time and Tide*. Her unpublished diaries and other papers are at the Houghton Library, Harvard. See Woolf's reply to this letter, dated November 7, 1929, *L*4 107 (2095).

37
Handwritten
November 7, 1929

THE DEANERY
BARNARD COLLEGE
THREE THOUSAND AND SEVEN BROADWAY
New York
U.S.A.

Nov. 7, 1929.

Dear Mrs. Woolf

I have just finished reading A Room of One's Own, & it has excited & delighted me so greatly that I cannot refrain from writing to thank you for it, & for the acute pleasure you have given me.

You express with such perfection, whimsically, imaginatively & so vividly, what I, with numberless other women, know to be the truth, that people – both men & women – may heed it, just because your ~~have~~ genius has clothed it in this delightful form.

I have taught young women – as well as some men – for nearly 30 years, & I have always had the profoundest belief in the potential powers – intellectual & artistic – of women, & in common with nearly all women who have tried to use their brains, have realised how incalculably these powers have been thwarted, cramped or extinguished by circumstances & convention. And you have shown it all in a few words, in the story of Shakespeare's sister alone.

Yet how amazingly women have risen above it at times – I wonder do you know that in full mid Victorian England, in addition to the greatest authority & innovator on army hygiene being a woman, & the greatest battle painter being a woman (Lady Butler) that the head of the Army medical service was a woman (disguised as a man of course) Dr. James Barry? (see D.N.B.)

My life goes back almost to mid-Victorian times. I began to educate myself at the age of 25, & 17 years later I was the first woman to be elected to a University Chair in England, (English Literature, Univ of London), so I know all about it, though my own small efforts are in the direction of scholarship, for I have no imaginative gift.

I can hardly tell you how much I admire & delight in your writings, & how proud you make me of being a woman.

I should so much like to meet you if you ever had half an hour to spare, but I don't want to intrude upon that 'room of your own'.

Someone told me you lived near me in Sussex – at Firle. I wonder is that true? I have a cottage nearby Old Postman's Cottage
Alciston, Polegate, Sussex
which is my permanent address, & where I hope to be in a month's time. With renewed thanks,
I am yours sincerely Caroline F. E. Spurgeon

Letters from readers, Letters about A Room of One's Own

By permission of Royal Holloway, University of London.

Caroline F. E. Spurgeon (1869-1942) was an English literary scholar whose *Shakespeare's Imagery and What It Tells Us* (1935) was influential and whose other work included a preface that joined Sir Walter Scott's introduction to Horace Walpole's *The Castle of Otranto* (1907), a study of five hundred years of Chaucer criticism (1925; rpt. 1960), and a study called *Keats's Shakespeare* (1929). She was head of the English literature department at Bedford College for Women from 1913-1929 and helped found the International Federation of University Women, serving as its first president from 1920-1924. Her papers are at the Royal Holloway, University of London, which was founded as a college for women in 1879.

38
Handwritten
November 22, 1929

---

55 High Street
Hampstead
November 22. 1929.

Dear Mrs Woolf,

May I say how delighted I was by "A Room of One's Own"? Not only by the argument and your exhilarating wit, but by the exquisite passages of description.

When one hears about people in the past, nearly out of their minds with excitement waiting for the new Dickens or George Eliot to come out, and compare it with one's own rapture on hearing that something more of yours is going to be published, it makes one feel that the past with all the Jane Austens and Charlotte

Brontës is not cut off absolutely from the present as one always felt it was as a child, and that to be alive at the same time as you is the same kind of excitement being given to us that the other contemporaries had. Although I first read some of your novels when I was too young to value them properly, I knew even then that they were in the same category as what we had understood to be great literature.

I am afraid this is clumsily put, and you have had it said very much better many times over.

Yours sincerely
Elizabeth Jenkins.

Farrell-Lubbock

Elizabeth Jenkins (1905-) became a distinguished biographer (see *D*3 182, n1), publishing studies of Lady Caroline Lamb (1932), Jane Austen (1938), Henry Fielding (1947), and Elizabeth the Great (1958), among others. She also wrote novels, including *Virginia Water* (1930), *Harriet* (1934), for which she won the Femina Vie Heureuse prize, and *Honey* (1968). Woolf mentions having had tea with her in a letter to Vanessa Bell, dated May 9, 1928, *L*3 495 (1893).

39
Handwritten
December 2, 1929

THE BURLTON INSTITUTE
MISS GLADYS BURLTON, B.A. (Lond.)
30 MANCHESTER ST., MANCHESTER SQ., W.1

Telephone: Mayfair 5663 Telegrams: Burlton Mayfair 5663
STAFF AGENCY (licensed by the L.C.C.) STAFF TRAINING SERVICE PUBLIC LECTURES CONSULTATIONS
SERVICE AND VALUE TESTING Author of RETAIL SELLING

December 2nd 1929

Dear Miss Virginia Woolf

I have just put down A Room of One's Own, the most exciting book I have read since Heloïse and Abelard.

You will not want to be pestered with letters from all the women whose minds you have set in a ferment, and I confess I am acting on a merely selfish impulse in writing to thank you.

There is a problem which faces women who earn your £500 & a room etc. It is how to conserve their energy so as to leave a margin for authorship. I myself earn by my wits a comfortable income, but at such a sacrifice that at the end of the day, I am too tired to concentrate on writing.

Yet the idea you seem to hold that ordinarily intelligent people can by writing exactly what they think about this and that pave the way for the advent of "Shakespeare's sister" is so delightful that I am encouraged to continue my efforts.

If tomorrow I have any left of today's courage – or is it impudence – I will post you this letter & also a copy of my one and only book, though it deals with neither travel nor research nor history nor philosophy nor science. It is merely an attempt to put down what I think about one branch of business life.

Yet you have, as I said, excited me with the thought that I may in some minute degree help to give Shakespeare's sister the opportunity she has been waiting for all these centuries.

Yours truly
Gladys Burlton

[enclosure missing, or perhaps not sent]

Letters from readers, Letters about A Room of One's Own

Gladys Burlton published *Retail Selling* with Jonathan Cape (1927), and it was reprinted by Burlton Institute (1937, 1946); it is not in the Leonard and Virginia Woolf Library at Washington State University, though that does not mean Woolf never received it. Burlton continued writing about business, publishing *Warehouse Selling* in 1940 and *Selling Textiles* in 1960.

40
Handwritten
December 4, 1929

TELEPHONE at 6 LOWNDES SQUARE,
SLOANE 4022. S.W.1.

December 4th 1929

Dear Madam

Believe me I am setting out to do something that I find very difficult. I am seldom moved to the desire to write to tell an author how intensely I have enjoyed a piece of work. On the few occasions when I have been so moved I have resisted the impulse, but the wish to write to you & tell you how sincerely I admire your work has proven too strong to be resisted.

When I read To the Lighthouse—soon after it first appeared—I thought it one of the loveliest things I had ever read.

Orlando appealed to me too, but not in the same way.

Now I have been enjoying A Room of One's Own, & all your amusing, imaginative & stimulating treatment of your subject.

Apart from your beautiful & individual English, it is, I think, the quality of mind that stirs me, & I feel very deeply your power & importance as a writer. To the Lighthouse moves me, of course, also by its perfect artistry.

May I offer my wholehearted thanks for the real pleasure (it is more than pleasure) that you have given me?

Yours faithfully
(Miss) Lois Jarred.

Letters from agents, editors, publishers, etc., Letters about various books

41
Handwritten
December 30, 1929

Villa Lorenzi
Dec 30. 1929 42 Via Taddeo Alderotte
Florence. 8R.

Dear Madam.

I have just read your book, A Room of Ones Own, and with most of it I deeply agree. What you say needed saying. I think with you that a century or two will be wanted before women's brains will reach a point of development when they can produce work comparable with that of men. But women are growing so fast that it may not need more than that; still, they have not only to achieve financial independence and a room of their own, but freedom from all those inhibitions which thousands of years have rubbed well into their minds, and of which they are commonly unaware. This is no more than you have said; also that the present tiresome obsession with sex, which obstructs so much more useful and constructive thought, must die away. Many of the books now written by women do suggest that they were written out of defiance, and these have earned from men the imputation that women are greater rather, not only at heart, than they are themselves.

But you cannot break habits without an effort, and the effort seems to be stirring up the mind which ought to lie at the bottom –

It is a curious thing, by the way, that there seems a twist towards femininity in many of the books written by men, at this time.

What one wants is fair play, and as yet one might as well want the moon, for the unfairness began, I suppose, when the cave man found that his muscles were tougher than those of his wife, and that by a whack on the head he could make her carry the loads. The balance is adjusted sometimes, and I am bound to say that I have a feeling of pleasure when I think of the female spider eating her husband when done with. "Ça soulage," as the mother-in-law said in the French play when she boxed her son-in-law's ears. But I believe as you do, that in women's work not much will be done until we have grown out of that feeling of antagonism, and are able to deal with art in a more disinterested way. We are still too personal, and general ideas are not vivid enough to us.

This will mean a shifting of points of view in men and women, and a number of material consequences, which ought to make for real civilisation; a thing which is only beginning to come to life.

I apologise for this letter, but it is entirely provoked by your most stimulating book, which says what I have been thinking for a good many years.

I am yours truly,
Eleanor D. Hill

Letters from readers, Letters about A Room of One's Own

This correspondent may be Eleanor Deane Hill, who published three books of poetry between 1918 and 1929.

42
Handwritten
[1929]

FLAXMAN 0606.

27 CHEYNE WALK
CHELSEA.

Dear Madam,

After reading "A room of one's own" I have found it too hard not to say thank-you – even at the risk of trespassing on the writer's privacy. For I read here, wisely & beautifully put, what many of us—who are trying to develop our 'androgynous mind' from that mind which springs naturally from our being ~~female ver~~ women – are confusedly thinking & feeling. It seems presumptuous to say this—yet I think you meant to speak for all of us who are not sufficiently subtle of mind or speech to be able to speak truthfully for ourselves.

Thank you for so wittily and beautifully and un-angrily crystallising the situation; for illuminating our capacity to ourselves & for making clear the distinction between chaff & grain in our particular kinds of work. It is easier to write now – if one is a beginner <in that line> – with a clearer head & fewer unhelpful misgivings.

It seems one of the hardest things in the world now to be an unselfconscious, independent woman – personally & spiritually. Our approach to work & to relationships is made extraordinarily confused & difficult because women (apparently) aren't people; they are suspicious strangers, or pets or performing animals. They are not given the right to hold that invisible passport which good men carry through the world simply on the strength of their being good people. Perhaps £500 a year & a room for each would give women this passport.

Till they have it, it seems hardly possible that they can, often, tangibly prove their worthiness of it. Some <women> do, even yet, with work which <does> spring from the 'incandescent' 'androgynous' lucid mind, & to these people the rest of us must be extraordinarily grateful: to you & to such a writer as Elizabeth Bowen, for instance - I can think of no others in England now living.

Meanwhile, while some of the rest of us are trying to learn how to ~~do~~ work ~~it~~, thank you for helping with 'A room of ones own'.

Yours truly -
Beatrice Brown

Mrs. Leonard Woolf.

Letters from readers, Letters about A Room of One's Own

Beatrice Curtis Brown (1901-1974) wrote novels based on historical figures, such as *Elizabeth Chudleigh, Duchess of Kingston* (1927), *Queen Anne: A Reading of Her Life* (1929), and *For the Delight of Antonio* (1932). She also wrote *Isabel Fry, 1869-1958, Portrait of a Great Teacher* (1960), which included a memoir and extracts from Isabel Fry's writing; see letter 129.

43
Handwritten; first page missing
[late 1929/early 1930]

715 Liberty Street
Clarion
Pennsylvania

Elizabeth's ambassador & am writing to ask you in which of the Voyages they are told of. Also what edition it is from which you worked.

You may be interested to know that a friend and I are having a Virginia Woolf winter! We read aloud first the book reviews in Books. Then the articles on Fiction in the Bookman. Next A Room of One's Own—And now we are all day in The Common Reader. We are enjoying the reading so much. Even when we most definitely disagree with you we are delighted with the stimulus and challenge that you have given to our minds! And we still have so much ahead to enjoy.

Very cordially
Edith Freelove Smith

Miss Edith Freelove Smith
715 Liberty St.
Clarion Pa

Letters from agents, editors, publishers, etc., Letters about various books

---

Edith Freelove Smith published a children's book called *Trading East: A Story Based on Hakluyt's Voyages to Russia, Turkeman, and Persia* in 1930. Reviews by Woolf appeared in the Books section of the *New York Herald Tribune* from 1924 through 1931, but most frequently in 1927-1929. "Phases of Fiction" appeared in the April, May, and June 1929 issues of *Bookman*. Smith's question seems related to "The Elizabethan Lumber Room" in the first *Common Reader* (1925). Smith also abridged *The Pilgrim's Progress* (1923) and *David Copperfield* (1938) for young readers.

44
Typed; signed
January 12, 1930

ELIZABETH COX WRIGHT
ROSE VALLEY ROAD
MOYLAN, PA.

January 12, 1930.

My dear Mrs. Woolf,

For several years I have thanked my husband for your books, Christmas gifts, until it now seems to me time that I should thank you. I made my first discovery with Night and Day a few years ago, and have just completed the list of fiction and essays with A Room of One's Own. Mrs. Dalloway remains for me one of the most thoroughly enjoyable novels I have ever read, and I read novels widely as a student and for pleasure. I am a little daft about London, and being an American, probably rather sentimental about it; Mrs. Dalloway, ever since I first read it, has been a great help when the nostalgia becomes too painful. The beauty and penetration of your treatment of the theme always strikes me with fresh admiration. It is a musical book.

It would be fun for me to go over the list telling you point by point the pleasure your books have afforded me, but rather dull for you. Besides, ~~the~~ my real motive for writing you is bound up with A Room of One's Own. It seems to me that you are one of the very few women who adequately realize the significance of the change which is coming over the position of women, and that dangers still hang over us. I am a student of English history, and if I had been a man would now undoubtedly be teaching in a University. If I had not married I would probably have gone back to my own college as a teacher. I don't think I would like teaching much, and I am really fitted, not for teaching, but research. I have been married for seven years, the first three years of which I spent getting my doctor's degree at the University where my husband is a professor, and where I have been working as time permits ever since. I now have two children of whom I take rather closer care than I would if I were English; our points of view about nurses, probably our nurses, being different. But on the whole I have quite as much leisure for my work as my friends, men or women, who are earning their living as teachers, and I think greater emotional satisfaction and stability than the women who are unmarried. Nevertheless, I am greatly hindered by the fact that my work is inextricably mixed with a sense of rebellion. It poisons my outlook.

I have to explain, or think I have to, to apologize, even to myself, when my children catch cold the day I spend at the University. I have a hard and fast rule that I can see no one from nine to twelve, yet the sound of the telephone which I can not entirely exclude from my study, which is my own, by the way, sets my mind astray excusing myself to the person who wants to speak to me about some inconsequential. I have a nagging feeling that if I were a man my study of fifteenth century humanism would some day amount to something; as it is I go through periods of nervousness about it which sap whatever ability I may have.

I do not intend this to be a diatribe, but a bit of evidence to support your point, that women have still, psychologically, a real barrier between them and attainment. I wish that you would write the novel that Mary Carmichael tried. I have been somewhat disappointed that your women have been uneducated women, technically speaking, for I have known, even before A Room of One's Own, that you must understand the problem. Show in a novel that women like women, and though interested in personal relationships, that they are also interested in ideas. I search literature for the woman to whom the theory of relativity is an exciting thought. There are plenty of us, and we do not all hate beautiful, sociable things, like Miss Kilman. I have half a dozen friends in London, women who are doctors, lawyers, writers, bank clerks, and what not, one of each, to be exact! and they would make fine central figures for the novel you ask for, and I ask you for. What about the woman historian? The reviews are full of the work of Jane Eileen Powers, and Helen Cams, and extraordinarily good work they do too. They have arrived, but they have struggled too, I am sure, although I do not know any of them personally.

This is enough to bother you with, even typewritten. Please forgive me if you have been bored. You see a writer inevitably makes friends that are hard to escape from, once they become articulate.

Yours very sincerely,
Elizabeth Cox Wright.

Letters from readers, Letters about A Room of One's Own

Elizabeth Cox Wright (1899-1973) completed a dissertation at the University of Pennsylvania in 1927 entitled *Common Law in Thirteenth Century English Royal Forests.* In 1951, she published *Metaphor, Sound, and Meaning in Bridges'* The Testament of Beauty. She married Edward Wright in 1922; he was a Quaker by birth, a conscientious objector in both world wars, and the author of *Conscientious Objectors in the Civil War* (1931). She taught English literature at Swarthmore College and the University of Illinois at Chicago.

45
Typed; signed
January 12, 1930

254 SEAMAN AVENUE
NEW YORK, N.Y.

January 12, 1930.

Dear Mrs. Woolf,

Even at the risk of being a great nuisance I cannot refrain from telling you how much I enjoyed A ROOM OF ONE'S OWN. I don't know when a book has seemed so intimately written for me alone. But that is exactly what my friends and some of the women students in my husband's lecture course in English literature at Columbia University to whom I have recommended it say too. After a year of sharing the dull food and what was for me the dull existence of English women in their colleges - with the dreariness occasionally lifted by glimpses of what the university gives men - I began to inquire into the reasons for the difference. The hours I spent in the British Museum and the Bodleian going over the miles of volumes written about women by men aroused more reflections and eventually the book VICTORIAN WORKING WOMEN, which your husband so generously reviewed in The Nation last summer. Will you please convey to him my belated thanks for his kindness?

Of your solid superstructure of fact, I was prepared to be appreciative, and for your historical approach to women's position in the arts. But the detachment, tact, and grace of A ROOM OF ONE'S OWN, and the deadly weapons of poetry, wit, and irony which compel the male reader to swallow unpalatable truth as if it were sugar are new in feministic writing. We ought now to be better mannered in our disputes forever.

I want to thank you also for the steady pleasure I have had for many years now from your books. Until this winter, when I reread them both, I could never decide whether MRS. DALLOWAY or TO THE LIGHTHOUSE was my favorite. Now I know it is TO THE LIGHTHOUSE - at least until your next novel comes along to upset my little system.

Very sincerely yours,
Wanda Fraiken Neff.

Mrs. Virginia Woolf
The Hogarth Press
Tavistock Square
London.

Letters from readers, Letters about A Room of One's Own

Wanda Fraiken Neff (1889-1961) published the still useful *Victorian Working Women: An Historical and Literary Study of Women in British Industries and Professions, 1832-1850* in 1929, and Leonard Woolf reviewed it in *Nation and Athenaeum* (8 June 1929: 338). Under her own name, she published two novels, *We Sing Diana* (1928) and *Lone Voyagers* (1929), and from 1932 on, continued to write novels under the pseudonym of E. M. Lovell. She was married to Emory Neff, member of the Columbia University English Department from 1916-1953.

46
Handwritten
January 19, 1930

Jan:19, 1930. 569. Sprowston Road,
Norwich.

Dear Miss Woolf,

Please do not be outraged by my writing to thank you for your joyous & beautiful essay 'A Room of One's Own'. You will probably think me mad or a publicity-fiend. I assure you I am neither, but only a humble admirer of your talent, who has the courage to believe that, though a successful writer, you may be human at the same time.

I wish there were some other way than trying to crystallize in words my feeling of gratitude for what you have done – for the amount of pleasure given by your Essay – for the thoughts of wisdom stored in it. It seems so abundantly time that someone had these thoughts, & stirred up others to have them and act on them too. If you will allow me to say so, without being thought impertinent, but just because, as in Miss Carmichael's novel, "Chloe liked Olivia," I do think, and I am sure many hundreds of other women think like me, that you have done our sex a great service, one which a part of them will not easily let die.

Perhaps I feel more strongly about what you say being right, because I had a few scattered thoughts myself on the very same subject a few years ago, as this extract I have copied from an old notebook will show you, if ever you have the patience to read it. I suppose we always like to see our own thoughts echoed in print. But apart from that, may I, very humbly, yet very sincerely, thank you from the bottom of my heart, for what seems to me to be one of the sanest, ablest & yet utterly joyous pieces of writing our language can boast?

Forgive my uncalled for intrusion, should this ever reach your eyes, & think of me only as some chance passerby, who has dared for a moment, to stop beneath your window.

Yours sincerely
E. J. Poignard. (Miss)

[enclosure missing]

Letters from readers, Letters about A Room of One's Own

47
Handwritten
January 22, 1930

STOCKA HOUSE,
COTTINGLEY,
NR BINGLEY,
YORKSHIRE.
22nd January 1930.

Dear Madam,

Though intrusive I would not like you to think me impertinent.

I have read so much of your work with joy that, acting on impulse, and in the fellow feeling of craftsman for craftswoman, I write to say so. Your latest book, "A Room of One's Own", is beside me as I write. I read it through, silently, myself, testing its beautiful prose in my mind by "ear" and thought. Having enjoyed it quietly, to enjoy it again, and to share my joy, I re-read it aloud to my wife. She on hearing much of it so enjoyed it too that, in turn, she has read it all to herself, in quiet, with renewed delight. I'm afraid not many books of to-day will stand such a test of quality, or invite such a test. What a happy marriage there is between your manner and your spirit. And how warm and persuasive are your words & phrases in the truth of that happiness. We love more than art when we write like that. And I think it is the lack of love for that "something more" which is the cause of that chill brilliance, and strutting crudeness, which is so characteristic of much of the literature and art of our day. To my thinking, you embody a real and central truth in Chap. VI. of your little book.

The truly creative artist, while at work, is unconscious of sex as of morals. He or she will work from the sum of themselves, – man-cum-woman, embodying in perfect poise the virtues, powers, and weaknesses of both.

Your opinions and feelings in the presence of Kipling and Galsworthy are exactly mine. I admire both men, and their books. But it seems to me they lack that totality – that poetry of the understanding heart, without which there cannot be a universal appeal or an artistic consummation. It is the "woman" within us or woman without who gives to man's austerities the warmth and the grace of triumphant art. <The male in her soul does as much for woman (vide the Brontë lecture enclosed.)>

You and I have this much in common. To me it seems we have much more. In the hope that you may find a little, I send to you a book and a couple of trifles.

The book, published in 1928, was almost quite ignored by the London press. I did not expect it would be <otherwise>, for I am quite outside all the "swims," and know nothing of the coteries. Perhaps, as you say, "Praise or blame means nothing": I have felt for myself, and thought for myself in silence for most of a lifetime, and I am not unfriendly to the silence of critics.

I need not steal more of your time; forgive me for the already large theft, and for the vast invitation to your patience enclosed with this letter.

Believe me, Madam, to be
truly & gratefully yours
James A Mackereth

[enclosures missing]

Letters from agents, editors, publishers, etc., Letters about various books

---

James Allan Mackereth (b. 1871), a Lake District poet, published his first book, *Lays of Love and Liberty*, in 1897. He published *Storm-wrack, a Night with the Brontës and Other Poems* in 1927, and on February 9, 1929, he gave an address to the annual meeting of the Brontë Society at Haworth. The book he refers to here is probably *Earth, Dear Earth* (1928). He has two books of poetry listed in *English Poetry of the Second World War: A Biobibliography* (1986).

48
Handwritten
January 27, 1930

Jan 27 '30
c/o American Express
Vienna, Austria

Dear Mrs. Woolf -

I want to write and tell you that what I found in "A Room of One's Own" and in "Orlando" have been real discoveries. I don't think I've ever felt like that about any books I've read. It sounds foolish to say that one gets strength from some ones' elses ideas, but still, that's the way I felt after reading "A Room of One's Own". It was a little like the old year going out and the new year coming in – I mean, the way it might be if the world were changed after midnight – sort of a moment of exaltation, I suppose, when one sees and feels everything much more clearly, and what one sees and feels is rather wonderful because one's aim, or what one wants to do becomes stripped of mist and wrappings and it stands before one crystallized and real.

I'm awfully grateful to the books, and as you've written them I wanted to tell you so.

I'd like to meet you some time and talk about a million things, but probably if I met you I wouldn't have a thing to say! Anyhow, I'll be watching for your books and I hope you'll write a lot of them.

Sincerely
Erika Wilbuch

Letters from readers, Letters about A Room of One's Own

49
Handwritten
January 31, 1930

The Barn.
Chalfont St. Peter
Bucks

Jan^ry^ 31st
1930

I have been reading your book 'a room of one's own' & it has interested me enormously. I wonder if it would bore you intensely if I express to you something of what I feel after reading it? Is it meant to hearten women on to effort? I wonder. Of course I know you were speaking chiefly to women who were able to attend lectures, who had every advantage – but your book is also read by those who labour under every disability of which you write.

You write with all the confidence of a woman who – to use a slang term – 'has got there'. You give the credit of that achievement to your £500 a year, & that room of your own. I somehow believe you would have done it without that; however, that is not the point in question.

Will you bear with me for a moment if I lay before you a case? A woman – (yes, I feel like you in that—call it [W.?] & have done with it!) who has <u>not</u> 'got there', who has struggled for years with that desire for expression, & has met with no success; – a short novel, written to please neither publisher, nor public, but merely to express an ideal which burnt to be expressed, & needless to say met with but scanty notice; a second novel, without ideal, which met with a little better luck, but not sufficient to secure a market for further publications. Since then – just a series of novels, written in the common sitting room, with a mind harassed by the need of money, by constant domestic difficulties, & interruptions, varied by operations & serious illness, finished, typed, sent to various publishers, ever with the inevitable return notice, interspersed here & there by a desire to see further work, but never with the longed for acceptance. You are more than right about the limitations, the need of leisure, travel, & unburdened mind. But are you right about the £500 a year & a room of one's own? Everything in me cries out that you are. All the cowardice & want of hope that for the last two or three years has called to me to give in agrees with you. "It is all useless, nothing of all I long to express is worth expressing", to write & fail is the direst of all failures, because it is failure complete – one has no audience, nothing anyone wants to look at – all is wasted effort; the artist can show his works & at least please an uneducated audience if his works do not hang at Burlington House; the would be musician can please at least the members of his own household; but the would be writer has only wasted hours, neglected house hold jobs, a chest of crumpled typescript!

Your book, therefore, seemed to come as the last straw to the fast dying hope of a Woman without £500 a year, without travel, without a room to herself with nothing of all that you say is essential to a writer! Still there remains that desire that killed the sister of Shakespeare, just the 'will' that says to her 'hold on'.

What would you say to such a one? One whose mind & reason, & logic agrees with you. Whose better judgment prompts over & over again. 'Give it up. Accept failure'. Whose hope, almost past mending found in your book very nearly the last straw, coming as it did the same day the postman brought two returned M.S.S. And yet, that same urge continues; 'you can't give up. As long as pencils & paper exist you will mar the cleanness of one by the black head of the other'!

What is your advice to such a reader of your work? Accept the inevitable with all the submission & meekness which should be woman's attribute?

Well, I have nearly decided to endeavour to attain those Victorian graces.

Have you time, I wonder to answer this? I ask it in all seriousness. Perhaps it is asking too much. But may not we women <u>sometimes</u> adventure greatly?

Yours truly

M. P. Thomasset.

Letters from readers, Letters about A Room of One's Own

Marjorie Phyllis Thomasset published a novel, *Gentleman Unafraid*, in 1921, *The Adventure of Life* (addressed to young people) in 1937, and what seem to be children's books ("The Fairy Spectacles" and "Princess Crystal," published by the Society for the Promotion of Christian Knowledge) in 1920.

50
Handwritten
January 31, 1930

61. Manchuria Road SW.11
7th February. 1930.

Dear Mrs. Woolf.

I may be taking a liberty – I don't know – I have just this evening read your book "A room of one's own" –

I am a woman living in "one of those long streets somewhere south of the river" – I have a flat of my own and I earn at present £300 a year – some day it will be £400.

I am not telling you these facts for any other reason but to say that we women are approaching your ideal conditions for literary development.

There is just a faint, very faint, possibility, that I may get a scholarship to Oxford – I want to write eventually.

Now I am sending you this letter to say how much I appreciated your book – and that your "peroration" is already taking effect.

You must be a very busy woman so please don't bother to answer this brief note – even out of [our?] politeness –

Yours sincerely,
E. G. J. Eastwood.

Letters from readers, Letters about A Room of One's Own

51
Handwritten
February 10, 1930

5 LONDOUN ROAD,
ST. JOHN'S WOOD, N.W. 8

Feby 10th
1930

Dear Madam,

I hope you will excuse a periodical prompting I receive to thank authors for their books, because it is too rare to be denounced as a habit. Your "Room of One's Own" is the most refreshing thing I have read for years and I feel that literature is under a great debt to you for your noble and penetrating insight into the mysteries of creative genius. I always remember a stray remark of one of the Goncourt's that "women of genius are men": you show that the converse may be equally true. I should like to see your essay in larger type on a large page, as Morris or Cobden Sanderson would have printed it, so that it might receive a binding worthy of the contents. But that is only an incidental comment and all I wish really to do is to pay you a tribute for your achievement.

I am

yours faithfully

Max Judge

Mrs Virginia Woolf.

Letters from readers, Letters about A Room of One's Own

Max Judge, with A. J. A. Symons, founded the First Edition Club in 1922. Thomas James Cobden-Sanderson (1840-1922) was an English book designer and binder who contributed to the Arts & Crafts Movement. See letters 52 and 53.

52
Handwritten
February 19, 1930

---

5 Londoun Road, Feb. 19. 1930.
St. John's Wood, N.W. 8

Mrs. Julia Woolf.

Dear Madam,

When I had read "A Room of my Own", I felt a great want of expressing my thanks to you for the splendid vindication of women you have given voice to. <u>All</u> women owe you an everlasting debt of gratitude. Before I could put my desire on paper, my son, I found had forestalled me, with his. All the same, I will not let that fact prevent my own individual duty, as well as pleasure.

Sixty years ago, my mother had a great, and broad conception of what is due to women. But she had not your gifted pen, nor any means of spreading her views broadcast. She predicted then that the day would come when women would sit in Parliament on an equality with men. She was jeered at as a lunatic, especially by men. Yet I have lived to see her assertion verified.

Your delightful book is the finest and truest exposé of the real position of women that I have met with, either as regards fiction or any other branch of mental development. I seem to find the air fresher now!

And I beg you to accept my heartfelt thanks.

Yours sincerely,
Emily S. Judge
(Mrs. Mark H. Judge).

Letters from readers, Letters about A Room of One's Own

Perhaps the Mark H. Judge referred to in the signature is Mark Hayler Judge (1847-1927), who published several books about labor laws, hygienic conditions, and politics. See letters 51 and 53.

53
Handwritten
March 16, 1930

---

5 LONDOUN ROAD,
ST. JOHN'S WOOD, N.W. 8

March 16. 1930.

Mrs. Virginia Woolf.

Dear Madam,

I hope you will not mind my troubling you with still another letter.

Your book " room of one's own" has given me food for thought—in more ways than one, and I should like to mention to you one of the ways.

Just over a year ago I inherited a fine old Chateau, in Eastern France, near Epernay, to be precise. What to do with it has been a problem, till now, when I have an idea. I did not want to sell it, for the sake of associations with the owner who left it to me, neither can I live in the huge place alone. I spent the whole of last summer there, with one some of my family, and, personally, I enjoyed the lovely peace of the place, and the inspiration it gave towards thought other than humdrum.

What I have in my mind is that it would make a splendid College for Women, on the lines originally started at Girton, etc. Of course, it should get its main support from France, and I am sure that French women would awaken to the call—they are striking out for individualism. But possibly some English women would like to come in as well, and I am venturing to ask you if you could tell me of anyone likely to be interested in such a movement, to whom I could communicate my idea of founding a College.

The place is so essentially it for the purpose, that I want to go in for it, and if I can do nothing more this summer than try to get some nucleus, just a kernel, in the shape of women writers to live there, with a room of their own, and nothing to worry about, that need not prevent my going on with possibilities of further development.

I really must apologise for allowing my project to inflict this long letter on you, but I think you will forgive me for the sake of what it deals with.

I am, dear Madam,
Yours sincerely,
Emily S. Judge.

Letters from readers, Letters about A Room of One's Own

See letters 51 and 52.

54
Handwritten
April 1, 1930

Villa La Havane
Le Tholonet
Aix-en-Provence
France
April 1, 1930

Dear Mrs. Woolf:

This is a note of appreciation. I have read "Mrs. Dalloway", "To the Lighthouse", "Orlando", always with the deepest pleasure, and as much for the poetry I found there as for the reflections of life. Your work to me is a room of mirrors. So now when I discover you in "A Room of One's Own" expressing directly all my hidden rebellions, choosing for a title the one phrase that matters most to a young person trying to write: I am too happy not to tell you so.

I have very understanding parents, writers themselves, who are eager that I should have the opportunities they missed; who have learned that the business of earning one's bread destroys slowly the other hunger to create. Yet they could not sympathize with me for wanting to escape from them, from the family circle. I persisted, and under the guise of studying at an university here, have had a year of freedom—with a room of my own. When I go back to my country, Canada, again, there will be another struggle. But my father has read your book: from a letter he wrote, I believe he understands.

It is for this that I thank you.

Very faithfully yours,
Dorothy Livesay

Letters from agents, editors, publishers, etc., Letters about various books

---

Dorothy Livesay (1909-1996) became a major Canadian poet. Her parents, Florence Randal Livesay (journalist, poet, and translator) and J. F. B. Livesay (general manager of Canadian Press), did encourage her literary efforts, starting with her first publication, *Green Pitcher* in 1928. Livesay was a welfare worker, newspaper reporter, and teacher, and she wrote journalism, short fiction, autobiography, and literary criticism along with her poetry. Among her best-known poetry publications are *Call My People Home* (1950),

Ice Age (1975), *The Woman I Am* (1977), *The Phases of Love* (1983), and *Journey with My Selves: A Memoir, 1909-1963* (1991). In 1979, *Room of One's Own* had a special issue on Livesay (5.i-ii), and her papers are at the University of Manitoba where her daughter-in-law has established a bursary for new writers in her name.

55
Handwritten
May 24, 1930

24.5.30.

Dear Mrs. Woolf.

I rang you up last Vac, to ask you if I might come & see you, but hearing that you were very busy, and not feeling well, I thought you would not be pleased to see extra visitors.

I wanted to tell you about an idea that I had, to make an Anthology of Cambridge Women's Poetry, similar to the "Cambridge Poetry", published by the Hogarth Press. I have been collecting contributions from Girton & Newnham, and it seems to me that some of the poems are good. I should like very much to show them to you, & ask you whether you think the Anthology would be a good idea, & if the Hogarth Press would publish it. Personally, though no doubt there may be a diversity of opinion concerning the merit of the poems, I am convinced that from many points of view, it will be worth while making this Anthology. Not only will it be an encouragement to creative work on the part of University Women, but it will increase the prestige of Girton & Newnham in Cambridge. These reasons by themselves are not sufficient, but are undoubtedly good ones. I think, moreover, that there are a great many people who will be interested in catching a glimpse of the point of view of the more cultured "Undergraduettes", & I must say, that I am amazed myself, how little I know about the minds of the people who walk about the corridors of Girton with me every day! The poems are all extremely interesting from this sociological point of view, and some of them seem to me artistically excellent. I have noticed two chief things about them. The first is that they are not "mannered" in the pseudo-T. S. Eliot tradition, and the second is that they are inclined to reveal a paucity of emotional experience. I am glad about the first point, and the second I think is a natural outcome of a rather narrow upbringing at home & at school. From this point of view the poems which show this most strongly, are to my mind some of the most interesting. I don't know what you think about all this. I should be most grateful if you would write to me, and tell me if you are interested in the idea, and would have time to see me or the poems, or both. I know that your time is very valuable, but I can assure you that these poems will interest you if you have a cool hour to read them in.

My Tripos ends on June 7th, after which, if you could spare the time, I should be delighted to come to you about this.

With many thanks for the interest you have shown in the past, & in hopes that you will look upon this idea favourably,

Yours sincerely
Margaret E. Thomas

Stephen-Turner

See letter 34 for biographical information. Hogarth Press published *An Anthology of Cambridge Women's Verse*, edited by Margaret Thomas, in 1931. Included in the fourteen poets were Kathleen Raine, Margaret Diggle, Gwendolen Freeman, and Margaret Thomas herself, who also wrote a preface. Later in her life, Margaret Thomas Bullard became a craftswoman, making jewelry and then furniture.

56
Handwritten
October 12, 1931

125 Queen's Gate, S.W.7.
Western 4871
– 12 . . 10 . . 31 –

Dear Mrs Woolf: I want to thank you for the intense and concentrated pleasure I felt while I read, and which I still feel after reading "The Waves". But I can think of nothing to say except: Thank you. They sound so feeble, those two words, and yet if a man came to me in the street and gave me a parcel labelled

"Happiness" and a cheque for a million pounds, I should have nothing better to say. I have never read anything that gave me the same kind of pleasure as The Waves. It is as if someone took a halfpenny out of a bag and, placing it on the table, said, "That is life, that is consciousness of living, that is everything"; and one suddenly realized that what he said was true, although he only had a halfpenny to say it with. It was a most extraordinary experience. I see that I have tried to say more than two words, and made non-sense.

John Hayward.

Letters from readers, Letters about The Waves

John Hayward (1905-1965) was a scholar, anthologist, critic, and editor, publishing editions of John Donne, William Blake, Robert Herrick, the Earl of Rochester, Jonathan Swift, and T. S. Eliot, along with titles such as *The Oxford Book of Nineteenth-Century English Verse* (1964) and *The Penguin Book of English Verse* (1956). He was a contributor and editor for *The Book Collector* from 1952-1960 and editorial director from 1960 until his death. John Smart, master at Gresham School in Norfolk, is writing a biography of Hayward. See Woolf's reply, dated October 13, 1931, *L4* 389 (2450).

57
Handwritten
October 13, 1931

ELMSTONE
NORTHWOOD
MIDDLESEX
Oct. 13, 1931

Dear Mrs Woolf.

You must long ago have lost interest in the praise of unknown readers - possibly of your own self-appointed critics. But please do allow me the egotistical pleasure of trying to express my quivering admiration for "The Waves."

I did not guess that the rhythm & flow, & the beauty & indifference &

unchanging variableness of the sea (& of how much else) could actually be cradled even by you in words. And so I feel a new breathless amazement.

"The Waves" seems to me to be a perfect & satisfying book. You must have had moments when you knew it to be as good a thing as it is – so one asks no reward – for you. It is not gratitude I offer, but – why should one not say it? – a kind of spiritual recognition & obeisance?

I write this at night, nervously glancing at the morning when it will have to be posted.

Yours, with sincere admiration,
Hilda Finnemore

Letters from readers, Letters about The Waves

Hilda Finnemore (b. 1891) was the author of children's stories published in *Boy's Own Paper*, two novels, *The Mountain Sides of Dreams* (1914) and *Storm so Ruinous* (1934), short stories in *Stories of Course* (1921), two foot-path guides to Aylesbury and Berkhamsted, and nonfiction, *Class Book of English Elements* (1922) and *A History of the Earth from Stardust to Man* (1924).

58
Handwritten
October 15, 1931

21, rue Luben Karaveloff
Sofia
Bulgarie.
Le 15 octobre 1931.

Madame,

Je viens de tourner la dernière page de "The Waves." J'ai tourné cette page avec le sentiment d'une profonde, presque inexprimable émotion que peu de livres out suscitée en moi. Et c'est cette émotion qui me fait vous adresser ces lignes, malgré que je sache parfaitement combien il est vain d'écrire à de grands écrivains, combien de telles lettres sonnet d'une note de fausse sentimentalité—aussi sincères qu'elles soient—lettres que vous devez recevoir par dizaine tous les jours et qui doivent, je n'imagine, vous ennuyer bien, si toutefois vous les lisez jamais.

Je ne vous écris pas pour vous répéter que « The Waves » est une grande, une remarquable œuvre ; je ne vous écris par pour vous conter les pensées et impressions que cet inoubliable livre a suscité en moi—cela ferait ma lettre trop longue et vous ennuyerait sûrement ; je ne vous écris non plus pour exprimer tout mon enthousiasme—nous, autres slaves d'Orient, sommes tellement sentimentales—combien d'ailleurs le mot enthousiasme semblerait vide s'il devait exprimer ce frémissement, cette émotion avec lesquels j'ai lu « The Waves. » Je vous écris simplement pour vous dire que dans un pays appauvri par les injustices – conséquences de la guerre – qui est arrêté dans sa possibilité de suivre les lointaines manifestations de la vie intellectuelle de l'Occident – et plus encore de l'Angleterre – dans ce pays, où votre nom est inconnu – et qui sait s'il y sera bientôt – vous avez une fervente admiratrice qui vous aime infiniment, pour laquelle tout ce que vous écrivez est très cher. Et si, même le temps d'une seconde, vous sentez que cela ne vous est pas indifférent, je ne trouverai pas que je vous ai écrit ces lignes en vain.

Milla Tcholakova

[translation by Helen Southworth]

Madam,

I just turned the last page of "The Waves." As I turned this last page I experienced a profound, almost inexpressible emotion that few books have inspired in me. And it's this emotion that has moved me to address these lines to you, although I know perfectly well how vain it is to write to great writers, how much such letters resound with a note of false sentimentality—as sincere as they might be—letters that you must receive by the dozen every day and which must, I imagine, bore you, that is if you read them at all.

I'm not writing to you merely to repeat that "The Waves" is a great, a remarkable work; I'm not writing to you in order to recount to you the thoughts and impressions that this unforgettable book has inspired in me—that would be too long a letter and would surely bore you; I'm not writing to you either to express the extent of my enthusiasm—we, other Slavs of the Orient, are known for our sentimentality—how inadequate besides the word enthusiasm is to describe the shudder, the emotion with which I read "The Waves." I am writing to you simply to say that in a country impoverished by injustices—consequences of the war—which have hampered its ability to follow the distant manifestations of the intellectual life of the Occident—and more still that of England—in this country, in which your name is unknown—and who knows if it will be known here soon—you have a fervent admirer who loves you infinitely, and who cherishes all that you write. And if, even for one second, this moves you, I will find that I have not written these lines to you in vain.

Milla Tcholakova

Letters from readers, Letters about The Waves

59
Handwritten
October 16, 1931

TELEPHONE: SHARPTHORNE 11.
TELEGRAMS: DALINGRIDGE, SHARPTHORNE.
STATION & PARCELS. WEST HOATHLEY. LB & S.C.R. 1 ¼ M.

DALINGRIDGE PLACE,
TYE'S CROSS,
VIA EAST GRINSTEAD.

16. Oct. 31.

My dear Goat

What a wonderful book your 'Waves' & a rare & exact title for it that no one but yourself wd have thought of. Madcap some will say. But not a bit of it, only a literal statement of feelings that all have had but as yet none but you have visualised & expressed in words & such words. A terrible fate awaits you. All the womens Colleges, some of mens, certainly all the male & female mixtures in the U.S.A will be up & doing to form 'you' Societies. Headed each one of them by the Oscar Brownings of the place. Lanky, sloppy young men with spectacled earnest & ill dressed young women will pore over & discuss hidden meanings where no such meanings exist while the philomaths (mathematically minded) will deal with your vocabulary & compare its extent & variety with Shakespeare & Browning & Meredith. Such is my forecast & you know what happens to prophets. How you will long to be free of them & know that some at least & those the least expected know that your book is not a whit imaginative but merely a statement of fact.

Yours v affect.
G. H. D.

Clifford-Eliot

See Woolf's reply, dated October 18, 1931, *L4* 392-93 (2454). See also letter 16 for biographical information.

See letters from Lady Margaret Duckworth (1870-1958) to Leonard Woolf and Vanessa Bell in *A* 16-17, 186.

60
Handwritten
October 21, 1931

TELEPHONE - KNOWLE 11. FOUR ASHES,
DORRIDGE,
BIRMINGHAM.

21 – 10 - 31.

Dear Mrs. Woolf,

I have read all your books with pleasure and admiration. 'The Waves,' I think, the most exquisite of them all. When I am wretched I shall turn to Bernard's final soliloquy for comfort and encouragement.

Yours sincerely
John Hampson Simpson.

Letters from readers, Letters about The Waves

John Hampson Simpson (pseud. John Hampson; 1901-1955) was self-educated, a voracious reader, and associated with the Birmingham group of working-class writers. He lived with the Wilson family at Four Ashes, taking care of their mentally handicapped son. His first novel, *Saturday Night at the Greyhound*, was published by Hogarth Press in 1931, and was very successful (see J. H. Willis, Jr., *Leonard and Virginia Woolf as Publishers* [Charlottesville: UP of Virginia, 1992], 187-89), and although he continued to write novels, none was as successful as his first. See Woolf's references to him in *L4* 221, 270, and 347, along with *L6* 338, n3. Simpson wrote to Leonard Woolf after Virginia Woolf's death, and later sent a friend's tribute as well; see *A* 90, 153.

61
Typed; signed
October 23, [1931]

Kings Coll Camb . Oct 23

Dear Virginia

I have been living the last week almost entirely in your company whether I have been actually reading you or not and I have kept up such a conversation with you that I am urged to try to put some of it down. But there is such a lot of it and what one puts down is dead as it touches the paper.

Your book is a poem and as I think a great poem. Nothing that I know of has ever been written like it. It could I suppose only have been written in this moment of time. And now I understand or think I do to what you have been leading up all these years. The beauty of it is almost incredible. Such prose also has never been written and it also belongs to here and now though it is dealing also with a theme that is perpetual and universal. Oh dear what words, and even so only touching the least essential. For there is throbbing under it the mystery which all the poets and philosophers worth mentioning have felt and had their little shot at. I have only read it once and I see and know that it ought to be read often though I don't know whether I shall do that since I brood more and more and read less and less except to get information which is not reading but mugging up. I am a old man now and find age curious. My mind is all right though I suppose it may go tomorrow as my memory is going fast. But oddly the imagination functions as never before and about things one cant write down. The worlds incomprehensible and must remain so to us anumalcules, though the best thing about us is our shots to comprehend it. You make no shots because you will not make the shallow and the stale ones. Possibly though you may agree with me (though very likely you don't) in this. The universe (or universes) is not without significance. It is apparently indifferent to our values; it is certainly indifferent to our happiness our well being our goodness or badness our morals our loves. "Our". But what are we? Waves, yes? But waves in the sea part of the sea inseparable from the sea bound too each of us to be this wave and not that (whence much if not all of our trouble) but able and increasingly able as we get older to perceive that the other waves have their life too and while we are clashing with them we are somehow they Those sort of things, which I find in your book (I don't think I merely put them in, though that is the most common thing we do with other peoples thoughts and makes us so recalcitrant to new truth.) Anyhow

I feel it like that. Also life seems like a dream as one comes to the end of it. Ones separate individual skin ceases to hold one, it cracks; all over nightmares come in and visions and terrors and ecstacies till finally one rides at death, like your Bernard at the end. Oh dear, words words words as you also so vividly feel. To change the tone, I walked down the river the other day. The eights were thick over the water, and the fours, a kind of inextricable tangle, and to every eight and every four a young man (what children they look now) shouting to them from bicycles or horse in every kind of tone, hortatory abusive encouraging desperately earnest. Among them of course Percival. Firmly but kindly he was saying "It isn't one of you, its all of you that are wrong!" How profoundly and everlastingly true! Then once more firmly and kindly – "Now I'll tell you the best way." But alas his words faded on the wind and before he knows or we hear the only way, the youth who was piloting an aeroplane will have dropped bombs neatly on him and on all the Percivals before he is brought down himself by a machine gun, falling with the last proud sense that he is doing his bit for the dear old country. Courses were being done, the coxes yelled, the October sun shone out in the garden by the river, where some dons wife entertains bored boys and talks gossip about the matrimonial affairs of the fellows of Kings, the dahlias and chrysanthemums burned; some one was upset in a whiff (as we used to call them) and came swimming in laughing (he too was Percival) a very old a disreputable man held open a gate and ourself under his breath when he was not tippled, Louis walked along the tow path ashamed because he could not row, and Neville, looking for new prey, and I thinking of you and your book, was aware in the back of mind that I was coming home to a cup of tea, that there was a fraudulent election on and how should I vote; that I ought to call on so and so and so and so, that I might be dead tomorrow and that nothing mattered except to break through this mesh as decently as one could into – what? At which point, as george meredith says somewhere my imagination "tottered in dots". Oh dear, too much of this. But my dear Virginia, you will pardon me, for it is the best and only tribute I can pay in return for what seems to me a great book. Leonards book still lies on the table and before I can get to it I have others to at least look into. Why will people send me their books? What do you do when they send them to you? Of course the simplest plan is to write at once saying one hopes to read it, and then not read it, but there are a few cases where this is impossible.

I don't think I shall correct this typing. I'm told it only makes it worse.

Yours always
G. Lowes Dickinson

Clifford-Eliot

Goldsworthy Lowes Dickinson (1862-1932) held a special place in Bloomsbury (Mark Hussey, *Virginia Woolf A to Z* [NY: Facts on File, 1995], 71), but his typing, as he notes, was indeed terrible. I have reproduced writers' letters exactly as they wrote them except in his case. To give just one example, and that a mild one, his last sentence above, as typed, reads: Im to;d it on;y males it worse. The letter above, then, is sanitized enough to be readable. It is quoted by E. M. Forster in *Goldsworthy Lowes Dickinson* ([New York: Harcourt, 1934], 230-32), where he calls it a "critical rhapsody" unlike anything else from Dickinson's pen (230), and partially reprinted in *Virginia Woolf, The Critical Heritage* (Majumdar and McLaurin [London: Routledge, 1975], 271). See Woolf's reply, dated October 27, 1931, *L4* 397-98 (2460).

62
Handwritten
October 24, [1931]

18, Cecil Court, S.W. 10.
Flaxman 8091
Oct. 24th

Dear Mrs. Woolf,

For a very long time, five years at least, I have been trying to pluck up courage to write to you. Even now I cannot help feeling that it would be much more sensible not to. It seems a kind of impertinence to say to a person that one passionately admires her work and really does live from one book of hers to the next and the most tiresome of all kinds of impertinence to say that one would like, just once, to meet her.

I suppose I could have scraped an introduction to you from people I know who know you, Logan Pearsall Smith, for example, but, for some reason, I felt it would be unfair to them and to you, and that this clumsier way does at least give you the chance to say "no". I haven't any reason at all for intruding on you except a very deep and solid admiration for your work. I think I have read everything you have published from early ones like "The Voyage Out' to the last and most lovely "The Waves". You are the only person writing to-day about whom I feel "This is it . . . the real, right thing." I read "Mrs. Dalloway" after I had been in an asylum for ten months and I saw that there was a reason and a pattern in being mad. Oh, it's so impossible to write to you. One says the stupidest, the most priggish, the most idiotic things.

I am trying to learn to write myself and produce little dry pellets at intervals in "The New Statesman" & so on. I once wrote something for "Life & Letters" that Logan said you had read. But I don't want to bother you with all that. If you do ever let me come to see you, I promise not to mention it at all.

Years ago I cut a photograph of you out of "Vogue" & stuck it up on my desk in an office and it used to comfort me while I wrote advertisements for corsets and disinfectants and baking powder. There – you see – when one at last breaks down and writes to someone for whom one feels a private and passionate devotion one writes exactly like a housemaid writing to Greta Garbo.

Oh dear, oh dear, it would have been so much more decent and sensible not to have written at all. I truly haven't done this sort of thing before.

By this time you are saying "But what is the poor mumbling, stumbling creature after?" Simply this. I want to be allowed to come and see you for one hour. If you say "no", I promise not to bother you again. And don't even trouble to write "no". If I don't hear in a week I shall take it that it is "no" and be reasonable about it.

Yours sincerely
Antonia White

Vaughn-Wylie

Antonia White (1899-1980) wrote a quartet of novels about her relationship with her father and with the Catholic Church, the most famous of which is *Frost in May* (1933; rpt. 1981). She also translated Colette and other French writers and was a tireless diarist and analyst of her own writer's block. Elizabeth Podnieks, in *Daily Modernism: The Literary Diaries of Virginia Woolf, Antonia White, Elizabeth Smart, and Anaïs Nin* (Montreal: McGill-Queen's, 2000), notes Woolf's diary entry about meeting Antonia White on November 3, 1936 (*D*5 29) and White's diary entry in 1970 (*D*2 216) about Woolf as "The great heroine-writer of my youth" (346).

See Woolf's query about Antonia White in a letter to Ethel Sands, dated October 28, 1931, *L*4 398 (2461). Jane Dunn quotes a few sentences from White's letter in "The Beauty of the Beast: Virginia Woolf, Antonia White and Mental Illness," *The Charleston Magazine* 20 (Autumn/Winter 1999: 22) and says there is no evidence Woolf ever replied.

63
Handwritten
October 27, 1931

14, Upper Park Road,
Hampstead, N.W.3.
primrose 0526

Oct. 27th 31.

Dear Virginia,

Please don't think me impertinent in writing to tell you how absolutely exquisitely lovely I think "The Waves." But I only do so because it moved me so much that I can't help it.

It seemed to me to convey all that is real & significant about life in a picture that was at the same time the most beautiful poetry. So that one both heard it & saw it & felt it all together.

yours ever
Faith Henderson

P.S. Thought you might like to know that Toby is now at boarding school. She seems very happy there.

Farrell-Lubbock

Faith Bagenal Henderson (b. 1889) was married to Hubert Henderson (1890-1952), the editor of *The Nation*. A letter from Woolf to Vita Sackville-West dated November 8, 1929, *L*4 107 (2096) mentions Faith's desire to call Sackville-West about a school. See also Toby Henderson's letter to Woolf about *Three Guineas* (*WSA* 6: 39-40).

64
Typed; signed
November 20, 1931

November 20, 1931.

My dear Mrs. Woolf:

Since I respect you more highly than any other living writer, the enthusiasm with which I look forward to the publication of your works is boundless. For me to criticize you may be as presumptuous as taking the Almighty to task, but I feel compelled to voice my disappointment in The Waves in this, the first communication I have ever addressed to an author. I almost wish all the copies of your new book could be recalled and that you might see fit to spend several months more in revising what could easily be an even finer thing than To the Lighthouse. Certainly, there are passages in The Waves which are magnificent, bits of prose-poetry which exceed in beauty and imagery any that you have offered us heretofore. But one leaves the book without having heard near enough of what one would think you would be so eager to impart, remembering details which might have been omitted and labored portions of the descriptive interludes which tended to throw the design as a whole off balance and destroy its singleness of effect. Sometimes I felt you were doing what I thought you totally incapable of doing: writing words which did not matter.

You were wise in including such an individual as Bernard to the throw the personalities of the other five characters into higher relief, but there was far too much told from his point of view. Your submerging yourself in him page after page (they seemed much longer than I suppose they really were) was like lowering a radiant, heavenly light into a Mason jar. Its glory never shone through. To have dwelt so long with him dimmed the gleam, flattered him to an almost unbearable degree. I could have wept when I found that it was necessary to learn the fates of all from his 'summing up'. Then I do not think even Bernard himself would have broken the news of Rhoda's suicide quite so bluntly. Why Percival played such a prominent part in the lives of all is beyond me.

I dislike Jinny, but I am forced to confess my belief that you have succeeded with her most completely. Rhoda and Neville, less tangible, are fascinating. And when he says, "I have signed my name" etc., Louis is magnificent.

To me you are the only real thrill in modern literature. The technical experiment you have attempted is rich in possibilities which you, and only you, would be able to attain. But . . . . Perhaps there never will be another To the Lighthouse.

Most sincerely,

Frank Hallam Lyell
(I am a student, aged 20)

935 Bellevue Place
Jackson, Mississippi. U.S.A.

Letters from readers, Letters about The Waves

Frank Hallam Lyell (1911-1977) earned a Ph.D. from Princeton and became a professor at the University of Texas, where Willie Morris was one of his students. He published *A Study of the Novels of John Galt* (1942), wrote for the *New York Times*, and taught until 1976. Eudora Welty and he were lifelong friends; they almost surely had a conversation about Woolf's novel before writing their letters! See letter 66.

65
Handwritten
November 20, 1931

November 23 1931

My dear Mrs Woolfe

May I tell you that the increase in one's emotional stature gained from reading "The Waves" is comparable to that received from studying the Bible or reading Shakespeare?

May I also ask you if you founded your title on Jeremiah 5:22? The mutual enhancement of the one by the other prompts me to take the liberty of making this inquiry.

Very sincerely
(Mrs. LN) Doris B. Borst
410 Broad Street
Oneida New York
USA

Letters from readers, Letters about The Waves

Doris Gregg Barnaskey Borst (?1893-1948) was married to Lauren Nelson Borst and was a professor of English at Utica College of Syracuse University. Jeremiah 5: 22 reads: "Fear ye not me? saith the Lord: will ye not tremble at my presence, which have placed the sand for the bound of the sea by a perpetual decree, that it cannot pass it: and though the waves thereof toss themselves, yet can they not prevail; though they roar, yet can they not pass over it?"

66
Typed; signed
November 23, 1931

1119 Pinehurst Place
Jackson, Mississipi
November 23, 1931

Dear Mrs. Woolf,

First let me say that I am yours humbly. To me "To the Lighthouse" is perfect and life- giving and yours the only inspired writing today. It was better to have read "To the Lighthouse" than to have written any other book, or, almost, to have lived any given life. It dissolved all the sediment of loneliness of my dull days into a perfect amorphous stream of motion and intensity that flows clear and penetrative over the mosaic of my imagination, or perhaps yours. It was light under a door I shall never open. It was alchemy, insinuating into my veins a drop of all too golden blood and into my ghost-like world (for nothing may ever happen) an integration of the elements of loneliness that clings through stretches of pointless time with a significance that could easily be the only beautiful thing about my life. One could become enslaved by the wonder of one's own impenetrable aloneness, since you have given aloneness its wonder, did not you yourself enter it by perfect recognition and prove such enslavement an insensitive act.

Feeling your power as I do, with perhaps more rhapsody than accuracy, I bought "The Waves" with a high heart, anticipating that its conception would be a development more intensely centerward toward the core of "To the Lighthouse", a development which your superb imaginative insight had further directed. Oh well, of course "The Waves" is beautiful; there are places in it where, one feels, only you would not fear to tread; but the sections of the book about Bernard close over the divine footprints and almost make one doubt what is now obscured and roughened away by lesser surges of inspiration. The flaw, one feels, is not in the fitness of Bernard's existence in "The Waves", or in his portrayal, certainly, but in your use of such an unworthy medium as Bernard's personality for your writing. It seems wrong for you to shine there within Bernard; the spirit has descended to inhabit at those times an object we cannot worship. And Mrs. Woolf, to end the book from his lips is cruel.

Forgive the impertinence of even the praise. It seems, already, an offensive attempt at precarious intimacy with austerity and greatness. But I probably have quite a long life ahead of me, and the fact that you will be writing other books which, like "To the Lighthouse", will stun me speechless is only too heavenly to contemplate.

Yours sincerely,
Eudora Welty

Letters from readers, Letters about The Waves

Eudora Welty (1909-2001) indeed had a long life ahead of her, a life in which she worked for the WPA in Mississippi (*One Time, One Place* 1971 includes her photographs), published several collections of short stories (see *Collected Stories*, 1980), wrote many novels (including *The Robber Bridegroom*, 1942, *Delta Wedding*, 1946, and *The Optimist's Daughter*, 1972), wrote essays and reviews (*The Eye of the Story*, 1978 and *A Writer's Eye*, 1994), did a critical study of Willa Cather, and wrote a memoir (*One Writer's Beginnings*, 1984). She was the first living author to have her works published by The Library of America (2 volumes, edited by Richard Ford and Michael Kreyling, 1998).

Suzan Harrison has done a comparative study of the two authors, *Eudora Welty & Virginia Woolf: Gender, Genre, and Influence* (Baton Rouge: Louisiana UP, 1997), and Suzanne Marrs discusses this letter to Woolf in *Eudora Welty: A Biography* (Orlando: Harcourt, 2005).

67
Handwritten
November 26, 1931

Melle F. Hélie
Professeur Agrégée d'Anglais
123 rue Brûle Maison
Lille. Nord. France.

Nov. 26.1931.

Madam,

It may be needless to say that I have always been greatly interested in your books. But they were such discoveries to me that it seems only fair that you should know what amount of pleasure, of durable enjoyment and what infinite widening in one's outlook, your works may mean to a foreign reader and admirer.

Some time ago, I happened to pass before your door on a weekend trip to London. I was then in the glow of a recent reading of The Waves and the temptation was great for me to try to meet you. I made bold to ring you up but I knew I could not expect much of a telephone call. Kindly excuse such blunt intrusion. Had there been a chance, I had no time to take it with due formality.

I had translated into French quite a part of Orlando when I heard that the work was being done. I have been wondering whether you have any engagement of that sort concerning The Waves. And, were it not so, if you would consent to entrust such a work to me. A three years' stay in the U.S.A. as a student led me to have a translation of Th. Dreiser (Twelve Men) published by Rieder & Co. in 1923. Since then, I have been busy with university work in Paris and for the last 7 years with teaching English in French public schools.

Whatever your answer may be, I am glad I had at least that chance to tell you of the respectful gratitude I owe you as the writer of books with which I feel enriched.

Yours truly
Fernande Hélie

Letters from readers, Letters about The Waves

Fernande Hélie translated *Douze Hommes* by Theodore Dreiser (F. Rieder, 1923) and *Le Diable Dans le Beffroi* by Edgar Allan Poe (J. et J. Vaucher, 1927). *Orlando* was translated into French by Charles Mauron in 1931, and *The Waves* was translated into French by Marguerite Yourcenar in 1937.

68
Typed; signed
November 27, 1931

OGDEN W. HEATH
139 NASSAU BLVD.
GARDEN CITY, N.Y.

Nov. 27, 1931

Dear Mrs. Woolf:

I have just finished The Waves. I feel so grateful to you for it and so full of the wonder of it that I must share it with someone. But I know no one to whom I can speak with any hope of being understood so do you mind if I tell you. It is a tragic, lovely, penetrating, poignantly moving, stimulating, true book—but what am I saying? Nothing really. All these adjectives give such an inadequate idea of what the book means to me. I took a long time reading it, limiting myself to ten, fifteen, at most twenty pages a day, so as to make it last longer. It is one of the four or five books I have ever read which I honestly hated to come to the end of. I continually found myself stopping to read over a sentence, a page, to read them aloud, rolling the words over my tongue and into every corner of my mouth, like wine, in an attempt to squeeze every last bit of beauty from them. But I know I must have missed a good deal even so. Like great music, it is impossible to absorb it all at one hearing, or reading. So in a day or two I shall start to read it over again.

I have read several reviews of The Waves but to my surprise not one of the reviewers seemed to be aware of what I began to suspect when about half through it and of which now that I have finished it I am all but convinced. All of them spoke of it as being the life story of six or seven, counting Percival, persons. But to me those seven characters, along with the old hairy fellow, not to mention innumerable others, minor characters scattered through the book, are the different selves of one person, the narrator, let us say, Bernard, whose soliloquy at the end is one of the finest things I have ever read. When Jinny kisses Louis, that is the end of childhood and the beginning of adolescence. Percival is the youthful ideal which during school days one longs and hopes to be, but of course he dies when one comes into contact with the world as it is. And Rhoda, the romantic dreamer, dies too when one reaches a certain age and desire is dead. Perhaps I read into it more than you intended but I could mention many other things which seem to bear out my suspicion.

All this strikes me very close because some time ago I started to write a book in which my various selves often become quite distinct, contradictory people. But I laid your book down with the feeling that there was no more to be said. The Waves presents the last words, anything else must be mere repetition. And I thought, What's the use of going on. But even as I write I know I shall go on because one must go on, or die. Because the demon is always lying there in the long grass and he never sleeps for long.

I hope I have not wearied you. Fan mail, as I have had reason to discover lately for myself, is not always a blessing. The impulse back of it is often commendable but to the receiver it is more often a nuisance. Well, you are under no compulsion to answer this. I hope you will tell me if my guess as to your intention is correct. But if you dont care to answer, that is all right with me. The sole impulse back of this letter is to say, as sincerely as I can, Thank you.

Ogden Heath

Letters from readers, Letters about The Waves

Although the last paragraph of this letter suggests popularity, no publications by Ogden Heath have been located. Heath also wrote to Lewis Mumford (Lewis Mumford Papers, University of Pennsylvania) and John Cowper Powys (Powys Papers, Colgate University); James Branch Cabell wrote to him (Cabell mss., 1915-1935, Lilly Library, Indiana University); and Dorothy Richardson wrote him three letters and a card (Special Collections, University of Iowa; see Gloria G. Fromm, ed. *Windows on Modernism: Selected Letters of Dorothy Richardson* [Athens: U of Georgia P, 1995] for two of the letters: 236-27 and 242-43). He was half-paralyzed, bed-ridden, and at work on a book, according to a letter from Richardson to someone else (236), but who he was and what he may have written remains a mystery.

69
***Typed**
November 27, [1931]

21, Lloyd Square,
London, W.C.1.
Nov. 27

Dear Mrs. Woolf,

It is ten years since the only time I met you, when I dined with you one night at Richmond, which you have probably forgotten, so I write to you with diffidence: but the impression The Waves made on me is so great I cannot help it. I have always admired you peculiarly, but in this book I feel you have achieved something quite unparalleled.

I was alone in Wales when I read it: but the pressure of so much harmonious beauty was so great that – even alone – I could not keep quiet about it, & lost my head, & became exclamatory.

I have yet to see a review that gives an inkling of the book's quality: but I suppose the reverse side of the respect a name like yours commands from reviewers is necessarily great slowness in discovering when you have excelled even yourself, as well as everyone else.

I am afraid letters like this one are uncomfortable to receive: so please forgive me for it.

Yours sincerely,
Richard Hughes

Farrell-Lubbock

Richard Hughes (1900-1976) wrote novels, including *A High Wind in Jamaica* (1929) and *The Human Predicament* (1961), edited collections of public school verse, wrote an introduction for William Faulkner's *The Sound and the Fury* in 1930, and wrote children's stories, so many that *The Wonder-dog: The Collected Children's Stories of Richard Hughes* was published after his death (1977). See *L*2 453-54 (1161 and 1162) for Woolf's description of Hughes and the meeting mentioned here and n1 for his own recollections of this dinner. See also *D*4 104, n12.

70
Handwritten
December 5, 1931

Crouch Farm House,
Crouch.

5th Dec. 1931.

Dear Mrs. Woolf,

Do not feel because I am writing again that you need trouble to answer me, but I want to tell you what deep pleasure your letter gave me. It has made me so happy to know I can express what I feel about your work, which I admire so greatly.

We cannot understand any one having been made ill by The Waves. Brian and I read it solidly for hours each day until we had finished it, we were so absorbed. Mother read it in smaller doses because her only time for reading is in bed before she goes to sleep. One can only think something must have been the matter with the people who read it and became ill, for we are convinced it was not the book. I found its very concentrated essence a stimulation; ~~[ ]~~ and <the> concentration, which was so penetrating, seemed to flow with the smoothness of water itself.

It is most kind of you to say you will try and borrow a copy of On Being Ill for me sometime.

I am so sorry you have been ill in bed; you must take great care of yourself. If ever you wished to escape from responsibility and have a few days rest, we should always welcome you here; and of course we'd ask no one else in all the time and give you a quiet time with walks around here. We know only too well how horrid it is to be ill, for we are none of us strong ourselves.

I myself am much better now.

On Monday Mother and I hope to find some more primroses in the woods, if we do we shall send you them.

I am wishing all the time for you to feel much better soon. Mother sends her kind regards and sympathy.

Yours, Joan.

Letters from readers, Letters about The Waves

Joan Easdale (1913-1998) published what she wrote with Hogarth Press: *A Collection of Poems (written between the ages of 14 and 17)*, 1931; *Clemence and Clare*, 1932; and

Amber Innocent, 1939. J. H. Willis, Jr. mentions a letter to Vita Sackville-West dated September 16, 1931, *L4* 379 (2436) in which Woolf mentions the odd juxtaposition in Joan of the "chocolate box flapper" who "produces those strange poems" (185-87). Her mother was Gladys Easdale; see letter 74.

See *A* 59-61 for her letter and poem to Leonard Woolf after Virginia Woolf's death.

71
Typed; signed
December 5, 1931

University, Virginia.
Dec. 5th 1931.

Dear Miss Woolf,

This letter is nothing more than a foolish expression of admiration for your latest work, foolish in that I have no intention of trying to analyze your book. (I need not add that I am in no wise connected with the Department of English Literature.) Perhaps I may best give vent to my enthusiasm by saying that, if a genius in the field of philosophy is to be defined as one who can ask questions nobody is able to answer, a genius in the field of literature may be regarded as one whose work produces in those of us who propose to write, a feeling of the utmost depression, culminating in a desire to destroy all that we have previously written and to retire to some convent, such as that of mathematics or the sciences. If I am ever cursed with a child who aspires to be an author, I shall do all in my power to prevent this hypothetical offspring from getting hold of your works; in the mean time, I shall reread them as often as possible. In short, I like your book.

Sincerely yours,
W. G. Weedon

Letters from readers, Letters about The Waves

W. G. Weedon (1908-1984) began his teaching career in mathematics, became a professor of philosophy specializing in oriental philosophy, and then went to the University of

Virginia in 1963 as a University Professor, which allowed him to teach in different departments throughout the university. He was an avid reader, and he helped found the Literary Seminars, the only interdisciplinary courses in the university at the time. He was interested in obsolete languages, helping found a Center for Obsolete Languages in California, and he read and spoke Chinese and Japanese so fluently that part of his military work in World War II was breaking the Japanese Code. He was also a wonderful gardener, and he and his wife Elizabeth often entertained distinguished guests to the university, including Gertrude Stein and Alice B. Toklas, W. H. Auden, Elizabeth Bowen, Stephen Spender, T. S. Eliot, and Irwin Panofsky.

72
Handwritten
December 15, 1931

TELEPHONE :
MUSEUM 4095.

THE PENN CLUB.
8, 9, 10 TAVISTOCK SQUARE.
W.C.1.
December 15th 1931

Virginia Woolf,
Dear Madam,

May I thank you for the beauty and truth of "The Waves." To read it gives me the keenest joy, and I am filled with exultation that such a lovely thing should be.

Yours very truly,
Grace Wilson.

Letters from readers, Letters about The Waves

Grace Wilson (1903-1991) taught English at Roan's School for Girls in Greenwich, London, from 1930 until her retirement in 1963. She met John Wyndham (1903-1969), the science fiction writer, at the Penn Club (which then offered permanent accommodations) in 1931, they began a relationship in 1935, and a large correspondence between them during the war years exists in the Wyndham archive at the University of Liverpool. They married in 1963 and lived in Petersfield, Hampshire, just outside the grounds of Bedales School where Wyndham had been a young student.

73
Handwritten
December 17, 1931

TEL: AMERSHAM 531.

WOODROW HIGH HOUSE,
AMERSHAM,
BUCKS.

Dec. 17. 1931
Dear Madam

All the wise and bookloving celebrities will have praised "The Waves", I know, so that perhaps you will be tired of appreciation, but I am writing as one of the public who picks up a novel to be entertained. I am quite sure you wanted to reach people like myself and will be glad that you have succeeded. It is very nearly a miracle to unlock the inarticulate soul.

I keep thinking what fun it would be to write – the outside sayings and doings of each sex, and put the two books side by side, and read from one to the other. It would be extraordinarily like living. The idea reminds me of some music I have heard but can't remember what.

Thank you for doing something so difficult and brave.

Yours faithfully
Harriette R. Campbell.

Letters from readers, Letters about The Waves

Harriette Russell Campbell (1883-1954) wrote romances and detective novels, including *The Mystery of Saint's Island* (1927), *The Sting Glove Mystery* (1936), *The Moor Fires Mystery* (1938), and *Three Names for Murder* (1940). Born in the United States and completely deaf by the age of 14, she married Nigel Campbell (who prospected for gold and learned the US banking system before returning to the UK) and was active in the suffragette movement.

74
Handwritten
[1931]

TELEPHONE
BOROUGH GREEN 66.
STATION: WROTHAM

CROUCH FARM HOUSE,
CROUCH,
NR. SEVENOAKS.

Thursday.

Dear Mrs Woolf,

Brian is conducting his own 'March Macabre' at the Royal College of Music public concert next Tuesday 27th at 4.45. He would like it so much if you & Mr Woolf happen to have time to spare to hear it. No tickets are required. But I am afraid the 27th is an impossible day, & I must confess I hardly like to tell you!

Thank you for your letter accepting 'The Castle.' I always felt that book especially belonged to you. It is 26 years since I read the books of 'The Upanishads' so I may be mistaken, but while I read 'The Waves' I am continually reminded of those great books with their rich & beautiful similes –

Yours sincerely,
Gladys. E. Easdale

Letters from readers, Letters about The Waves

Gladys Easdale (1885-1970) published a memoir entitled *Middle Age, 1885-1932* (1935) in which she described having tea with Virginia Woolf. Woolf's reaction is in *D*4 345. Although Kafka's *The Castle* had been published with a translation by Thomas Mann in September 1930, Horace Walpole's *The Castle of Otranto* is the more likely candidate for the book mentioned here. Neither book is in the Library of Leonard and Virginia Woolf at Washington State University. See letter 70.

75
Handwritten
[1931]

This is anonymous, and tiresome no doubt. An old, undistinguished, but moderately discerning man may now be pictured as swinging a censer before your image. He has read your wonderful poem called 'Waves' – has been taken and shaken and hoovered by it to such a degree that he must pay his debt of recognition somehow.

He takes no credit to himself for recognising it as a poem, an epic of life in fact – that is so clear.

Accept, please, this blend of gratitude and apology.

Letters from readers, Letters about The Waves

76
Typed; signed
January 8, 1932

83 Tuam Road,
Plumstead Common.
London. S.E.18.
8th January 1932

Dear Madam,

I want to tell you how much I love your books - I have only read "The Voyage Out", "To the Lighthouse" and "The Waves".

I think I envy you more than anybody in the world. Everybody is suffering from something, and to my mind one of the worst sufferings is inarticulateness - it is simply awful - to feel bursting with a terrible desire to express yourself and to be sort of paralysed, it can grow into an anguish.

When I read "To the Lighthouse" I realised how stupendously you were gifted. All the thoughts that accumulate and press on one's brain seemed to tumble out quite naturally on your pages - it is wonderful - I was filled with real ecstasy when I read. That evening meal for instance, and all the thoughts buzzing about - "She let it uphold her and sustain her, this admirable fabric of the masculine intelligence, which ran up and down, across this way and that, like iron girders spanning the swaying fabric, upholding the world, so that she could trust herself to it utterly, even shut her eyes or flicker them for a moment, as a child staring up from its pillow winks at the myriad layers of the leaves of a tree" and this too "Her eyes were so clear that they seem to go round the table unveiling each of these people and their thoughts and their feelings, without effort, like a light stealing under water that its ripples and the reeds in it, and the minnows balancing themselves, and the sudden silent trout are all lit up hanging, trembling." Just fancy being able to get one sentence like that quite clear and whole from you brain - and yet you get thousands - I envy you passionately. When you have finished a book I wonder if you feel most completely physically exhausted and gorgeously satisfied - you simply must.

I was filled with bitter rage when I read that thing called "The Flames" in Punch. Why are people allowed to make their living by swooping down on lovely things and picking at them. I hate critics, I would draw them all as vultures with horrid gleaming eyes waiting to swoop. There can never be any criticism anywhere – it is a foolish and conceited profession.

I have not read "The Waves" properly, I bought it for a friend and skimmed through it before I gave it. The ecstasy I feel when I read your books gives me almost tears in my heart - nothing to do with my eyes. I have still to read all your other books thank goodness.

I simply had to tell you all this
Yours sincerely,
(Miss) M. I. Rowell

Mrs. Virginia Woolf,
52 Tavistock Square.
W.C.1.

Letters from readers, Letters about The Waves

The parody "The Flames" appeared in *Punch* on 18 November 1931: 552-53. Mr. Smith, Mr. Brown, Mr. Jones, and Mr. Robinson are all sitting in front of a fire that has "just been lighted." The parody uses italics for the interludes and ends with "*The flames shot up and then sank. The fire glowed.*"

77
Handwritten
January 9, 1932

Dublin: Saturday 9 January 1932
(as from King's College Cambridge)

Dear Virginia,

At last I have ~~got~~ had the opportunity that I have been long waiting for – two quiet <whole> days for "The Waves." I had read the first chapter in the middle of term, & rightly decided that here was a book that ~~requir~~ demanded the fullest mental <spiritual> activity & could not be taken as a substitute for Bridge. And so I did not attempt it immediately after term when I was tired & jaded. My patience ~~has~~ (& forbearance) has been rewarded.

Dear Virginia, you have gloriously succeeded. ~~If~~ There ~~can~~ <could> be no half-way about "The Waves": it must be either a great success or a great failure: & it is a great success. It is much the best novel that you have written - & (in my opinion, though I know that comparisons are foolish as well as odious) the best English novel since "The Return of the Native."

You have succeeded, by your imagination & your ~~Puritan~~ economy, in conveying your own vision ~~of~~ (audition would be the better word) of the rhythm of life.

Susan gives me something similar to what I get from Natascha at the end of "War & Peace" (the part that so many people object to) and Jinny at the beginning something like Natasha at the opera. You have been marvellously successful over Jinny – the "perfect whore" has sometimes been managed externally successfully (e.g. by Somerset Maugham in Cakes & Ale), but internally never before.

I like Louis very much. Neville is a little vague in parts – but this is chiefly my fault, because I stupidly identified myself with him early on & then had to de-identify him. Bernard <l'homme moyen litteraire?> is terrific & the last soliloquy, especially the very end, the best part of the book. Apart from this, I like the section after Percival's death best.

You are the only writer I know who can describe the subtleties of bereavement truthfully ~~&~~; and I prefer you here to the end of "The Voyage Out" which before I had considered the best that had been done.

"The Waves" will be criticised – I have heard it so criticised –, as "Mrs Dalloway" was criticised, on the ground that its subject matter is unimportant. It will be complained that Rhoda's living with Louis, & her suicide, are dismissed in sentences, that Bernard's wife, ~~(~~though he is obviously the sort of man to whom the character of his wife mattered, is only alluded to, that they are all grossly sentimental about Percival, etc. I think that this criticism doesn't realise that your novel is, to use the language of mathematical logic, a novel of a higher logical type than the standard narrative (or reflective) novel. What you are concerned with is, not the importance or unimportance of situations or behaviours, but the importance <u>of</u> the importance & unimportance of etc. i.e. the Importance of ~~Life~~ <Being Important>. (At least this is how it appears to me.) And since this second-type importance is, to me, more important than ~~the~~ first-type-importance-in-itself, it makes "The Waves" seem to me such an exceedingly good & important book. (It is better than "Mrs Dalloway" essentially because in the latter you have one first-~~order~~ type scale of importance to play with, whereas in "The Waves" you have six – or perhaps only five because Rhoda has got something different which I ~~don't think~~ don't understand sufficiently to intellectualise about.)

Your affectionate admirer
Richard Braithwaite

Letters from readers, Letters about The Waves

By kind permission of the Provost and Scholars of King's College, Cambridge 2006.

Richard Braithwaite (1900-1990) was a Fellow of King's College, University Lecturer in Moral Science, 1928-1934, and Knightsbridge Professor of Moral Philosophy at Cambridge, 1953-1967. His first wife, Dorothea Cotter Morison, had died in 1928. He coordinated a survey on belief done in *Nation & Athenaeum*, the results of which were published by Hogarth Press as *The Nature of Religious Belief* (1927). His work was in the philosophy of science (*Scientific Explanation: A Study of the Function of Theory, Probability and Law in Science*, 1953) and games theory (*Theory of Games as a Tool for the Moral Philosopher*, 1955). Braithwaite worked to admit women to membership of Cambridge University and thus to its degrees; his second wife, Margaret Masterman, whom he married in 1932, was a Newnham graduate who had read Modern and Medieval Languages and Moral Sciences.

78
Handwritten
February 16, 1932

9 St Edmund's Terrace.
N.W.8.
Feb. 16. 1932.

Dear Mrs. Woolf,

I was dining a few nights ago with my old friend, the classical tutor at Somerville, H. L. Lorimer, and talking of The Waves. She had sent it out to a sister, married to some one who is investigating mosquitos or something of the kind in the jungle, and had had this letter of thanks in return. I asked if I might have it to send to you. Because in spite of all that has already been said in print, there is something in the manuscript word and in the circumstances of the writing that makes it valuable.

Yours sincerely,
Helen Waddell

78a
Handwritten enclosure; incomplete (no signature)
January 4, 1932

<From Mrs. K. B. Williamson>
Tanah Rata
Cameron Highlands
via Tapah F.M.S.
4th Jan. 1932

My dearest Hilda

I can't find your last letter, but I don't think at any rate there was any business matter to reply to in it. Perhaps the one that did have business matters which I answered just before we went off for Xmas was really your last. But now I have "The Waves"! I am in the middle of it: I am in the midst of all that "Mysterium tremendum" feeling that overwhelms one in a new and powerful work of imagination, and can write nothing that's not ecstatic about it now. I read "Mrs. Dalloway" with interest and appreciation some years ago: but this with its new unfathomable technique, its possibilities that can never have been imagined before of subtlety and truthfulness, & of being at the centre of each personality, seems an unheralded and unsurpassable achievement. One (I haven't read Joyce though, except Anna Livia Plurabelle which is unintelligible) feels there is no other way of writing novels now! The prose is really imaginative prose, and not "poetic prose," I think; there is a wonderful wealth of images of sensation and feeling, and accumulations of such often bore or annoy me, but here they seem rightly used, for significance and beauty. As to the characters, perhaps I've a regret that so much is given to the two typical, purely typical, women, Susan & Jinny: without any Rhoda in them. There are Susan-Rhodas & Jinny-Rhodas in life, and it wouldn't have spoilt the typical quality of the book, its character as a general picture of life, to have had them rather than the plain types. None of the men were plain types. As to the whole philosophic imaginative feeling of the book, its whole feeling about life, and about man, I haven't got on to that yet.

Letters from readers, Letters about The Waves

Helen Waddell (1889-1965), a well-known Medieval scholar, brought the middle ages to a wide audience in *The Wandering Scholars* (1927) and in her novel *Peter Abelard* (1933). She wrote poetry, translated works from Chinese, Latin, and French, and was an assistant editor of *The Nineteenth Century* during WWII. See D. Felicitas Corrigan's *Helen Waddell: A Biography* (1990).

Hilda Lorimer (d. 1954) was Classical Tutor at Somerville College, Oxford from 1896-1937 and published *Homer and the Monuments* (1950), but little can be found out about her sister. Tapah is in Malaysia.

79
Handwritten
February 17, 1932

TELEPHONE NO.:
ST. AUBIN'S 87.

OAK GLEN,
ST. BRELADE'S
JERSEY.

Feb. 17. 1932.

Dear Virginia Woolf -

You, the bard, sweeping your fingers across the strings and chanting of life and thought tell us when Percival passed he 'was flowering with green leaves and was laid in earth with all his branches still sighing in the summer wind.'

In 1922 I dreamt that I was driving with my husband along the dark road he had chosen until we came to a high black rock which barred our way entirely. He said "we can go no further; You must find our way back".

When I woke I thought "this is a warning I must try and counteract the course he is taking with Clive" (our son). Soon after I dreamt I was in a house with my husband and daughter Winifred. While I was standing at a window I saw a fine young tree near by fall and disappear entirely into the earth. We said "There must be a fissure – We must leave the house for it will perish."

When I woke I had no doubt that this dream referred to Clive and thought it meant he might be utterly estranged from us. I worked unceasingly to prevent this and thought all was well when his motor-bicycle skidded & he was thrown & killed. No suffering. With him the house has perished.

I wonder why you thought of Percival as a young tree.

Yours very faithfully,
L. C. Rose.

Letters from readers, Letters about The Waves

80
Handwritten
June 23, 1932

['Quentins']
Rodmell,
Nr. Lewes,
Sussex.

23-6-32.

Dear Mrs. Woolf,

I have just read 'The Waves.' Please forgive my presumption, as a stranger, in writing to tell you my appreciation of your strange & lovely book. I have read it twice, but this is only a beginning, because in it are a thousand lovely things that will exist for all time to be read and re-read, for inspiration, for music, always new, always unique.

I imagine that the book must have been written gloriously & exhaustingly in an hour's mood, or through many separate recurrences of just that mood. The book's atmosphere is so constantly & consistently rarified & inspired, tense with the concentration of perception and understanding, that it seems impossible to associate with it all the labour of 'composition,' the pen-chewing, altering and despairing, exhilaration & sense of futility & frustration, & final measured accomplishment. Each sentence in it seems to have been netted intact & perfect from the elves from a flying chariot of inspiration – a mood that lives like a flame for a little while, & then dies. As if the Muse were with you, & returned again, & again. One feels that of ninety-nine per cent of the books one reads no Muse ever visited the author at all. Muses are, after all, hopelessly archaic, like Santa Claus. Nowadays one just writes.

So I am clamorous with admiration, & make no apology! I love the sorcery with which you have frozen the filmy wisps of minds into lovely stalactites for ever; & your wealth of comparison – simile linking with simile, like the iron rings the Conjuror plays with, magically linking & interlinking & parting again, none knows how, so that one is fascinated & bewildered, aware only of purpose & pattern & hope.

And the petty tribute I would pay you, the highest of which I am capable, is that I think the egoistical adorable Charlotte Brontë would have loved your book, not thinking of it as 'literature,' but poring over it over the fire as she sat lonely at Haworth, learning from it, adding from it to her pitiful store of world – & people – knowledge, & with it oiling her own stiff puppets.

This probably sounds rubbish to you. But, I am only trying to say thank you for a tremendous rich pleasure.

Sincerely yours,
Elizabeth Read

Nash-Rylands

Elizabeth Read was a social worker in Stepney (*D*4 170, n12); in a letter to Quentin Bell dated July 26, 1933, *L5* 206-07 (2767), Woolf says she's "a virgin, living with a large dog, rhapsodical, slim—about eighteen; now lodged in an Inn—but for the past six months at Quentins, in the village" (206). She later married Gilbert Denny, and they had a son, George. The fullest diary description by Woolf is on March 27, 1935, *D*4 292. See letters 81 and 91.

81
Handwritten
August 14, [1932]

Harveys,
Glynde.

August 14th

Dear Mrs. Woolf, Thank you for these books. I enjoyed three of them immensely. Forster is very good indeed, isn't he? And 'Jacob's Room' – I wish I didn't so much enjoy reading what you write. It is discontenting, now that I know you a little. But I can't read Gogol. I can't read Tolstoy, either. Nor any of them. That condemns me for ever, but there it is. I'm not sure enough on my pins for even the quietest set-to with dark & dangerous minds; they terrify & oppress me. Their tortures are not the sort of tortures I like, & their laughter echoes round gloomy caverns – I shut the book with a slam (not your copy) & thank God for my fat sleeping dog, & rush to the passionate, but safe, bosom of Charlotte, or the silver calm of Jane Austen. – This will not interest you, but I have confessed.

Small Marie of Stepney still talks of 'the tall lady.' You made her happy, &

somehow it wasn't the chocolate cake or the goldfish. Children are true democrats & nothing counts at all to them but kindliness, & until their eyes are clouded with Reason & Thought, they see true. We discuss these matters nightly in her tub, when she ceases to be Marie & becomes Child.

I want to talk about your writing, but it seems an impertinence & I couldn't when I was with you. I suppose all commentary is tedious unless it comes from people who either admire or love, & I think you must labour under a heavy burden of other people's words, words. I used to think that imagination plus sensual pleasure at the contact of pen with paper were enough to make a writer; then I grew & now I am annihilated at the realisation of how drilled & strong a mind must be to produce a readable book. Someone lent me 'Orlando' (the magic of 'The hand' having eaten deeply into my bones), & then I stole 'The Waves,' & then most of the others followed naturally, & now – I'm sorry – but I have an idol. I love your books because you are so clear & strong, & can pin down to the bench not only reality & fact, which journalists can do, but also their shadows, fancy & probability, & the full meaning of the whole, as far as any of it has meaning. And with such clarity. Searchlights you have, to turn from every angle upon a thought, so that when it is presented one marvels at the simplicity & visibleness of the crystal-pure thing, not obscured with words & a clot of implication, like a limb in plaster of Paris. You lift curtains on different scenes, & indicate them with a pitiful, satiric gesture, drop the curtains & away you go. There is no reply.

It isn't enough, really. One wants more. Doubtless the most interesting thing in life is Life; also, having caught your spirit (or thought one has), it is definitely beneficial in times of un-balance or bloody woe to remember how you were bitter-honest, comprehending, & at the end of your commentary ever so slightly shrugged your shoulders. You are an astringent memory, as against the Russians who seem to me to bludgeon the futility of everything with loud moans. But yet one needs more. One wants your searchlights on bigger issues. Are there any? I don't know. I can't bring it down to a practical matter, because my mind stops several hundred miles before yours begins. In any case I'm being impertinent. I loved you best in the Common Reader.

Oh, forgive me. It's worse than anything – it's sheer tedium nonsense what I write. But I've nothing else to send you.

Thanking you for everything,
Elizabeth Read

Nash-Rylands

See letter 80 for biographical information and letter 91.

82
Typed; signed
September 6, 1932

Bloomfield Hills,
Michigan,
September 6, 1932

To Virginia Woolf:

I have just finished reading "The Waves" and though I never write letters to authors, I feel that I must write this letter. And the must that impells me, is not of course the same which tells me that before this letter is finished I must leave it to prepare the vegetables for supper. I must write it because in these phrases, in these chapters, in this book, more than in any of the others (which are benefit enough, heaven knows), you have written my own feelings that live on the edge of thought, articulated them in phrases of which I am not capable.

With the cumulative momentum of a wave, your words, your phrases heap all of life together, and slowly let it ebb, leaving one alone facing the enemy with the short, sharp challenge of the ant that rises up against the foot ~~that is~~ descending to crush it.

It is no comfort that you know the enemy as I do, though there is a slim satisfaction in it. But there is a certain pleasure in seeing the ebb and flow eye to eye with you for a moment. For I do not follow you always; often you brush beyond me because you are subtler and fuller of knowledge. But the feeling is the same; life comes to us along the same nerve paths - yours so much more complicated and sensitive than mine. You see a more intricate fabric than I see, both above and below the surface. With the glow of yours upon it, my imagination can follow a little way, and the rich texture of your words gives me more pleasure than I am able to explain to you.

Seven years ago in "Mrs Dalloway" you expressed for me the moment, the now, that forever torments me: - "what she loved was this, here, now, in front of her; the fat lady in the cab." The book delighted me so much that I have used it since as a test, a measure. I loan it to an acquaintance, and in his comment when he returns it, is drawn, usually, the chart of our future course. I know him then for a stranger or an intimate, and in the back fly leaf of my copy are written the names of ten people (I like to keep a record of those to whom I loan the books I most like) and only two of these caught you - your style that so perfectly - more than poetry - catches the rhythm, the ebb and flow, the thought that fringes every act, and the past that is always an overtone. It pleased me that my half-brother, at twenty, delighted in you; knowing you a little helped us to know each other better.

Of course in "A Room of One's Own," you spoke to me directly (as to how many others?) because, like Bernard, I have always made phrases, written them on scattered sheets, or watched them wing through the ceiling as I lay in bed of a morning, knowing it impossible to call them back. There is obviously no loss in the fact that I have never had a room of my own, except to me, but to me my whole life seems lost because of that small thing. As I read you again, now, I realize that I do not rise up and demand a room of my own because never, never could I write as you write. Your writing is what I should have liked mine to be, and with you in the world why can I not, now, after years of scribbling on scraps, why can I not now enjoy this summer afternoon - as I am enjoying it with one side of my mind - wholly, give up phrases, give up trying to fit the moment into words, feeling it unfulfilled and nothing if I cannot "retrieve it from formlessness with words?"

It is the urge you know so well, but weak in me; too weak to form into a steady stream as it washes back and forth over every occasion in my life, ubiquitous as this knowledge of death that you make so definite, so tenuous, so - just as it is.

Perhaps it will mean nothing to you, perhaps something, that in America, in Michigan, in the country near the ugliest city in the world, Detroit, is this woman sitting in the late afternoon sunshine writing to you in words that do not say what she wants them to say. It does not greatly matter. I shall send the letter because it wrote itself after I had put down The Waves, with the clock saying it is forty-five minutes since the impulse took root enough to make me drag the typewriter toward this couch and begin to write.

Neither does it greatly matter that the clock, which has ticked off more than a hundred years of time, sits on a huge desk whose little drawers and pigeon holes are stuffed with scribbled scraps of paper; nor (except to those who will come in hungry, presently) that the clock says the vegetables should have been prepared some time ago, and cooking, now, for supper.

Faithfully yours,
Marion Holden Bemis
Mrs. Elden J. Bemis

Letters from readers, Letters about The Waves

Marion Holden Bemis (b. 1893) reviewed *Orlando* in the *Detroit Free Press* (6 January 1929: part 4), where she had been art editor from 1921-1925. She was a public relations executive, free-lance writer, and editor. She married Elden Johnson Bemis in 1922; he died in 1949.

83
Handwritten
October 4, 1932

COLLINGBEAMS,
DONHEAD ST. MARY,
SHAFTESBURY,
DORSET.
4 Oct. 1932

Dear Mrs Woolf,

I apologise for having kept M. Delattre's book so long. My friend, A. M. Allen, & I have both read it with much interest, but our chief pleasure came from the re-reading of all your books, necessary so as to judge of his opinions & see how far we agreed with him. It puzzles me that he should regard the lives of the people in the "Waves" as unclear. After one hasty preliminary reading, I found that not only the characters but the lives of your six were far more clear to me than the people expounded through several volumes of most novellists, not to speak of real people of one's own acquaintance. A. M. Allen read "The Waves" first with such delight in the language that she needed a second reading to see the people themselves.

As you see, we are both great admirers of your books & we cannot miss this opportunity of thanking you for all the delight you have given us in reading them.

If only we were French we could end up with Homage.

Yours sincerely
Sophy Sanger

Letters from readers, Letters about The Waves

Sophy Sanger (1881-1950) graduated from Newnham in 1902 and was involved in politics (child labor, political and economic science). Her books include a *Report on the Legal Limitation of Hours of Work in Industry and Commerce in the United Kingdom* (1906), *The Permanent Court of International Justice and "Labour Cases"* (1921), and *The International Labour Organisation of the League of Nations* (1920). Her companion, Alice Maud Allen, wrote *Sophy Sanger: A Pioneer in Internationalism* in 1958; see Allen's letter to Leonard Woolf in *A* 146-47.

84
Handwritten
October 15, 1932

Burnhams,
Naphill,
Nr. Gt.Wycombe,
Bucks.
October 15th 1932.

Dear Miss Virginia Woolf,

May I tell you how grateful I am to you for "The Waves." I have been reading your work since I was at school and it has always helped me to have an unmuddled attitude to life, to see the vividness and importance of every minute, the significance of every action.

"The Waves" was a tremendous adventure. I have just read it a second time. So rarely, in prose, is anyone so keenly appreciative of individual words. It is like a symphony. Suddenly the English language is translated into fluid music, like Greek, so that a man who knew not a word of it, ~~coul~~ could listen to it and realise its force and beauty and liquidity.

I felt compelled to write to you, because I do ~~fe~~ believe in gratitude, and even from a very young and unimportant person it must give you a warm feeling to know you are so valued.

Yours very sincerely,
Elizabeth Coles (aged 20.)

P.S. I shall never forget the sight of Susan's little screwed handkerchief lying, with her hate knotted in it.

Letters from readers, Letters about The Waves

Elizabeth Coles Taylor (1912-1975) was the author of sixteen novels (among them *At Mrs. Lippincote's*, 1946, *A View of the Harbour*, 1947, and *The Wedding Group*, 1968) and short stories (such as in *The Blush*, 1958 and *The Devastating Boys*, 1972). Virago Press re-issued several of her works in the 1980s, and she has been praised for her "subtle observation of women's lives and the morally significant details of social manners" (*Feminist Companion* 1057). Taylor once gave a lecture on Woolf at Oxford, and in *Current Biography* for 1948, she names Austen, Flaubert, Compton-Burnett, Turgenev, Sterne, and Woolf as her favorite authors (614).

85
Handwritten
[1932]

ASHTON WOLD,
PETERBOROUGH.

Dear Mrs. Woolf,

The Common Readers have been a great worry to me. Barbara may have told you that I am a scientist, and, as you know, we outdo even those mediaeval angels in keeping our eyes firmly on the pinpoint – in my case the frog's egg before fertilisation. Some of the essays to which I turn for recreation I appreciate at the time, and a few stimulate me to further reading. But the trouble about your Common Readers is that all the essays compel me to investigate further and God knows where my Biophysics will go.

When I open my Common Reader it is pleasant to remember that you have known that it is one of my favourites, and I am duly grateful to you.

Barbara tells me that you have invited me and her to dinner with you next week which also will be delightful, but I am perplexed about the brown homespun. I have a furry Austrian and a special-occasion London, but brown homespun defeats me. So don't be displeased when I turn up in something else.

Victor Rothschild.

Nash-Rylands

Sir Nathaniel Mayer Victor Rothschild (1910-1990), zoologist, public servant, and book collector, married Barbara Hutchinson in December 1933; they divorced in 1946. In a letter to Vita Sackville-West dated June 23 (?), 1933, *L5* 198-99 (2755), Woolf mentions that Victor and Barbara are coming to dine, so it is possible that the above letter should be dated 1933 instead of 1932.

86
***Typed**
March 22, 1933

The Victoria
University of Manchester.
March 22nd 1933

Dear Mrs. Woolf,

I have much pleasure in writing to inform you that the Council and Senate propose to ask the Court of the University at its Meeting on May 17th to authorise the conferment upon you of the Degree of Doctors of Letters (honoris causa).

It is proposed that the Degree should be conferred on the occasion of the Celebration of the Jubilee of the admission of Women to the University. The Degree Ceremony will be held on the evening of Saturday, July 8th, in connection with a Reception to be given by the Council of the University.

I shall be glad to know, as soon as possible, whether you will be able to be present at the Ceremony on that occasion to receive the Degree.

Will you kindly regard this information as strictly confidential until the Court has approved the Degree? As soon as this has been done I will communicate with you again.

Believe me,
Yours very truly,
Walter H. Moberly
Vice-Chancellor

Mrs. Virginia Woolf
52 Tavistock Square
London W.C.1.

Letters from agents, editors, publishers, etc., Fan mail

Published by kind permission of the University of Manchester.

Walter Moberly (1881-1974) was a highly respected administrator who served the University of Manchester as Vice-Chancellor from 1926-34 and as Chair of the University Grants Committee from 1935-49. See *L5* 171 for Woolf's reply, dated March 26, 1933 (2719), and letter 87. Although Woolf consistently refused such honors, such letters (see also letters 94, 109, and 110) reveal the high level of public esteem accorded to her. See S. P. Rosenbaum, "Virginia Woolf and the Clark Lectures," *Charleston Magazine* 22 (Autumn/Winter 2000: 5-10) for a somewhat different refusal.

87
***Typed**
March 29, 1933

The Vice-Chancellor,
The University,
Manchester.
March 29th 1933

Dear Mrs. Woolf,

I have received with much regret your letter of the 26th inst. We shall all be disappointed at your decision but we understand and respect the grounds on which it is based.

It would, none the less, have been a great pleasure to have had the opportunity of testifying in the way proposed to the very high regard in which your work is held here.

Believe me,
Yours sincerely,
Walter H. Moberly.

Mrs. Virginia Woolf,
52 Tavistock Square
London W.C.1.

Letters from agents, editors, publishers, etc., Fan mail

See letter 86 for biographical information.

88
***Typed**
April 3, 1933

Eight East Sixty-ninth Street
New York
April 3rd

My dear Mrs. Woolf -

Your letter arrived, and caused a great deal of happiness. I never really allowed myself to believe that you would not have already promised the manuscript of Flush to someone you knew. As it is, I feel as though I had been given the piece of the birthday cake that contained the ring - That is, you must know, cause for excitement to bachelors of nine.

(My engagement was announced this very April third, so I shall not long, thank God, remain a bachelor of twenty-three.)

I don't know what to say about the business end of your letter. As an innocent connected with INDUSTRY in New York, I should drive a very hard bargain. As a foolish boy who has spent a great abundance of his happiest hours reading, I should be anxious and willing to give you anything you might suggest. As a combination of the two, I call you at 40 pounds and retire to hide behind the screen with Lady Teazle. There you will find me, awaiting with shudders (delicate conventional shudders) the outcome of your interview with Mammon. (I interview him every day on 42nd St. so that now I am less than afraid of him.)

Please be frank with me. I may have insulted you; I may have suddenly become a plutocrat in your eyes. Please tell me honestly how you feel about the price I mentioned. The fact is, you have never sold and I have never bought a manuscript. Perhaps you would be willing to consult one who professes to know. Whatever I should have said, it just seems that I can't evaluate a manuscript in pounds. It's like weighing a soul before invoicing it to St. Peter, or trying to collect damages from a railroad that has crippled your wife. If £40 is all right, then the great transaction's done, and I shall be a proud god-father. If not, tant pis, I shall try again, if you permit me another chance!

I am, of course, delighted at the idea of it's being really a manuscript, not a typescript! That makes it a thousand times more real and living - a modern machine has not had a hand in its making.

Your mention of the Browning letters reminds me of an incident that I have always enjoyed remembering. Last autumn, when I was at Corpus Christi in

Cambridge, I was arguing with a friend about the frequency of the letters that Robert wrote to the invalid Elizabeth. This took us to the D.N.B., a copy of which we found in the Corpus Library – But this edition contained no "Robert Browning." It had been published before his death. He was later discovered in an appendix! After several years of efficient study in Yale's new factory of the mind and book, this made me very happy, leisurely, peaceful, and interested. It was a symbol of the spirit, perhaps, that prompted your father's Hours In A Library, the spirit that pushes time and temporality into the noisy street, and is content to leave them there, wrestling.

I read your letter to my mother and she was more than relieved to know that Flush was "red." That is the color our cocker was once (during the War, I think), but now he is nearly all white, when he is not too dirty. He is the perfect example of the country gentleman who has kept his physique and kept his form.

Very sincerely yours,
F. B. Adams Jr.

Letters from agents, editors, publishers, etc., Correspondence about publications

---

Frederick Baldwin Adams, Jr. (1910-2001) was an antiquarian, bibliographer, and collector, particularly of works by Thomas Hardy, Robert Frost, and Karl Marx. He was the Director of Pierpont Morgan Library from 1948 to 1969 and President of the Association Internationale de Bibliophilie from 1974-1983. This letter replies to Woolf's, dated March 14, 1933, *L5* 167-68 (2715). Her reply to this letter is dated April 24, 1933, *L5* 179 (2730). The manuscript of *Flush* (3 holograph notebooks) is in the Berg Collection, and the proof copy was first owned by Hugh Walpole and then by P. J. Allen.

This letter was first published in Lola L. Szladits' "The Art and Craft of Collecting Manuscripts" in *Book Collecting: A Modern Guide* (1977), edited by Jean Peters, 74-75.

89
Typed; signed
June 26, 1933

11 West 107 Street,
New York City, U.S.A.,
June 26, 1933.

Mrs. Virginia Woolf,
c/o Messrs. Harcourt, Brace and Company,
393 Madison Avenue,
New York City.

Dear Mrs. Woolf:

I have recently approached Messrs. Harcourt, Brace and Company with the request that they put me in touch with you, in order that I might approach you in the matter of my doing a critical study of your work for publication in this country. This they have consented to do, and they believe, as I have for some time believed, that such a study would fill a very definite need in our literary world, provided, of course, it were capably done.

It seems to me that a critical study of a living author should not be undertaken without some co-operation by that author. For that reason my first step has been to obtain your own reaction to my plan. First of all, I feel that I must know whether you have any objections to a long study, as such, of your work. Not, as yet, having published any fiction myself, I do not know how it feels to have one's literary creations raked over by a total stranger.

Perhaps your answer to this question will depend on who this person is who thus approaches you. I cannot refer you to any published work, as I am not yet twenty-one, and am only now beginning to enter the literary and critical world. My chief qualification for doing a study of your fiction is an intense love of every word of it. I put that first because I feel that the subject of criticism should be an integral part of the critic's intellectual make-up. Your work stands in just that relation to me; it has stood in that relation since I first began to read and study literature of any pretensions. I have felt since that time that, of whatever I myself might create, a large part would be a direct heritage from Virginia Woolf. There are doubtless hundreds of other writers who feel this way about your books, writers better equipped than I to make an interpretation of them. But the impulsion which I feel toward writing about you and your work is so strong as to make me believe that I could do as well as anyone.

Beyond that I can only say that such critical work as I have already done has been well received by persons whose opinions are of some significance. For the past six months I have been doing book reviews in a small magazine, and as a consequence have been offered an important position in the literary department of a large magazine to be started in the Fall. My education is good, and I can say in all modesty that such start as I have already made in the world of letters is promising.

I tell you all these things, and I seek your reaction to my project because, if I undertake it at all, I wish to do so with your full knowledge and co-operation. It is possible that I shall go far astray in my interpretation of your work, and it will be a waste of literary effort if the divergences I make are not corrected by the only real authority. Furthermore, it is one of my own critical tenets that a writer's work cannot be considered entirely separate from the writer's personality, and while I do not intend to make my study in any sense biographical, I do not feel that I should be able to do my best work without some references to your actual life. Such references, of course, could not be made without your own full co-operation.

Your reply to this will be eagerly awaited. It is a matter of great importance to myself as a writer, for, while I have a number of things projected for work in the near future, none of them is as attractive to me as the matter discussed here, and on none of them am I so keen to begin work. I shall be inestimably grateful for your assistance in this matter, and, if the idea meets with your approval, shall count it a high honor and a most auspicious start for a critical career.

Yours most respectfully,
Richard Greenleaf.

Please address all communications to:
Mr. Richard Greenleaf,
Marks Memorial Camp,
Red Hook, New York, U.S.A.
Until September 1. Thereafter:
11 West 107 Street,
New York City, U.S.A.

Letters from agents, editors, publishers, etc., Letters about various books

---

Richard Greenleaf (b. 1913) wrote reviews and occasional essays, such as "The Social Thinking of F. Scott Fitzgerald" and "British Labor against American Slavery" for *Science and Society* between 1951 and 1972; he also wrote for *People's Weekly World.*

Woolf received a great deal of attention in the early 1930s. Winifred Holtby's biography, *Virginia Woolf*, appeared in 1932 (London: Wishart; rpt. 1978), as did Floris Delattre's *Le Roman Psychologique de Virginia Woolf* (Paris: J. Vrin; trans. and rpt. 1994), and Ruth Gruber's *Virginia Woolf: A Study* (Leipzig: Tauchnitz), based on her 1931 dissertation, would appear in 1935 (rpt. *Virginia Woolf: The Will to Create as a Woman* [NY: Carroll & Graf, 2005]).

This interest continued after her death, as the Hogarth Press files at the University of Reading clearly show. Letters to Leonard Woolf from students in Masters and Doctoral programs as well as from those interested in doing biographical or critical studies include requests for everything from copies of her books (which were scarce after the war because of limited paper supplies) to information about her life.

90
Typed; signed
June 26, 1933

TÉLÉGR. POSTOTEL-ROUEN
TÉLÉPHONE 77-79
INTER 11-03
MÉMES MAISONS
ROYAL HOTEL
PARIS
GD. HOTEL DU PARC
CHATEL-GUYON
(P. DE D.)

GRAND HOTEL DE LA POSTE
ROUEN

August 20th, 1933

Dear Mrs. Woolf,

You are very kind to write about my book, and what you say is especially welcome for I have hoped that it would have some slight interest for persons who are not specialists in economic history. It was all in print before I read your second Common Reader last winter; otherwise I think I might have done better with it. I remember thinking that economic historians could learn a great deal from you, and I remember taking copious notes. Your chapter on the Two Parsons, bringing out as it does how the Industrial Revolution changed the way of life of even the remotest villager, is worth a great many volumes of competent but uninspired economic history. And, indeed, the whole of your Common Reader, both the first and second series, deals again and again with what ought to be, but seldom has been, the central theme of historians: how the problems of life and the manner of living have changed through six centuries of English history.

We were very sorry to learn that you had been ill, and hope that you are now completely recovered. May I tell you how great a privilege it was for my wife and me to see you and Mr. Woolf.

With many thanks from us both.

Yours sincerely,
John U. Nef

Letters from readers, Letters about specific books

John U. Nef (1899-1988) wrote interdisciplinary studies, including *The Universities Look for Unity: An Essay on the Responsibility of the Mind to Civilization in War and Peace* (1943), *War and Human Progress: An Essay on the Rise of Industrial Civilization* (1950), and *Towards World Community* (1968). He founded the Committee on Social Thought at the University of Chicago in 1941. The book mentioned here is *The Rise of the British Coal Industry* (1932); see Woolf's letter, dated August 16, 1933, *L5* 215 (2779), which then prompted the above reply. See also *D4* 171-172 and *L5* 212, n4. *His Search for Meaning: The Autobiography of a Nonconformist* (1973) includes several passages about Woolf.

91
Handwritten
September 5, [1933]

Harveys,
Glynde.
September 5th

Dear Mrs Woolf,

Very many thanks for these. Have you written, or are you writing, a book about Elizabeth Barrett's spaniel, or have I been dreaming more than usual? Did you see the twaddle Vachell has written in today's 'Post'? 'Cultivate your garden,' sez 'e. Literally & to the exclusion of all else. 'Get under God's own sky in God's own country (the west of England, apparently), soak in rain & sweat & cease to think, O intense Youth of Today. Thought, except about rock gardens & ale, I mean cider, is a sign of sluggish lives. Get back to nature, & be Better Youth. Wash your face in dew.' Doesn't he know about Stepney & things? Hasn't everybody got to think like fury? Not that it's of any use whatever; only every time I go on the downs & walk for hours with my dog & meet no one & my whole body sings with delight, I see garbagey gutters & lousy babies playing in them & women giving birth to hundreds more in the hovels behind the gutters. And then Vachell – 'Civilization isn't rotten, everything will be quite all right, you'll find, without any precocious pessimism on your part, youth of today.'

Honestly, what is one to do? Personally, I can't think because I don't know how to; but my mind kicks frantically in all directions like a beetle on its back between the fat complacency of people like Vachell & the extremes of Communism which one wants to hit him with, but which, I am certain, wouldn't do away with the gutters for more than a generation or two.

I hope the new fish is well. I dreamt he was a reincarnation of Marie Antoinette – poor lady, in your pond of all ponds!

Thank you again for the books.

Yours sincerely,

Elizabeth.

P.S. Please permit this. I feel 101 & an ass when you call me Miss Read.

Nash-Rylands

See letter 80 for biographical information and letter 81. Horace Annesley Vachell (1861-1955), a prolific and saccharine writer who loved to explore the past, had a column titled "It's Good to be on Earth" in *The Morning Post* on 5 September 1933: 10.

92
Handwritten
November 14, [1933]

SHERWOOD TERRACE
YONKERS, NEW YORK

Dear Mrs. Woolf

I have rejoiced in your splendid press concerning "Flush", even as I revelled in the installments as they appeared in the Atlantic. I understand there are valuable notes in the book which I am sorry to say I have not yet seen. I shall hope to do so soon.

I am wondering if you solved the question as to when and how Flush died, or if you used invention barring the existence of any record. It has always seemed strange to me that there is no mention of his passing on in her printed correspondence. One cannot tolerate Arabel's destroying her letters!

And I wonder also if you found the portrait at Balliol? I heard from the librarian early in August that the Browning treasures were in the safe during repairs but he would write me later and that hasn't eventuated. I must write to remind him.

I found E. B. B.'s own sketch of Flush's head in the Thomas J. Wise Bibliography of her writings, privately printed, opposite Page 46, but it was merely a profile of the head. However it was the head of a cocker as the one purporting to be of Flush in R. B.'s Album certainly was not unless taken in extreme puppyhood—and Flush was no puppy when R. B. first knew him. So one couldn't feel sure Dean Hood, who has edited the letters, has not assumed the identity.

If it will not be an imposition, I shall be so glad to know when you solve the mystery, if indeed you do. All success be yours!

November fourteenth Sincerely, Harriet Gaylord

The volume of R. B.'s letters was published in April, Yale University Press. Your book is utterly delightful. [postscript written down left margin]

Letters from agents, editors, publishers, etc., Letters about various books

---

Harriet Gaylord, an instructor in English literature and a free-lance writer of fiction and literary criticism, published *Our Boys in Blue and Brown* and *Pals* in 1918 (both poetry) and *Pompilia and Her Poet* in 1931, about the Brownings. She also wrote verses for music composers. Arabel refers to Arabella Moulton-Barrett, Elizabeth's sister.

93
Handwritten
February 6, 1935

Bronxville, New York
February 6, 1935

My dear Virginia Woolf,

For years in Minnesota, in Illinois, I have been writing you letters in my mind. It seems a little strange that all that time when I was pursuing the leisurely peripatetic pace behind cloistered walls I should never have confided any of these messages to paper – & that now when I am still dizzied from the futile attempt to fit into the New York time-pattern – (and I think no mid-westerner ever really puts his roots down & grows in the East!) – I should at last get down to it. I suppose that is partly explained by the fact that I now have a room of my own (and $1200 a year!), where last night & this morning I have been propped up in bed reading you again – No leisure for my own pursuits comes legitimately with my room & stipend, since these are rewards for handling 150 different students every day in a highly organized, nervous public school. But I am indulging in the luxury of a sore throat today – & whether my classes stood on heads or heels, there is for me this morning sun flashing in my window from the gleaming snow fields, and that tranquil sense of isolation that comes on stolen holidays. (You remember how Eustacia Vye never felt she was really enjoying herself in a holiday unless everyone else on the heath was at work?!)

There is something precious about smoking & drinking tea in the morning sun & following the beautifully weighted sentences of Virginia Woolf when this is done despite the clamor & insistences of one hundred & fifty people who are going about the business of accomplishment in a pious fashion! It would not be at all the same experience of a Saturday or Sunday!

Just outside my window a little black spaniel is sniffing the bright snow crust. I remember how you brought Flush aware & snuffing out of Elizabeth Barrett's letters. How you did define his sense of smell – how your inimitable notes at the end of the book twitted the scholars! That was a wonderful bit, too, where Flush & Miss Mitford scuttled & stalked thru the fields.

You have very few outdoor scenes in your writings, do you know? I have the impression that you have never walked much. Oh, down city streets (I wish you had to fetch lead pencils more often!) and in parks – I have forgotten the name & appearance of the young man in Night & Day who was in love with your secret astronomer, but I remember feeding the pigeons in the park with him – and I can see his room – enter at tea time with her her crowded drawing room, watch with him her silent swift tea-pouring, still feel his discomfiture in the presence of her mother's graciously planned & 'literary' talk. And I can see & hear again (though I have not so much as beheld the cover of the book for three years) his family talking around the Sunday night supper table the night he suddenly brought her home.

Yes, it seems to me your people are always in rooms. Walls are clearly defined: – Orlando in his small chamber at his writing desk, or kneeling in the great hall to kiss Elizabeth's hand. Bernard waiting for doors to open or shut in the café – or if your people are moving between rooms, there are the walls of long corridors or of city streets defined by buildings – or the sliding evanescent walls of consciousness.

I think of you, too, within walls — receding deeper & deeper into the background of whatever room you inhabit, & of that room of your own, & defining each mutation of the atmosphere as you move. You were not sitting near the hearth, within flip of Johnson's coat tail, at Fanny Burney's party. You were stilled in the farthest corner (almost into the next room), noting, feeling your mind wrinkle with laughter though your face, except your eyes, I think, was passive. Yet it seems as if, had the party lasted another instant, you would have risen & moved swiftly & noiselessly to the hearth and said something in Dr. Johnson's ear—I can see his heavy quizzical expression & hear his sudden snort of laughter.

I often try to picture the house you live in. I can see you so vividly as you live at certain moments. Never in the morning, somehow, but in the afternoon or evening. Over & over I have imagined having tea with you. (For I would rather meet you than any one alive in the world today) There are so many things I want to ask you. But I recall Pound's doleful "I had over-prepared the event," & content myself with awaiting your next book, knowing that I shall meet you fully there while you could never meet me freely anywhere.

It's this "next book" of yours that preoccupies me chiefly. I think it must be in process of evolving since we have not had any word of you over here for so long. (And I wonder if your English public prizes you as much as we Americans do? I am twenty-three, so it is natural that I explore the literature of experimentation. But a few months ago a conversation at tea with a southern woman fifty years my senior reached its crisis, after a long discussion of Bridges' Testament of Beauty & of Plato, with her question: "and you have read Virginia Woolf?" Upon my allowing that I had & do, she admitted me into the inner circle! And you have created other friends for me. I daresay you do not realize how many people you have drawn together.)

But that "next book"! Is it to be, at last, that novel for which all of your others are studies? Will you become now, wholly & authoritatively, your own Orlando? There is no one else to do it. I remember the glow I felt when I happened on Katherine Mansfield's "We are both trying to do the same thing, Virginia." For she was given time only to prefigure what she would have done. And it seems as if it should be yours to write that humble great book that shall be 'true' in the Keatsian sense of the word.

Your essays have a kind of perfection that must be inimitable. I wept over your On Not Knowing Greek when I first read it. Wept quietly as one must sometimes on discovering a new & unexpected beauty. "English prose is not dead," I said (reacting against Stein's narcissive "sentences", which sprawl like fat white pythons in a fatuous sunlight) – "not while Virginia Woolf still writes like this." And you have done more to write the past into the present, for me, at least, than has any other writer.

But it is your next novel which I await. You who can so readily now contrive whatever atmosphere & whatever states of consciousness, you wish to evoke; you who have relived & revived with such immediacy the evolution of our amazing English world of letters; who are conscious of time as only the Elizabethans before our own day were conscious of it & have experimented with logical & emotional & temporal sequences; you who are conscious not only of the dilemmas of consciousness in this age but of the larger economic & social questions — it seems to me you should at last bring forth a novel which should be immediately of this time & indirectly of every time. Till now you have belonged to a group rather than to an historic period it seems to me.

T.S. Eliot has somehow betrayed us. He has asked & then damned our questions. And finally turned back to the thirteenth century for an answer to his own impossible questions. And so he fills the air with his 'supernatural vermin'. "Clean the sky, purge the air, work the mind" indeed! Lot's husband, he! When they put him in Westminster Abbey they should stand his effigy in a corner with his head turned half round & his chin sculpted into his left shoulder. The honestest of our writers seem to have got stuck on the Magic Mountain, either because they asked the wrong questions or because the age refused them a living answer.

But not you!

Oh, there are so many things I want to ask you! But you have been patient enough of my illiterate scrawl.

God send you [happy?],

Isabel Forbes Milton
(Mrs. Edwin Cerney,
Bronxville Schools,
N.Y. USA)

Letters from agents, editors, publishers, etc., Miscellaneous fan mail

94
Typed; signed
May 15, 1935

Personal & Confidential.

10, DOWNING STREET,
WHITEHALL,
15th May, 1935.

Madam,

I have the honour to inform you, at the Prime Minister's request, that it is his intention in respect of the forthcoming list of Birthday Honours to submit your name to the King with a recommendation that he may be graciously pleased to approve that you be appointed a Member of the Order of Companions of Honour.

Before doing so, however, Mr. MacDonald would be glad to know that this mark of His Majesty's favour would be agreeable to you, and I am therefore to ask if you will be good enough to communicate with me accordingly at your earliest convenience.

Yours faithfully,
H. G. Vincent

Mrs. Virginia Woolf.

Nash-Rylands

Woolf drafts her refusal on the verso of this letter. See Woolf's letter to Ethel Smyth, dated 2 June 1935, where she notes she was "offered a red ribbon" which would have allowed her to call herself a Companion of Honour and "walk into the room behind you, the Dames." She continues, "I said No thanks; I don't believe in Honours, though Ethel Smyth, I said, does" (*L5* 396 [3025]). See also letters 86, 87, 109, and 110.

95
Handwritten
December 2, 1935

2 Décembre 1935.
Beauvais.

Madame,

Je viens à vous charger des hommages d'une vielle dame, qui n'a pas encore passé plusieurs siècles dans l'adoration de la littérature – elle re se vante que d'un siècle – occupé par d'illustres amitiés – celles de Musset et de George Sand, de Renan et de Taine, de Flaubert, de Mérimée, de Tourguéniev, de Loti, de France, de Barrès. Elle s'appelle La Revue du Deux Mondes. Elle me prie de vous dire qu'elle vous aime.

Ce message elle me l'a confié un jour où ayant l'honneur de causer avec elle, je lui parlais de l'admiration et du goût émerveillé que j'ai pour quelques uns de vos livres – ceux que j'ai lus. Elle – il – je dois changer de genre ! – par un phenomène qui n'a rien de secret pour vous, La Revue des Deux Mondes était devenue un vieux monsieur très distingué – il abonda dans le sens d'une passion si vive qu'elle s'attendait plutôt à combattre et s'étonnait presque de se voir partagée. Je demandai alors à La Revue de Deux Monde – alias M. René Doumic – s'il me donnerait une chance de parler de cette admiration et de l'œuvre qui l'inspire à ses lecteurs ? Il parut enchanté de cette idée – ce qui comportait pour moi une part de compliment dont je fus un peu étourdie. Mais pour parler de votre œuvre, Madame, combien je souhaiterais d'abord vous voir, vous entendre, être orientée ou confirmée par vous. Même dans les progrès d'une compréhension qui je n'ai pas l'impertinence de tenir pour achevée !

Vous avez écrit qu'il y a tout Pope, tout Addison, tout Swift, jusqu'à la manière de tenir la canne et de croquer le chapeau dans douze lignes de chacun d'eux. Et cependant – est-ce la preuve que je ne sais pas lire ? Je ne vois pas Virginia Woolf. Je pense à elle – je voudrais la voir.

Si ce vœu ne vous est pas importun, Madame, vous avez la bonté de me faire savoir où et quand il vous conviendrait de l'exaucer. De chers amis qui le connaissent m'attendent à Londres. Si j'apprenais que je puis vous y trouver – vers la fin de cette exposition chinoise qui a tout de quoi faire rêver, je me sentirais comblée des faveurs du sort. Je dis vers la fin, car je suis engagée actuellement dans la composition d'une nouvelle promise à cette Revue des Deux Mondes et je préférais beaucoup ne pas me distraire de ce travail avant de l'avoir fini. Un rendez-vous dans la seconde quinzaine de Février serait la récompense que je voudrais entrevoir.

Mais voici que je parle de mois Madame, ce qui est une grande faute pour le porteur d'un message d'amour. La Revue des Deux Mondes me chargeait de vous dire qu'ayant eu le privilège de publier la traduction de Flush, elle songe à ceux qui suivront, et espère vous persuader de prendre sa maison pour la vôtre en France et le lieu de votre rencontre avec le public français.

J'espère, Madame, qu'une autre fois il me sera donné de vous dire un peu de ce que sont vos livres – le sentiment de délivrance que j'éprouve quand je lis The Lighthouse, comme si une œuvre qu'on doit vraiment aimer, était préformée en vous sous forme de souffrance et de besoin, de telle sorte que lorsqu'on la trouve, ou la reconnaît, on sait profondément que c'est elle qu'on cherchait. Aujourd'hui je m'en tiens à mes messages, à ma requête et n'y veux ajouter que la reconnaissance avec laquelle je suis votre attentive admiratrice.

Camille Mayran

Cette signature est mon pseudonyme – mon nom et mon adresse sont :
Madame Pierre Hepp
14 rue de Boyer,
Beauvais (Oise)

[translation by Helen Southworth]
Madam,

I come to heap on you the homage of an old woman, who has not yet spent several centuries in the adoration of literature – she can boast of only one century – busy with illustrious friendships, those of Musset and of George Sand, of Renan and Taine, Flaubert, Mérimée, Turgenev, of Loti, of [Anatole] France, of Barrès. She is called The Review of Two Worlds.

She asks me to tell you that she loves you. She confided this message to me one day when having the honor to chat with her I told her I admired and enjoyed some of your books – those that I've read. She – he – I must change the gender – via a phenomenon which holds no secrets for you, The Review of Two Worlds had become a very distinguished old man – he felt so strongly himself that he expected to have to put up a fight and was almost astonished to see his views shared. I therefore asked The Review of Two Worlds – alias Mr René Doumic – if he would give me the opportunity to talk about this admiration and about the work which inspires it to his readers? He appeared very pleased with this idea, which represented for me no small compliment which took me aback. But before talking about your work, Madame, I would very much like first to meet you, to hear your voice, to have my ideas directed or confirmed by you. Even on the way to an understanding which I do not have the impertinence to consider finished!

You have written that there's all Pope, all Addison, all Swift up to the point where one can hold one's cane and eat one's hat in 12 lines of each of them. And yet – is that the proof that I don't know how to read? I don't see Virginia Woolf – I think about her, I want to see her.

If this request does not inconvenience you, Madame, please let me know when and where it would be convenient for you to see me. Dear friends who know it expect me in London. If I learnt that I might find you there – towards the end of this Chinese exhibition which has everything you might need to dream, I would feel overwhelmed with the favors of fate. I say towards the end because I am currently involved in the writing of a short story promised to this same Review of Two Worlds and I would prefer very much not to distract myself from this work before having finished it. A meeting in the second fortnight of February would be the reward that I'd like to entertain.

But here I am talking about myself, Madam, a great mistake for anyone carrying a message of love. The Review of Two Worlds asked me to tell you that having had the privilege of publishing the translation of Flush, she is thinking about your next book, about those which will follow, and hopes to persuade you to assume its house for your own in France and to make it the place where you meet the French public.

I hope, Madam, that at another time I'll be able to tell you a little bit more about what your books represent – the feeling of deliverance that I feel when I read The Lighthouse, as if a work that one must truly love, had already taken shape in you in the form of suffering and need, in such a way that when one finds it or recognizes it, one knows deep down that it is that which one has looked for. Today I'll keep to my messages, to my request and want only to add the recognition with which I am your attentive admirer.

Camille Mayran

This signature is my pseudonym – my name and address are:
Madame Pierre Hepp
14 Rue Boyer,
Beauvas (Oise)

Letters from agents, editors, publishers, etc., Miscellaneous fan mail

---

Camille Mayran (1889-1989) wrote several novels, including *Hiver* (1926), *Dame en noir* (1935), and a book on Alsace with her husband Pierre Hepp (1945). *La Revue des Deux*

Mondes was founded in August 1829 by François Buloz and published work related to literature, fine arts, history, science, and politics.

Flush was translated into French by Charles Mauron and published in the *Revue* in three parts as *Vie de Flush* on November 15, December 1, and December 15, 1934. In its entirety, *Flush* appeared in French in 1935, translated by Charles Mauron.

96
Handwritten
[1935]

5 Hereford Square
S.W.7.

Dear Virginia,

Did you really seriously mean me to think about your position as a writer, & about writing generally? I feel it is a gross presumption on my part to do so – but at the same time I can't avoid short thinks in buses & trains on the subject. Nobody, having attained one sort of excellence, can forbear hankering after another. Kings turn monks, airmen turn poets & people like myself turn socialists. {This sounds conceited: what I mean is this: that when the ladylike qualities are attained fairly easily, one of the normal reactions is So What.} I wonder whether your sort of excellence bores you. Your books are so pleasant to read. They are about the pleasantest subject on earth – love & his disguises. They must be pleasant to write. But I must suppose that the quails fall into your mouth too easily. Or else why would you be worrying about becoming a bogus classic, being labeled, & given Alphas by the reviews? I suppose there is always a friction between a writer & his work – quite apart from the ordinary tension between ideas & material. I mean [corner of letter torn off here, so words left out] easiest & most plumb-successful way to write is two or three years behind one's new theories. And that while one is making up the lee-way, there is an irritating discrepancy between the new raw ideas & the old sweet fluency. (When I was at school I could write nice Yeatsian verse – but though I could do it now, I'd feel smothered in mud & treacle). And it is by brooding over this discrepancy, I imagine, that one invents new forms & styles, finds literary ways of sublimating literary desires. And this doesn't involve throwing over the old way, but broadening it by really grasping what one's increased knowledge involves, & realizing where & what the old falsifications were.

I'll try & put this more concretely. X can write delightful erotic poetry – & goes on writing it – it is called 'the modern Catullus' by the Sunday Times etc. Thousands of adolescents like myself buy his books. He gets older & older & his public younger & younger, relatively. At 35 the maturer ideas he has gotten by experience start a running fight with his lyrical facility. His poetry doesn't necessarily get worse, but he thinks worse of it. If he sticks at the old game, he'll eventually get whimsy, because he writes without the accelerator full-on. Say the emotional equivalent of the maturer ideas is Anger. The poet's problem will be to alter his technique to allow for a heavier strain on it.

I don't really know what your new values consist of. Does it take the form of wanting to laugh at luncheon-party life, being angry at literary bogus [ ]? If I were you – i.e. if I had written really good romantic novels, was skilful with words, & had quite got over my ambitious feelings – I should, pseudonymously, write a racy book about myself, & my godawful friends, my loathsome books, my flatterers – A satire with an attempt in it to show that the ridiculous people are not those who make mistakes but those who avoid them – a satire which promised a big constructive book to follow about the people who make mistakes, are victims of maladjustments – why they are so etc.

This is just a fantasy & a rather impertinent one. May Miss Pearn & I come to see you sometime?

yours affectionately
Sally G.

Farrell-Lubbock

Sally Graves Chilver (Elizabeth Millicent Chilver) (1914-), niece of Robert Graves, edited a journal called *Lysistrata* at Somerville College, Oxford University, and had solicited Woolf for a contribution. She published *A History of Socialism* with the Hogarth Press in 1939. A civil servant during World War II, she was Principal of Bedford College in London from 1964-71 and Principal of Lady Margaret Hall, Oxford from 1971-1979. Nancy Pearn represented literary agents; see *L5* 73, n2 and Naomi Black, *Virginia Woolf as Feminist* (Ithaca: Cornell UP, 2004, 132, 221, n10). See letter 102.

See her letter to Leonard Woolf in *A* 54.

97
Typed; signed
December 15, 1936

INTERNATIONAL ASSOCIATION OF WRITERS FOR THE
DEFENCE OF CULTURE
Executive Committee: British Section
Ras Mulk Anand, Lascelles Abercrombie, Charlotte Haldane, Rayner Heppenstall, James Hanley, Cecil Day Lewis, Rose Macaulay, Kingsley Martin, Geronwy Rees, Montagu Slater, Christina Stead, Hugh Walpole, Rebecca West, Amabel Williams-Ellis
~~ROMNEY'S HOUSE, HOLLYBUSH HILL, LONDON N.W.3~~

CENtral 1654. 4, Crane Court, E.C.4.
15th December, 1936.

Mrs. Virginia Woolf,
52 Tavistock Square,
W.C.I.
Dear Mrs. Woolf,

The Executive Committee decided at the last meeting to send out a questionnaire to about 100 leading writers of this country with the intention of finding out their attitude in the face of the present social disaccord. We hope to make this a basis for a new critical study of aesthetic viewpoints in England and further, to rally to us the friendly writers who are yet hesitating, or who are unconscious, still, of the direction they have taken; and again, to sharpen for others, the prejudices they still cling to . . . . We should be most happy if you would sign the questionnaire, as one of its proposers.

These are the questions: -

1. For whom do you write?
2. Do you think the writer suffers as an artist by taking part in political debate?
3. Do you consider any state of society ideal for artistic creation, as – Athenian, monastic, aristocratic (patronage), free competition; communal or collective; of living as, coffee-house or bucolic. Would any social state, except political repression, cramp your creative powers?

This is a tentative wording of question 3 . . . . The questions, with a short preamble, will be printed on cards, post-card size, and circulated shortly after Christmas. Four literary weeklies will receive copies, as a matter of literary interest. Mr. Kingsley Martin will publish in "The New Statesman and Nation" any replies of particular interest . . . . The material will be used further.

Will you kindly let me know if you will allow your name to be put at the foot of the questionnaire (with Mrs. William-Ellis, Rose Macaulay, C. Day Lewis, Mulk Raj Anand)? We hope also that you will answer the questionnaire.

Yours very truly,
Christina Stead
C. Stead

Letters from agents, editors, publishers, etc., Letters about articles

---

Christina Stead (1902-1983) wrote short stories (*The Salzburg Tales*, 1934) and novels set in Australia (*Seven Poor Men of Sydney*, 1934; *The Man Who Loved Children*, 1940), France (*The House of All Nations,* 1938), the United States (*A Little Tea, A Little Chat*, 1948), England (*Cotter's England*, 1966), and Switzerland (*The Little Hotel*, 1973). Woolf did not sign or answer the questionnaire, but according to Christine Froula, she was receiving this sort of letter more and more often (*Virginia Woolf and the Bloomsbury Avant-Garde* [New York: Columbia UP, 2005], 395, n1). Kingsley Martin published *Fascism, Democracy, and the Press* as a *New Statesman* pamphlet in 1938.

98
Handwritten
July 22, 1937

Woodgreen
Fordingbridle
22 July 37

Dear Mrs. Woolf

Your notice of Janet is most lovely & delightful and has given me intense pleasure. How like her – how understanding.

I remember so clearly my first sight of her as a charming little girl of nine or ten – an old friend is very grateful to you. R Nash

Nash-Rylands

Rosalind Nightingale Nash had written to Virginia Stephen in 1910 to ask her to support women's suffrage by doing some research and writing about women's rights in New Zealand; see Bell (I 161 and II, 269n.). The tribute to "Miss Janet Case, Classical Scholar and Teacher" appeared in *The Times* on the same day and on the same page as the announcement of Julian Bell's death in Spain, 22 July 1937: 16. Nash, a cousin of Florence Nightingale, wrote *A Sketch of the Life of Florence Nightingale* (1937) after having published *A Short Life of Florence Nightingale* (1925), an abridgement and revision of the life written by Sir Edward Cook. But she also wrote reports on the Accidents Compensation Act in 1897, about life and death in the potteries in 1898, and on "The Co-operative Housewife" for *Labour and Protection: A Series of Studies*, edited by H. W. Massingham in 1903.

99
Typed; signed
August 19, 1937

REIGATE 3520

MOTLEY,
ST. ALBAN'S ROAD,
REIGATE, SURREY.
August 19, 1937

Dear Mrs. Woolf:

This letter does not ask for anything, not even for an answer. I write to ease my own conscience, because I have had so much from your books and value them so dearly that I must thank you.

They are helping me now to keep from running quite to seed during the intellectually lean years (entirely satisfying though they are in other ways) when my baby, my house, and my garden leave me so little time for the other world. There are always socks to mend, a pudding to make, dishes to wash; the baby has a pain, and the garden wants weeding. But there is one oasis in the day when my husband, who is a good one, gives me breakfast in bed, and then I have half an hour of one of your books. I always get from them a feeling of rest that comes from absolute rightness, and at the same time exhilaration from their bracing stimulus.

"The Years" sustained me through the first weeks after my son was born in April, when I had to make myself fly from the almost too absorbing interest of very new maternity.

This family also had occasion to bless you when, three years ago my husband spent two months chasing whales off South Georgia in the Antarctic. I joined him there, and we were pretty well starved for books, music, and pictures. We had, however, "Orlando", "The Voyage Out," and "To the Lighthouse" and squeezed them as dry as we could.

It is like coming home to read your books, but a home brightened and made infinitely exciting.

Yours gratefully,
Margaret Laurie

Letters from agents, editors, publishers, etc., Miscellaneous fan mail

---

An Alec Laurie (b. 1907) served with the *Discovery* investigation of whale behavior, biology, and distribution in South Georgia, Antarctica, from 1930-33, and he published studies of whales in 1933 and 1937 and the ocean in 1972.

100
Handwritten
November 12, [1937]

HUDSON STRODE UNIVERSITY ALABAMA
November twelfth

My dear Mrs. Woolf:

The letter which you so kindly wrote me and sent to Newton Mearns, Scotland chased me about two hemispheres and finally caught up with me. It was indeed most gracious of you to write before you received the copy of my book South By Thunderbird. Alas I'm afraid something went wrong with those two copies I ordered sent to England. A notice came back to me here saying that a shilling or so was due for extra transportation. I wrote my friend Maurice Colbourn, the theatrical director, asking him to attend to the matter, again gave him your address and sent the fee. No word since from him. I fear my letter went astray and there somewhere in some office for the lost remain the two books. They are twice as handsomely produced as the English edition too. But to make sure you do get a copy of my book, I asked Harriet Hamilton to send you a copy as soon as the first of the editions came from the press. I received a copy yesterday – so I trust South by Thunderbird has reached you in one dress or another. If both copies turn up, you might be good enough to send one to Dame Katharine Furse.

If you do get time to read the book, I should be so grateful if you would let me know if you found any pleasure in its pages. You will see that I was often hard put to try to make information palatable. The critics over here have been wondrous kind – even the violently anti-Roosevelt papers. I cannot hope for as enthusiastic reception in England, because the book is definitely pro-Pan-American.

Random House has asked us to prepare an anthology of English lyrics from Wyatt to Housman – only the cream – less than a fourth of the Golden Treasury could be included. In my introductory essay I am mentioning favorite lyrics of ~~the~~ twelve most important living men and women of letters of England and twelve of the United States. Since I consider you the foremost person writing in the English language today, I want you to head the list. Would you be so very gracious as to tell me two, three or four of your favorite lyrics? And would you even do more and tell me the qualities you desired in a lyric? I shall be profoundly grateful if you find you can grant my request. Random House promises to do a superb job of printing.

Again my warm thanks for your kindness in writing me.

May you live long and have strength to write much. In my out of town lectures this fall I have ~~been~~ continued to speak of The Years as the most important novel of 1937.

Sincerely yours
Hudson Strode.

We recently had the pleasure of a visit from Vera Brittain who brought us a letter of introduction from her husband.

Letters from agents, editors, publishers, etc., Letters about various books

---

Hudson Strode (1892-1976) taught Shakespeare and creative writing at the University of Alabama from 1916-1963. He wrote a three-volume biography of Jefferson Davis, travel books about Scandinavia, the Caribbean, and Latin America (*South by Thunderbird* was about his travels there), and a memoir. His review of *Between the Acts* for *The New York Times* on 5 October 1941: section 6, I: 30, is partially reprinted in Majumdar and McLaurin, *Virginia Woolf: The Critical Heritage* ([London: Routledge, 1975], 446-47).

In the introduction to *Immortal Lyrics: An Anthology of English Lyric Poetry from Sir Walter Raleigh to A. E. Housman* (1938), Strode writes to Woolf for "enlightenment" into why some poems are "the cream of English lyric poetry" (9). But characteristically, she does not help him much: "As for your request that I should give you an opinion upon English lyric poetry I am greatly flattered that you should think it worth having. I began to think which are my favourite lyrics and why, and have been debating the question. The result, however, is as usual when I start reading English poetry—I am led away into hours of reading, find new lyrics as well as old ones, and in the end can no more say which I like best than I can say why I like them" (10).

101
Handwritten
December 22, 1937

---

60 Harrison Street, Princeton, New Jersey, U.S.A.
22 December 1937

Dear Leonard & Virginia,

This is our Princeton address, but I am writing in New York—not on Manhattan itself but very near it. From where I sit now I can see the water of Harlem river glittering in the sunshine through the trees of the surrounding gardens; we are staying with friends for Xmas, Max is off shopping, our host & hostess are in their respective offices & their child & ours are both asleep (for the whole afternoon, I hope, as the coloured girl, Rowena from Georgia, has gone out). I promised to tell you whether I thought you ought to come to see America,

& after 3 months, although I haven't seen so much of it myself, I feel quite sure you would be immensely interested. We are very much attracted as well as interested. The noise & vulgarity which one hears such a lot about only constitute a comparatively modest part of this enormous & varied country. About seven miles from Princeton there are little valleys among the hills & woods quieter & less frequented than anywhere I know in England, & even outside New York itself you come very quickly to totally wild unspoilt country with just a few farms & scattered log shacks among the woods. New York of course is amazingly solid with people & buildings, but (whether it is the air & the climate or the ability to rush up in a few minutes to a thousand feet or more above the crawling pavements, I don't know) I do not feel at all overwhelmed by the congestion of everything. We have no abode in Princeton after February 1st & our plans are for Max to stay at a club or in rooms there for February & March while Edward & I come up here to these friends, & I should enjoy that very much. Whether we do it depends largely on the problem of Edward's schooling – yes, Edward "commenced school" a little before his 2nd birthday, & is doing so well & enjoying life so much at the little nursery school we found in Princeton that we are reluctant to move him. There is a very good, similar type of school here attended by the small girl in this house, but it has reached its limit of scholars—sixteen—& has a long waiting list. I am so impressed by the American nursery school that I hope to start something of the sort in Cross Farm when we return, with the aid of some other mothers who have children between 2 and 4. Sometimes the mothers employ a permanent teacher or two, but quite often, to cut down expenses, they take it in turn to look after the children themselves for a week at a time. It has been a tremendous help to me this autumn at Princeton because I have been able to work at the University Library from 9-12 every morning while Edward was at school, & thanks to the time & the hospitality of the Library, my book on Fanny Kemble has gone ahead pretty well. There is a lot of material available here for it that I couldn't get even at the Brit. Mus. And I had one rare book borrowed for me & another filmed, as the Library of Congress could not lend it. Filming of books is very cheap & all the libraries have had installed small projectors for the use of readers, and there is a good deal of talk of this being the way to solve the space problem. But it isn't at all an easy or comfortable way of reading a book – it's a great nuisance not being able to flutter back the leaves. I am hoping to complete my researches by making a visit to Georgia to the plantations which Fanny's husband owned, when she made her short but famous acquaintance with slavery. I can't get away for more than 6 or 7 days. The journey will take 24 hours each way, or more if I get off & see Washington on the way there & perhaps Charleston on the way back, but I think it will be worth doing even in that hurried way.

Our chief complaint about America is that we meet so few Americans. The Institute of Advanced Studies, to which Max is attached, is packed with distinguished German exiles who have created a social group of their own, very interesting & intimate but not in the least American. In New York I see mainly old Cambridge friends married to or otherwise combined with men of varied nationalities but none of them American. It gave me quite a shock the other day when a friend of one of these friends said that when he was a boy his father used to take him to a certain good old-fashioned restaurant, down town in New York – I had grown so used to assuming that everyone I met had known a European childhood.

The States aren't dear to live in. Rents & wages are very high, but almost everything else much less than in England. You can buy a nice car for £10 – we did – and get six gallons of petrol for a dollar; cigarettes are half the price they are in England, & all clothes, except woollens & men's suits, are half the price. I don't know how I shall get reconciled to London shops after the shops of New York & Philadelphia. And the apples! A basket of 4 or 5 dozen apples for half a dollar. The food stores, which save so much trouble by providing everything except milk & bread, are full of wonderful vegetables & fruit all the year through – peas & beans, egg-plant, squash, lettuces, everything we have in the beginning of summer & so much besides. But it is a profound deprivation that nice bread cannot be found anywhere on this side of the Atlantic. No one can explain to us why – nor why in every house there are horrible yellow blinds which must always be pulled down to the top of the lower sash, although someone in Princeton assured us it was a very ancient custom, a relic of some form of protection against the Indians. Occasionally we see people, both white & brown with unmistakable Indian in their faces, & it is both striking & melancholy to see.

I hear one or other of the children squeaking upstairs. My best wishes to you both for 1938. I wish you would begin it by coming to New York, but the Autumn is the best time. Virginia, you would get a tremendous welcome, you are much read & appreciated. I bask from time to time in the glory of having known you both.

Yours

Lyn Newman

Nash-Rylands

Lyn Lloyd Irvine Newman (1901-1973) was at Girton from 1924-1927, and she struggled to maintain a reading and writing life as the wife of a Cambridge mathematician. She reviewed Woolf's *A Room of One's Own* for *Nation and Athenaeum* on 9 November 1929: 201-03, and she published *Ten Letter Writers* with Hogarth Press in 1932. The book she mentions here, however, the biography of Fanny Kemble, was never completed. She published a memoir of her childhood, *So Much Love, So Little Money* (1957), and published two other books, one under her own imprint, Monologue Books. See William Newman's "Married to a Mathematician: Lyn Newman's Life in Letters," a description of the papers she left to Cambridge, in *The Eagle* (2002): 21-26, at <www.joh.cam.ac.uk/johnian/publications/eagle>. The Newmans were staying with Vera and Pierre Damann, who had emigrated to the United States; their daughter Jacqueline was the same age as Edward.

See her letter to Leonard Woolf in *A* 128-29.

102
***Typed**
[1937]

83, Fellows Road N.W.3
Tuesday:

Dear Virginia,

No, I can't lie down under your accusation of scurviness: If you can think what I say about 'The Years' is of any value – here goes.

In the first place I have a monstrous prejudice in favour of dramatic word-writing – and a great shyness of the linings of people's minds. Dickens is the sort of writer I read for real pleasure, and Peacock too. So long as human beings are regarded as social types, or wits, or rational beings, or grotesques, I can read on without discomfort. It's when they begin to come to life, when the cadres of the novel ceases to be a stage proscenium, when, in fact, the writing invites you to be a participator rather than an onlooker that I frown and stamp and pretend to feel ill. 'The Years' had just that effect on me, and all your books do – more than most 'interior' novels because the twist and the outlook is more recognizable to me than Joyce's or anyone else's. I felt, after reading 'The Years', almost as if I were a school-girl caught reading a sex encyclopaedia. A mixture of fear, guilt, and exultation on one hand, and an effort to pooh-pooh and distract myself on the other. A few minutes after I finished the book I felt very angry. I felt got at, and hit under the belt. I thought – hell take it I could have been going on with reading for Leonard's book, I could have gone on trying to mend the light, – anything

– but now I've gone and got myself firmly stuck in a particularly potent sentimental reverie – B-F-H- ect ect. So I went round and argued at poor Baba (who staunchly defended you) till she was haggard and speechless, – and then went and found a worthy bolshie friend and made her drink more sherry than was good for her complexion. After this anti-social behaviour I felt very relieved – and less like a Hemingway heroine. (Bloody Christ I gone all to pieces inside Mike – etc.) So how can you expect a sober criticism of 'The Years'?

I read 'The Years' again later in little sips, keeping a mental pin in my leg to prevent myself going off again. I thought then that its only failing was this: that the characters were in a too rarefied atmosphere – moving too absolutely according to the pleasure-pain principle. Whenever you did allow the everyday comment, the effect was remarkable. When the man in the 'bus sizes up Eleanor for instance. Apart from that I thought it not only a tour de force on its own merits, but, with 'Orlando', your best book. I suppose you must have felt that you'd missed the mark when you'd finished it. Impossible not to, I should think, with such a large project. And the reader is never conscious of the mark at all unless you miss it now and then. And you ought to, like a good romantic.

It would be lovely to lunch in Regents Park or anywhere next week. Do you think it would be nice to make an assignation with Mrs. Cameron {Elizabeth Bowen} in the park? I'm supposed to be going to Salzburg with her and two of her friends and I should like to approach her again under your batteries. I think she's extremely nice but I'm still rather shy of her.

You must treat tortoises with the same respect as rabbits but on the opposite principle. Your barricades must have more under than above ground – like icebergs. I had a tortoise once, and it died on me. It was a dull beast.

Richard's got office mopes, but he sends his love, as I do.

Sally.

Farrell-Lubbock

See letter 96 for biographical information. On June 1, 1937, Woolf mentions in her diary that in private, Sally Graves and Stephen Spender say they like *The Years* (*D*5 91). *The Years* was published on March 15, 1937. B-F-H probably stands for "bloody foolish." Baba (Anastasia) was Helen Anrep's daughter. In a letter to Julian Bell, dated November 14, 1936, *L*6 83-85 (3189), Woolf had mentioned Sally's upcoming marriage to Richard Chilver. Probably the original transcriber, not Sally Graves, inserted Elizabeth Bowen's name.

103
Typed
April 28, 1938

McAllen, Texas
April 28, 1938

To Virginia Woolf,
Author of "Women Must weep".
c/o The Atlantic Monthly

Dear Remarkable Woman:

First, in my humble way I wish to thank you for this article. Being born a Quaker 68 years ago on an Ohio farm, it is easy to endorse your doctrine of Passivity at any Price, but I am sorry to say that finding none of this in this dogma-ridden world I have almost lost my belief in God or spirituality.

As I see it we are hopelessly enmeshed in the slimy folds of this anaconda of Greed and viciousness, that hourly reproduces itself in the sickening strife and jealousies of our modern life from the cradle to the grave.

I have but recently suffered a severe sick spell with an attack of heart trouble but had hoped to regain enough of my old strength to leave some kind of scar on the rotting body of our social system. I had that religious background and it has turned on me. Can I say in sincerity that God or Good Prevails, when facts laugh at faith?

I had hoped to rewrite in serial form that bible of mine, "Looking Backward," I hope you have read it and with your fine strong mind will catch the theme of Economic Salvation, a salvation that MUST come before the human race can shed its incisors for tearing human flesh, and its blood thirst bred of the demands of our entire social, or I should say our anti-social conception of life.

I thank God for Virginia Woolf. You must keep up the education. The mother of four, the grandmother of eight physically sound human beings, everyone of whom are on the skids of this insane system, can you wonder I am calling upon you for help?

Please set a fire to all these fine churches with their falsity try to revive the simplicity of the Christ life with its Peace unfolding a world of beauty in art music and research set free from the blighting curse of Commercialism, Competition and Greed. They begin before childbirth and breed it into the innocent babes. Well I can only say, yours is a Great Responsibility, more power to you. My body is wornout but I KNOW.

Faithfully Your Well wisher.
Mrs. Lillian A. Bray

Letters from agents, editors, publishers, etc., Miscellaneous fan mail

---

Lillian Arvilla Williams Bray (b. 1872) published *Hands Across the Border: A Brief Story of Mexico, Her People and Her Chief Attractions for Visitors from the United States and Elsewhere, Who Wish to See and Understand This Foreign Land that Shares Our Shores of Two Oceans* in 1941. Edward Bellamy's *Looking Backward* was first published in 1888.

104
Handwritten
May 25, 1938

ANNA B. CAROLAN
712 PUTNAM AVENUE
BROOKLYN, NEW YORK

May 25th 1938.

Dear Virginia Woolf,

It is difficult to express in words the effect of your article "Women Must Weep" in the Atlantic Monthly on a person like myself who has strong convictions but is seriously hampered by difficulty in expressing them. It is four o'clock in the morning when all good Christian ladies should be dreaming pleasant, peaceful dreams but here am I sitting bolt upright on my cot, ominous thoughts pounding madly in my brain, suffering the same emotions a hen must sense when immobile her canny eye watches the gyrations of a soaring hawk.

I am taking the liberty of enclosing a poorly written epistle published in a village paper where I have my studio. Were it possible I should write a humorous letter to the New York Times suggesting that the time is ripe for women to avail themselves of the late invention popularly called "test-tube babies"; but place in said "   "s only the seed of peaceful males and let all the others go fully armed to a huge plain and annihilate each other. If one survives, offer him hemlock.

One of my reactions to your remarkable article is to hope that you can reach down among the daughters and men of uneducated folks. Tell us how we can help make the world a safe place to live in.

Merci mille fors
Anna B. Carolan

[enclosure missing]

Letters from agents, editors, publishers etc., Miscellaneous fan mail

105
Handwritten
July 10, 1938

TELEGRAMS,
CASE MINSTEAD.

HEWER'S ORCHARD
MINSTEAD,
LYNDHURST
HANTS.

July 10. 1938

My dear Virginia -

I am now deep in £3.3 – and I wanted to ask Janet all about Lysistrata: I'm still smiling over the "tuft of horsehair" –

You are wonderful Virginia – I shall finish it tomorrow on the train on my way to see Essie – Would you like to see a letter from one of the younger generation (ie younger than Janet's & mine) about you and your books – I was tearing up old letters & came on this one to Janet – She (the writer) was so thrilled to find Janet knew you! I thought it might ~~amuse~~ interest you! You can read &

destroy –

Dear Virginia can you tell me when it was that Ka died? I can't think how I missed the Times notice – and about what date were the notices by Nevinson and A.S. I've looked through many old ones in vain –

Are you taking things easily now that this little yellow book is out? I hope so. Love to you both – How glad I am you came last year when you did.

Always your affectionate

E. S. Case.

I have read – so far. Vol I of The Amberley Papers – There is a mistake in the Index. Uncle James Stansfeld's first wife (Caroline Ashurst) was never Lady Stansfeld – that was his second wife She was Mrs H. Severn before she married him –

Another P.S. We were earning that [6d] a good long time before 1919!

Of course you know it was Uncle James (Stansfeld) who – after a fight – got women admitted to the Medical School (R. Free Hos[l]) and he appointed the first woman as 'Poor Law ~~Guardian~~ Inspector.'

[enclosure missing]

Bosanquet-Cecil

Emphie (Emma Sophia) Case (c.1860-c.1943) was the sister of Janet Case (1862-1937). Woolf associates 1919 with women's being able to earn the "sacred sixpence" (*TG* 16), and Emphie uses a symbol for that in her second postscript. James Stansfeld (1820-1898), Radical politician, fought to repeal the Contagious Diseases Acts, a repeal that finally succeeded in 1886.

See also her letter to Leonard Woolf in *A* 9.

106
Typed; signed
August 23, 1938

HARCOURT, BRACE AND COMPANY, INC.
PUBLISHERS
383 MADISON AVENUE, NEW YORK

TELEPHONE: ELDORADO 5-3610
CABLE ADDRESS: HARBRACE.NEW YORK

August 23, 1938.

Mrs. Virginia Woolf
52 Tavistock Square
London, W.C.1.
Dear Mrs. Woolf:

We shall be publishing THREE GUINEAS the day after tomorrow, August 25th. The enthusiasm of those who have read it in advance and the orders we have received in advance of publication indicate for it a success here similar to that which I gather it has received on your side. The enclosed leaflet, sent out by the Vassar Bookshop, a bookshop conducted by women at a women's college, will perhaps interest you.

What a delightfully brilliant, stirring, and significant book it is! I do congratulate you on it. I hope it will be widely read here, not only for your sake and ours, but for the general good.

With kindest regards,
Yours sincerely,
Donald Brace

DCB:CMc

[enclosure missing]

Letters from agents, editors, publishers, etc., Letters about articles

---

See letter 22 for biographical information. See Woolf's reply, dated August 30, 1938, *L6* 268 (3436).

107
***Typed**
October 29, 1938

THE FORUM
570 Lexington Avenue, New York.
October 29, 1938.

Dear Mrs. Woolf,

My talk with you was a memorable event in an altogether memorable week. Thank you for receiving me so graciously at a time when you must have been under an unusually severe strain. The soft glowing colors of your drawingroom stand out against the sombre background of London in crisis, and I am wondering if you would be good enough to let me know the name of the manufacturer of the unusually lovely carpet and chintz. I have seen nothing to equal them over here, and if the prices are reasonable I do not see why an excellent market could not be built up in this country.

By the way, it might interest you to see what Mary Colum says about Three Guineas in her next Forum article. I enclose a proof.

I returned to find American riding high on a wave of pro-war, anti-Chamberlain emotion. All the old slogans of national honor, preservation of democracy etc. etc. in circulation again. America seems to have learned little if anything from the last war. It was not long enough, I suppose, to teach her the things we learned so painfully in those four terrible years. The radio commentators, headed, I am sorry to say, by Dorothy Thompson are filling the ether with outcry against the betrayal of the Czechs. In fact I think this country is very much disappointed that after such a magnificent full-dress rehearsal we refused to raise the curtain on the real thing! There are many aspects about the peace that I dislike, but from the bottom of my heart I am thankful that it is still peace, and not war. We shall probably have to go on paying a very heavy price for peace, but my Scotch sense of values tells me that it is nothing compared to the unthinkable cost of war. I wish you could talk to these emotional women. Why not a lecture tour this winter?

Cordially yours,
PHYLLIS MOIR.
Managing Editor.

Mrs. Virginia Woolf,
52 Tavistock Sq.
London. W.C.1

P.S. I hope you have not forgotten the Forum article idea we discussed.

[enclosure missing]

Letters from agents, editors, publishers, etc., Correspondence about publications

---

Phyllis Moir, born in Staffordshire, began her career as a secretary, publishing *I Was Winston Churchill's Private Secretary* in 1941, moved into editorial work at *Forum*, and then managed a lecture bureau. Monks House Papers contains other letters from Phyllis Moir, one of which, dated November 17, 1939, reminds Woolf that she had promised she would boil over at some point. Moir's letters, along with letters such as 115 and 116 from Motier Harris Fisher, probably led to "Thoughts on Peace in an Air Raid."

Mary Colum's "Life and Literature: Are Women Outsiders?" appeared in *Forum* 100 (1938): 222-26. Dorothy Thompson (1894-1961) was a journalist who broadcast over the radio and wrote a syndicated column about the threat of Nazi Germany.

108
***Typed**
February 9, 1939

---

37 Cranley Gardens,
London, S.W.7. 9:II:39.

Dear Mrs. Woolf,

Since January the Thirtieth, I have made many attempts to write you a really appreciative letter! But all the attempts were discarded, one by one – They seemed either too gushing, or too reserved!

I find it so difficult to tell you how grateful I am for the helpful, encouraging, advice, and happiness, that you have given me!

Up to the present, I have only written Poetry when 'the spirit has moved me,' and it has been a spontaneous outlet for my feelings. So far, I have not worked over it, I have not experimented, I have hardly thought about it, – I have merely let it come. Now you have inspired me to think more, and to try try again, until I succeed in 'getting over' exactly what I mean.

I mean, one day, to prove myself worthy of your letter!

Yours sincerely
ANN McKNIGHT KAUFFER.

Letters from agents, editors, publishers, etc., Fan mail

Simon Rendall for the Estate of Ann McKnight Kauffer.

Ann McKnight Kauffer Rendall (1920-1996) is replying to Woolf's letter, dated January 31, 1939, *L6* 313 (3484). Kauffer was at Roedean, with plans to go to Grenoble University, but because of the war, studied only a few terms at Manchester University before joining the WAAF. She married Peter Rendall in 1944 and continued to write poetry until her death. She published 3 chapbooks of verse, *Loose Leaves* (1971), *New Leaves* (1975), and *Manuscript* (1984), all printed on her son's handpress, a practice she may have learned after visiting the Hogarth Press when she was young.

109
***Typed**
March 1, 1939

From
THE VICE-CHANCELLOR
The University of Liverpool
March 1st, 1939.

Dear Madam,

At a meeting of the Senate of the University, held to-day, a recommendation was received from the Council, and unanimously approved, that you should be invited to accept the Honorary Degree of Doctor of Letters of this University at a Special Congregation for the Conferment of Honorary Degrees to be held in St. George's Hall at 3 o'clock on Thursday, May 18th. It gives me great pleasure to convey that invitation to you, and to express our hope that you will honour us by accepting the Degree.

In the event of your acceptance, you will in due course receive an invitation from the University Association for Dinner in the evening.

Yours very truly,
ARNOLD D. McNAIR

Mrs. Virginia Woolf
52 Tavistock Square,
London, W.C.1.

Letters from agents, editors, publishers, etc., Fan mail

Sir Arnold D. McNair (1885-1975) was the Vice-Chancellor at the University of Liverpool from 1937-1945. Author of many books on international law and of *Dr. Johnson and the Law* (1948), he was elected a judge of the International Court of Justice in The Hague in 1946 and was its president from 1952-1955. He then served as the president of the European Court of Human Rights from 1959-1965. According to the University of Liverpool Senate minutes, the other people invited to receive honorary degrees were Arundell James Kennedy Esdaile, Martin Knudsen, Baron Atkin, Thomas Harrison Hughes, Horace John Wilson, and Leonard Bairstow. See letter 110 and letters 86, 87, and 94.

110
***Typed**
March 3, 1939

From
THE VICE-CHANCELLOR
THE UNIVERSITY OF LIVERPOOL
March 3rd, 1939.

Dear Madam,

Thank you for your letter of March 2nd. I am very sorry that you feel that you must refuse, because I know that your decision will disappoint a large group of your admirers here. At the same time I entirely understand and sympathise with the view upon these matters that you adopt.

Yours sincerely,
ARNOLD D. McNAIR.

Letters from agents, editors, publishers, etc., Fan mail

See letter 109 for biographical information. Woolf mentions the offer from Liverpool in the context of visiting a class of book-production students at a Polytechnic with Leonard on March 2, 1939 (*D5* 206-07): "No it wasn't formidable. It was rather cheerful. And free & easy. Better much than Oxford & Cambridge: which reminds me that Liverpool today offered me a Doctor's Degree; which I refused."

111
***Typed**
March 3, [1939]

---

56 Curzon St W.1.
March 3rd.

Dear Mrs Woolf,

Here is the copy of "Black Narcissus" which I said I would send you. If you could spare the time to read it I should be delighted; she hasn't got a noisy voice and wasn't heard at all till I started shouting. And she isn't anything to shout about, I know, but she does seem to me to have a delightful talent and a sense of humour.

It was a very great pleasure to meet you. Your books have meant so much more to me than those of any other living writer that it was surely extraordinary not to be disappointed.

Yours sincerely,
TANGYE LEAN

Letters from agents, editors, publishers, etc., Fan mail

Edward Tangye Lean (b. 1911) had been at school with both Julian and Quentin Bell (*D*5 207). He wrote *Storm in Oxford, A Fantasy* and *Of Unsound Mind*, two novels, in 1932, a book about the European radio war (*Voices in the Darkness*) in 1943, and an historical study, *The Napoleonists: A Study in Political Disaffection, 1760-1960* in 1970. Rumer Godden's *Black Narcissus* was published in 1939.

112
***Typed**
March 19, 1939

3 Bardwell Rd., Oxford.

19.iii.39

Chere Mrs Virginia Woolf.

Il m'est difficile de vous décrire quelle joie et quelle angoisse en même temps j'éprouve à venir vous importuner de mon admiration. J'ose à peine ajouter à cette audace celle de me trouver des excuses : la chance m'a donné Philippa et Marie comme élèves à Oxford High School où je suis « assistante » pour un an – Phillipa a été tres amusée de mon enthousiasme et m'a « conseillé » de vous écrire!

Je dois faire cette année un « memoire » sur Katherine Mansfield et je la sens si proche, si vivante que son amitié pour vous la grande admiration qu'elle vous portait me semblent en quelque sorte une « lettre d'introduction » auprès de vous. J'espère que vous m'excuserez de ma hardiesse.

Votre admirable livre: « The Waves » aurait personnifié à ses yeux cette « intégrité » qu'elle a cherché toute sa vie, il me semble. Mille autres gens de tous les coins du monde vous ont dit, avant moi, leur émotion, leur admiration; beaucoup ont pu vous en en exprimer l'écho avec bonheur. Pour moi, c'est une désespérante expérience aujourd'hui de constater combien les mots sont futiles, creux et sans vie – Permettez moi tout de même de vous balbutier mon enchantement. C'est le plus beau livre de poésie que j'ai lu. Vous nous mettez, comme par un miracle, en possession de nos pensées, de nos rêves, de nos émotions, non pas comme nous les possédons à l'ordinaire, mais avec une conscience chaude et immédiate et vivante. Vous nous restaurez notre grain de sincérité et pour un moment, nous sentons une merveilleuse union en nous-même et note union avec le monde. – Comme ce doit être beau pour vous d'avoir atteint l'Idéal que vous vous fixez à votre art! Excusez moi de vous citer : « Life is not a series of gig lamps symmetrically arranged; life is a luminous halo, a semi-transparent envelope surrounding us from the beginning of consciousness to the end. Is it not the task of the novelist to convey this varying, this unknown and uncircumscribed spirit whatever aberration or complexity it may display, with as little mixture of the alien and external as possible? » — To « attempt to come closer to life » et lorsque vous citez : « Learn to make yourself akin to people . . . But let this sympathy be not with the mind – for it is easy with the mind – but with the heart, with Love towards them. » Il me semble que c'est Katherine Mansfield qui parle – mais un Katherine Mansfield plus claire, plus sereine, plus consciente de son idéal – N'était-ce pas là en effet le grand but de son constant effort vers cette intégrité, « wholeness » qui la fuyait? « I have always been disunited » dit-elle vers la fin de sa vie. – Elle est morte avant d'avoir pu consciemment réaliser son rêve d'art – « getting the deepest truth out of the idea. » Il me semble que vous êtes arrivée au sommet même de la voie qu'elle s'était tracée – votre œuvre – et particulièrement ce livre que je ceris entre tous : « The Waves » – est transparente comme le crystal – « crystal clear » — Ce sont des notations de lumière ou de musique qui me viennent à l'esprit lorsque j'essaie de trouver le secret magique et recuielli de votre art – Il y a un clair matin dan The Waves qui a la parfaite et sereine limpidité du « Lever du jour » de Ravel, dans Daphnis et Chloë. Rien ne semble ternir la pureté, l'ingénuité, la simplicité poétiques que vous jetez sur le monde – C'est exactement l'image que je me fais de la « liberté » de l'artiste : une liberté qui le conduit directment à la nature profonde et essentielle des choses de la vie, et le laisse disponible –

Je vous prie, chère Mrs Virginia Woolf, d'avoir beaucoup d'indulgence pour cette trop longue épître et de m'excuser de ma hardiesse.

Permettez moi de vous addresser ma plus respectueuse, ma plus enthousiaste admiration –

SIMONE ROHR

[translation by Helen Southworth]

Dear Mrs Virginia Woolf.

It is difficult for me to describe to you with what mixture of both joy and anguish I impose my admiration on you. I hardly dare to add to this audaciousness that of finding excuses: good fortune gave me Philippa and Marie as pupils at Oxford High School where I am an "assistant" for a year—Phillipa was greatly amused by my enthusiasm and "advised" me to write to you!

This year I have to write a "memoir" about Katherine Mansfield and I feel her so close, so alive that her friendship for you, the great admiration that she had for you seemed to represent for me in a certain way "a letter of introduction" to you. I hope you'll excuse my being so forward.

Your admirable book: "The Waves" should have personified in her eyes the "integrity" which she sought throughout her lifetime, it seems to me. Thousands of other people from all corners of the world have conveyed to you, before me, their emotion, their admiration; many have been able to express the echo of it happily. For me, it's a despairing experience today to recognize how futile words are, hollow and without life — Allow me all the same to stumble through the expression of my enchantment. It's <u>the most beautiful</u> book of poetry that I have ever read. You put us, as if by miracle, in possession of our thoughts, of our dreams, of our emotions, not as we possess them normally, but with a warm, immediate, living conscience. You restore to us our grain of sincerity and for a moment, we feel a marvelous union in ourselves and our union with the world — How beautiful it must be for you to have reached the Ideal that you intended for your work. Permit me to quote you: "Life is not a series of gig lamps symmetrically arranged; life is a luminous halo, a semi-transparent envelope surrounding us from the beginning of consciousness to the end. Is it not the task of the novelist to convey this varying, this unknown and uncircumscribed spirit whatever aberration or complexity it may display, with as little mixture of the alien and external as possible??" To "attempt to come closer to life" and when to write: "Learn to make yourself akin to people. . . . But let this sympathy not be with the mind – for it is easy with the mind – but with the heart, with Love towards them." It seems to me as if Katherine Mansfield is speaking—but a clearer, more serene Katherine Mansfield, more conscious of her ideal—is this not the great aim, this integrity, this "wholeness" toward which she constantly aspired but which escaped her? "I have always been disunited" she said toward the end of her life. She died before being able consciously to realize her dream of art—"getting the deepest truth out of the idea." It seems to me that you have arrived at the very pinnacle of the trajectory that she had traced for herself—your work—and particularly this work that I cherish above all: "The Waves" is transparent like crystal—"crystal clear"—These are notations of light and music which come to my spirit when I try to find the magic and contemplative secret of your art—there is a clear morning in The Waves which has the perfect and serene limpidity of Ravel's "Lever du Jour" [Daybreak], in Daphnis and Chloe. Nothing seems to tarnish the poetic purity, ingenuity and simplicity that you shower upon the world—it is exactly how I envision the "freedom" of the artist: a liberty that drives him directly to the profound and essential nature of life's things, and leaves him available—

I beg you, dear Mrs Virginia Woolf, to indulge me for this too long letter and to excuse my forwardness.

Yours faithfully
SIMONE ROHR.

Letters from agents, editors, publishers, etc., Fan mail

Simone Rohr would have been the French language assistant at the school. 3 Bardwell Road is now an address within St. Clare's at Oxford, but it was not part of Oxford at the time of this letter. Philippa and Marie were Leonard Woolf's nieces, daughters of Philip and Marjorie Woolf. See Philippa's letter to Woolf, dated September 18, 1939 (*WSA* 6: 153-54), where she mentions this school and the staff there, and Woolf's reply, dated September 29, 1939, *L*6 360-61 (3554).

113
***Typed**
April 19, 1939

THE YALE EDITION OF HORACE WALPOLE'S CORRESPONDENCE
Editor: Wilmarth Sheldon Lewis, Fellow of Yale University
Farmington, Connecticut

19 April 1939.

Dear Mrs. Woolf,

I trust you don't mind my bursting in on you without ceremony. I am just back from a holiday in California to find the current Yale Review waiting for me and I cannot be ceremonious with one who has been so extraordinarily kind to me. Miss MacAfee had told me you had written an essay on Cole and Walpole, but she had carefully kept from telling me more so that my delight might be all the greater. My delight is very great indeed!

Oddly enough, you are the only reviewer of the two volumes who has pointed out that questions like the christian name of Cole's cook are really worth all the time and trouble they take. The pundits on both sides of the Atlantic have been very nice indeed about these two volumes, but you alone have said that this sort of thing is worth doing. (I am mortified about the cook's christian name! We probably could have got it from a parish register somewhere). This much I know, the satisfaction one gets from answering one of these minute questions is prodigious, out of all proportion to the importance of the thing discovered.

I wish I might call on you in Tavistock Square this summer, but my wife and I are taking a Sabbatical from England this year. (We decided to do so a year ago, before the Horror had come to you). I'd like to thank you in person for this perfectly intoxicating paper and I'd like to put your mind at rest about HW and Chatterton. HW was no more responsible for Chatterton's death than I am responsible for it. And I think our next six volumes which contain Madame du Deffand's correspondence with HW, and which will be out this autumn, will reassure you about his alleged ill-treatment of her. I have no desire to whitewash HW. The monkey in him was vain, but not cruel; it was sedulous and capricious; it was timid and hyper-sensitive, and it chattered hysterically when it pelted the too-inquisitive with mud, but it was not a sinister monkey and it loved having its ears scratched.

I hope some day we may meet. Until then, please accept my grateful thanks.

Yours sincerely,
W.S. LEWIS

Mrs. Virginia Woolf,
52 Tavistock Square,
London, W.C.1.

Letters from agents, editors, publishers, etc., Fan mail

Courtesy of the Lewis Walpole Library and by permission of Yale University.

Wilmarsh Sheldon Lewis (1895-1979), collector and bibliographer, was the editor (along with Alva Dayle Wallace) of the mammoth Horace Walpole Correspondence (48 volumes,

1937-1983) for Yale University Press, but he also edited *The Castle of Otranto*, published studies about Walpole and other literary figures of the 18th century, and wrote two memoirs, *Collector's Progress* (1951) and *One Man's Education* (1967), among many other publications.

"Two Antiquaries" appeared in *The Yale Review* for March 1939, even though the journal's usual policy was not to review Yale publications in its pages, and it featured *Letters of Horace Walpole to the Rev. William Cole*, volumes 1 and 2. See Woolf's reply to Lewis, dated April 30, 1939, *L6* 330-31 (3510).

114
Handwritten
[November 1939]

10 Eynsham Road
Oxford

Dear Miss Woolf,

You are in 'the trade'; I am not. Presumably, therefore, you know far more about it than I do, – the omissions in your pamphlet on reviewing are intentional. But permit me to recount: the early 18th c. essayists endeavoured to guide the public taste not only in manners, but in reading—Cf., for example Addisson's Comments on Paradise Lost in the Spectator. This was not reviewing in the special sense; it was criticism. But it was a public attempt to guide taste. Later in that century, the earliest reviews were founded: The Critic; The Monthly, the first Edinburgh Review. But these were bookseller's organs; little more really than extensive blurbs, & the public had little faith in them. In 1802 Frances Jeffrey & his colleagues changed the whole face of the matter by founding the second Edinburgh Review which was so completely free from the booksellers that although it was published by Constable, it could damn Scott's Marmion which the luckless Archibald also published! Here began modern reviewing. Once more a conscious effort to guide public taste, & to relate the book to the moral & social currents of the time. And as much as possible to relate it to literary history, the 'eternal standards.' How successful the E.R. was I need not tell you, for the whole nature of the periodical—'policy'; payment; editorship; etc—was therein founded. The reviewers discussed the books. Unlike the overworked modern reviewer, they did not review all, but only the best books, & that slowly (quarterly publication) & at length (many articles over fifty pages). They too addressed themselves to the author—Jeffrey above all. They gave him this competent advice which he so much desires. But most of all, they reached a wide public. They publicized the books!

How much does an advertisement cost in the Times newspaper? A review costs a copy of the book. You know, surely, how little effect advertising has upon book sales. But you also know that irate authors clamor because their publishers have not sent more copies for review, have not appropriated more money for direct advertising. This aspect of the matter is very unliterary, no doubt, but it is one of the actualities. Will your proposal meet the demand?

Secondly, have you sufficiently considered the readers? Your private conference would tell me nothing, however much it told the author. Even Mr. Woolf's note does not stress this enough. To me the Times Lit. Supp. is a digest; it acquaints me at least with the multiplicity of books I simply cannot read. How are you going to give me that knowledge if you abolish the reviewer? 'Gutter' he may be, but this function he does perform.

Last of all, would this saved space be hoarded until the end of a period & then be devoted to adequate criticism? Is that not rather like saying "I will put aside ten minutes every day until I've saved a week"? The periodical press has other things to do. Is the issue 'burning'? Good—discuss it. Is it a week old? It's ancient history.

You have two alternatives, it seems to me, to the present inadequate system. The first you say will not prosper financially: that is, a return to the quarterly review wherein the outstanding books of the quarter can be criticised by competent authorities at length. The second I say the public will not trust – the publisher's prospectus (cf. Jonathan Cape's Now & Then). The former would (one hopes) support itself – or why not have it subsidized by the Booksellers Association? – & the second would be supported by publishers with money now spent on advertising. But the present author is free! Is the problem a literary or a financial one?

Pardon me for talking so long; thank you for raising to the light a problem which interests every serious reader. I hope something comes from your initiative.

Sincerely yours,
W. Denham Sutcliffe

W. Denham Sutcliffe (1913-1964) was a 1937 graduate of Bates College (where he had to interrupt his studies for a year and a half to earn his tuition) and was a Rhodes Scholar, which explains his Oxford address. According to Harley Henry, who edited a collection of Sutcliffe's essays (*What Shall We Defend?* 1973), Sutcliffe taught at Kenyon College in Ohio from 1946-1964, grew up in Blackpool, England, and Richmond, Maine, and wrote a doctoral thesis at Oxford on English book reviewing in the 18th century. He also edited the letters of Edwin Arlington Robinson to Harry de Forest Smith (*Untriangulated Stars*, 1947).

Sutcliffe is responding to Woolf's "Reviewing," which had appeared as a Hogarth Sixpenny Pamphlet (#4) on November 2, 1939. Woolf's reply to Sutcliffe, dated November 16, 1939, is in *L6* 370-71 (3567).

115
Typed; signed
May 14, 1940

May 14, 1940
MOTIER HARRIS FISHER
OBERLIN, OHIO

Dear Mrs. Woolf:

This is not an American "fan" letter, though if I were ever to write one to any of the people I have greatly admired you would be the most likely recipient. It may turn out to be a begging letter, for we cannot be sure than any significant amount of money will come from the literary venture for which we greatly desire a contribution from you. I can only hope that you are <not> so accustomed to requests of the kind that your insulation is <~~not~~> complete, because there is no one else who can supply what is needed. There may be money, of course, the usual, and unpredictable, ten percent royalties. Let me tell you at some length what is planned.

A group of eminent women in the United States are planning a Centennial Congress to be held in New York this coming November. I am not quite sure that I know its exact purpose, as no one has thought to inform me, and after a certain point of involvement it takes courage to ask. Perhaps it is to mark "Woman's Coming of Age," with particular reference to the American woman during the century 1840-1940. There will be an effort, I have heard, to blaze some trails for the future, though I cannot think who would have the courage for that. At any rate, we are planning a book to be published by the Woman's Press shortly before this congress. Although it will have no official connection with the celebration, the publisher is chairman of the executive committee for the Congress, and she believes that such a book may ride off on the wave of publicity arising from the occasion to a wider distribution than could otherwise be arranged, and that it might even prove profitable.

It is to be a symposium, with contributions from many obscure writers and from women who are not writers at all but who can supply vivid personal material illustrative of typical features of life in this country. We should like to emphasize anonymity as a distinctive feature of the book, for we hope to record a sort of chorus of articulation which may approximate the voice of feminine America, if there is such a thing. Only a very few distinguished women will contribute to the volume. Mary Beard, who has established herself here as a historian in collaboration with her husband, will write a historical sketch. Pearl Buck has been asked for a short article. You are the only person outside this country who is being asked to contribute, and we shall wait in some anxiety for your answer. We should like something within the range of three to seven thousand words, and I have even thought of several subjects, but you are at liberty to choose any other which strikes your fancy. My first thought was that, since small groups of women in various parts of the United States have read your "Three Guineas," they would be interested in knowing whether its analysis of a constructive attitude of women toward peace in time of peace still seems valid in wartime. If you chose to write frankly on such a subject it might be possible to arrange for your manuscript to be delivered by personal messenger. Such a timely word from you might have tremendous influence.

Perhaps you can see, in the light of recent events, a need for new emphases on the part of women, or indications of unexpected trends. After the wars are once again cleared off the center of the board there will still be women, I suppose, and meals and babies. Peace has a way of coming around again bringing back the hum-drum questions which war can brush aside but never solve. (That bit of speculation you may have for a penny.) What we want, I suppose, is a word from on high combined with intimate human revelation!

If this seems too exacting for one involved in crisis, you could always write of us, for we are eternally interested in ourselves. Pearl Buck from her perspective of half a lifetime spent in China, believes that we have shamelessly neglected the richest field of opportunity ever open to women. Surprisingly, we do not seem to resent her accusation that we have not achieved as we might; it would almost seem that we like being goaded. Perhaps that bears out the contention of orthodox Freudians that women are naturally masochists, but I think it only an indication that they are pathetically eager to find worth-while outlets for their energies and believe they are more likely to receive sound guidance from those who are bold enough to dispense with usual amiability. This is not to invite disparaging remarks from you, but it is an announcement that perfect sympathies are not required. If we seem to you unspeakably shrill and callow, we seem so to ourselves also at times. And yet, I believe that preparation for the coming of your "Sister of Shakespeare" is definitely further along here than elsewhere. (Why should this sound sentimental when it didn't in your book?) There is now a young woman in Chicago - but you will hear of her in time.

Our contemporary problems are quite like yours except that we probably have them on a larger scale. There is the woman who must support an un-employed husband and children while at the same time receiving a smaller salary than her husband would receive doing the work less competently. Her problem, I think, is chiefly that of keeping intact family morale and bolstering the self-respect of the man. In our book we hope to give expression to her difficulties. We have our millions of industrial workers who must carry two jobs with no opportunity of going forward in either. This is only one aspect of the larger problem of labor, but it has important feminine angles. There is quite a large group of educated women who, for the sake of "biological fulfillment", have chosen to carry two jobs. These women - doctors, lawyers, professors, artists, writers, musicians - are really the envy of all the others, for they are endowed with intelligence and unusual energy. There are other thousands of educated women who have forsworn marriage for the sake of their work. No one seems to envy them or the great army of women teachers (85% of our teachers below the college level are women) who, for the most part, are not permitted to marry though an increasing number in the cities are contracting secret marriage.

One problem which is peculiar to this country, I think, is that of the great numbers of girls who are being almost deliberately trained for maladjustment. For example, although our institutions of higher education graduate almost as many women as men, many with higher degrees, these same institutions refuse to employ the women so trained. College faculties continue to be male except on the lowest levels, and all the good technical jobs elsewhere go, almost without question, to men. A symbol for women in 1940 might be a woman Ph.D. awkwardly mopping up after the baby or stirring the pottage in surroundings far from aesthetic. Is this tragic or comic? At any rate it is something new under the sun, a nation which ventures to give the finest technical training, largely at public expense, to immense numbers of persons who have practically no opportunity to put the training to use, and at the same time seems incapable of facing the problem realistically. What do you think of that?

We have another problem which is unique: that of the negro woman who has developed responsibility and resourcefulness simply because our society has not forced negro men to assume responsibility for wife and offspring. You will be hearing from her, too, in time, and her voice will be vivid, confident, encouraging.

This is the merest suggestion of what we would like the book to express, but it may serve to fire your imagination a little, if the stress of your moment is not too severe, and to induce you to write some little thing as the spirit moves you. Whatever you send will be treated with respect born of admiration and – at least on my part – affection. If you are tired of the feminine emphasis, so am I, but this, you see, is a woman's occasion. It is by no means the vogue here now to separate the woman's struggle from that of the human race, and the word "feminist" is in distinctly bad odor. College girls, even while submitting to the leadership of men on almost every campus, assume equality. It is a paradoxical situation - the bland expectancy on their part of self fulfillment, and the equally bland expectancy on the part of the college men that their wives will be trained to see wider horizons and at the same time attend to the mending, cooking and general traditional tasks with the same poise and competence that their mothers and grand-mothers exhibited. Disillusionment is due to strike too many of these, though we shall not know how serious the dilemma really is until imminent war, or actual war, ceases to be the focus of attention.

This has been a difficult letter to write. I have a sensation of trying to convey a faint echo across a tremendous uproar. It began as a clear inspiration, but now I begin to question the possibility of its significance for you. At any rate I am going to add that we hope (Is this the hope of every writer, editor, and publisher who produces a book?) that not one page of the volume will be dull or beyond the comprehension of any averagely literate woman and that at the same time not one page will be unworthy of respect even from those who appreciate your own definition of integrity.

Unless you answer this almost as soon as it is received - at the above address - your reply will reach me more directly addressed:

Mrs. Motier Harris Fisher
Care of Miss Rhoda McCulloch
The Woman's Press
600 Lexington Avenue
New York, N.Y.

Very sincerely yours,
Motier Fisher

Letters from agents, editors, publishers, etc., Letters about articles

---

Motier Harris Fisher (1896-1991) was a teacher and freelance writer; she also had a pilot's license! Her husband, Raymond Henry Fisher, was a professor of education at Oberlin College most of his career; they had a son and a daughter. She was a delegate to the Woman's Centennial Congress, held to honor the women of 1840 and their successors, on November 25-27, 1940 at the Hotel Commodore in New York City. The Congress opened with women from China, Spain, France, Canada, and Argentina speaking to American women and Carrie Chapman Catt speaking for American women. Five commissions—Economic and Social Welfare, Education of Women, Ethical and Religious Values, Government and Politics, and World Peace through World Organization—met and prepared reports, and the Congress ended with the adoption of a Declaration of Purpose for the future (*Woman's Centennial Congress* 1940).

When "Thoughts on Peace in an Air Raid" appeared in the *New Republic* on October 21, 1940, the editors included this note: "This article is expected to be published shortly in "Women's Forum," a symposium on current matters concerning women. The forum will be edited by Mrs. Motier Harris Fisher of Oberlin, Ohio" (549; see also Naomi Black, *Virginia Woolf as Feminist* [Ithaca: Cornell UP, 2004], 220, n55). Fisher's papers include a note saying "This is a partial list of contributions to the symposium which I edited," and Karen Horney, Virginia Woolf, Pearl Buck, and Margaret Mead are among the 23 authors listed, along with the titles of their articles, but so far, the symposium has not been traced.

116
Handwritten
July 12, 1940

MOTIER HARRIS FISHER
~~OBERLIN, OHIO~~

295 Convent Avenue
New York, N.Y.
July 12, 1940

Dear Mrs. Woolf:

Your letter came this morning, two days after I had sent one by air to you. Yours was delayed in reaching me by failure of someone at the Womans Press to follow directions.

After reading your kind answer, I find myself still retaining a little hope that you may feel like writing some small thing meant only for this book which I have described. If you feel that you really cannot do so, then of course we should be glad of book rights to your magazine article. I have been speculating as to which magazines may have bid for what would now be daring material if written in the same vein as the Three Guineas. Most of what is being published about women in the ~~most~~ commercially successful magazines now would be equally acceptable in a fascist country. The Atlantic Monthly is perhaps the most reactionary of all, with Harper's following in a more sprightly and contemporary style, a close second. Such publications as the Ladies Home Journal, and the Woman's Home Companion are almost frankly media for advertising and little else, though in order to hold a certain position of prestige in the publishing world they pay fabulous sums for slight material from well-known people. Last month in the Ladies Home Journal, for example, Dorothy Thompson wrote what was used as a reply to the Beards' indictment of the "best sellers" among women's magazines for not touching any vital economic or social problem. In the latest volume of their historical series ~~they~~ Charles and Mary Beard charged that these magazines included, over a certain period, no major articles on child welfare, unemployment, social security, etc. Dorothy Thompson justified this on the grounds that women can create comfort and beauty, can feed the family adequately and arrange flowers artistically, but are not able to do much about the "cosmic" problems. In that one adroit piece of writing, I suspect, she has nullified the work of large numbers of earnest men and women who feel that it is time for all of us, regardless of sex, to take our places as full-fledged citizens in a distressed world.

However, your contribution, for whatever magazine intended, cannot fail to carry some thought that will have more than contemporary value for women and for all. The chief difficulty would appear to be that of time. We have been forced to delay plans already because material from the "hinterlands" has been slow in arriving and has required considerable editing in order that some unity might be achieved.

What is the earliest time that the piece of writing that you may finally decide to designate to our purpose can be made available? Would you let us know your subject, or your exact title, quite soon? A manuscript from you would be worth waiting for, naturally. Perhaps we could still arrange to publish in late November or early December.

With deep appreciation for your cordial response, I am

Sincerely yours,
Motier Fisher

Letters from agents, editors, publishers, etc., Letters about articles

---

See letter 115 for biographical information. On August 28, 1977, Motier Harris Fisher wrote to her granddaughter that she wished she'd "taken the trouble to meet Virginia Woolf, who was easily available at one time. I have some of her letters." But those letters, perhaps replies to letters 115 and 116, have not been located.

117
Handwritten
July 18, 1940

July 18th 1940.

TELEPHONE 20
BOURNE END

FIELDHEAD,
BOURNE END.
BUCKS.

Dear Virginia Woolf,

I feel I must send you just a word to tell you of the enormous pleasure I have had in reading your biography of Roger Fry. You have given such a completely fascinating man so natural, so true. How happy one would be if there were many more like him!

Since my foolish accident, I have been reading you again with greater delight and admiration than ever.

I am glad to hear from John that Roger Fry is to be published now.

I am hoping that you will believe me when I say please do not trouble to acknowledge this note.

Yours most sincerely,
Alice Lehmann

Letters from readers, Letters about Roger Fry

Alice Lehmann (1874-1956), county councilor, was the mother of John Lehmann, who became a partner at Hogarth Press in 1938. Woolf's biography of Roger Fry was published on July 25, 1940, but several correspondents must have received copies before the publication date. See Woolf's reply, dated July 24, 1940, *L6* 407 (3618).

See her letter to Leonard Woolf in *A* 71.

118
Handwritten
July 21, [1940]

---

c/o J. E. Fry

Lac la Hache
B. C.
Canada.
21st July –

My dear Virginia –

If this letter ever reaches you which seems doubtful as posts are incredibly slow, it is just to tell you I found the rest of yr. M.S. here and have been delighted to have the opportunity of finishing it.

Even if I hadn't known Roger I should still think it one of the most wonderful biographies I had ever read – but knowing him, I have constantly wondered how you managed to divine his character so wonderfully, and to show him to us even better than we had seen him ourselves.

I think you have found the exact balance of the underlying characteristics and the details most wonderfully.

I hope you feel very pleased about it yourself, I am convinced it's a great work of art as well as a fascinating portrait.

I am very sorry Mrs Nicholson did not send her Barbara with us as I could easily have got her onto that boat with us, & I fear that most schemes for sending children over have been held up since our departure.

It feels incredibly peaceful and calm here 100 miles from the nearest station, with only 2 posts a week, though we listen to the cracky radio for every scrap of news we can get from England. It is wonderful to have the children here and no longer to feel that every remark of little Roger's is a stab in one's heart. We are terribly lucky. Julian's boys are perfectly friendly and natural and unspoilt and all five play and bathe endlessly together most happily. It's a marvelous sight to see a dozen children, all as brown as Indians (many are half cast) splashing in and out of the lake all the day. Julian is very busy with the hay, and Eva seems quite happy & balanced in a society which she can cope with & dominate. The most important thing now is whether they can shoot the 'kioty' who has been helping himself to the chickens – in fact if there were {not} such a total lack of civilized thought, it would be the most perfect life out here – maybe such things take centuries to develope.

We wonder so much about you all in England I was so glad of a cable from Micu saying all well yesterday. I often wonder if you & Vanessa are still in Sussex. I hope this will find you there safely, don't bother to answer. Yrs very afect^ly Pamela

Letters from readers, Letters about Roger Fry

Pamela Fry Diamand (b. 1902) was Roger Fry's only daughter; she married Micu Diamand, a Rumanian painter, in 1923. Her typed recollections and reflections about the Omega are in the Victoria and Albert Museum. Her brother, Julian Fry, had emigrated to British Columbia after World War I, and at this time, people in England were being urged to cross the Atlantic, which Pamela and her three children had just done; she returned to England in 1944.

119
Handwritten
August 11, 1940

TELEPHONE: FRAMPTON MANSELL 38.

FAR OAKRIDGE,
STROUD, GLOUCESTERSHIRE.

11 – 8 – 40

Dear Mrs. Woolf – I found yr life of R. F. at the Club & read ¾ of the book. You have done a fine & convincing portrait. I expected, of course, a discerning appreciation of Roger's distinguished qualities & had confidence in the fairness of yr attitude to others with whom he was concerned. The book is likely to remain as a convincing biography of a character, of a man who played a notable part in his time. The next generation will place him & the rest of us – how & where we cannot foretell.

There is one phrase you use, unless my fallible memory deceives me, wh. suggests judgment has already been possible, wherein you assert that those of us who didn't follow Roger have been left behind. Is it not possible that R. F's position as an artist was insufficient to effect those who had vision of their own when he wished to establish a new center? Painters are influenced by other painters who have greater powers & vision, by such men as Whistler, Degas, Manet & Cezanne, but not by cognoscenti, however learned & vital. The artists who influenced the younger men on whom Roger used his attractive & fertile mind also influenced younger men in Tokyo, New York, in fact everywhere, without R. F's intervention. Are you sure that his influence didn't deter some of the younger men from following their natural bent? I coined a phrase about Ricketts wh., if there is any truth in it, is applicable to R. F. to BB & others perhaps—einflusslust. One thing is undoubted, that Roger had a unique influence on contemporary criticism & patronage.

To return to the phrase on wh. I allowed myself to comment – Roger's views, much less his painting, had no effect on Steer, John & Sickert – are you sure they will really suffer in the eyes of future critics, as you suggest, because they didn't throw in their lot with him?

Forgive a letter wh. may seem carping. Yr biography has evoked memories of a friendship wh. was for some years a close one, & a character wh. still has for me touching qualities. Sincerely yrs Wm. Rothenstein

Nash-Rylands

William Rothenstein (1872-1945) published several books of portraits and was a painter, teacher (among his students were Henry Moore and Barbara Hepworth), and writer. Best known as a war artist in both World War I and II, he recorded the devastation of war and created portraits. He published two memoirs, *Men and Memories: A History of the Arts 1872-1922* (1937) and *Since Fifty: Men and Memories, 1922-1938* (1940). See Woolf's reply, dated August 15, 1940, *L6* 416-17 (3630).

See his letter to Leonard Woolf in *A* 84-85.

120
Handwritten
August 11, [1940]

116 Portland Rd
Nottingham

Sunday. Aug 11.

My dear Virginia

I must write and tell you what a pleasure it has been to read your life of Roger. How cleverly you have constructed and jointed it! And how neatly you have manipulated the transitions!

I am so glad you have done it. He was so worth 'doing'. I have the happiest memories of Dalmeny Ave and of visiting him in Cambridge and in other places. Perhaps one of my clearest recollections is the time when I found him in the South Kensington. I had been wafted into the building by one of those gusts of snobbery to which in those days I was only too responsive. I had gone to see a collection of ikons which had had their metal veils removed and their faces washed. Alas, they were the dreariest old bits of painted wood to me as I went dutifully round – and then I saw Roger. All was changed. In ten minutes he caused me to enjoy what I was looking at. The objects themselves became vivid and intelligible, and my own response quickened into appreciation.

There must be many people like me. People with scales on their eyes and wax in their ears, who are capable of spirited enjoyment if only someone comes along and removes the scales and digs out the wax. Roger Fry, I. R. Richards (does that surprise you?) Lytton and Desmond, and also, if I may say so, you yourself have performed that operation over and over again for me. I believe you have, of recent years, been a little hard on the critic, but I think you said that nothing could shut him up – and 'Thank God for that!' I say, when it came to [operative?] critics like yourself & Roger. I owe for such a debt of gratitude.

Your book came into my hands at the right moment.

I have been seconded from the University to the Ministry of Information in this Region. I have to arrange meetings for the areas from the Humber to Northampton, from the Peak to the West. People ask "whether we should be so much worse off under Hitler," and I think it is of vital importance that they should have an answer, so I don't mind the job itself. But the difficulties! You would scarcely believe the difficulties. Local Committees are established. "We all want to help," they say, and then one has to fix up a series of open air meetings in a hurry and they are furious because they have not been consulted in time. You fix up a campaign for Northamptonshire, and Chesterfield shrieks that it is being neglected. A good speaker is [appointed?], the [nights?] draw in, he must get on with his work as soon as possible. Where shall he go? [Surely?] he can start in the district in which he lives & which he knows. This is fixed up. Screams from London. "Mr [Baum?] must not operate in the [ ] parliamentary division of Leicestershire, because he is a political agent there. He must be sent to the furthest part of [ ] Region – anywhere he is unknown and where he himself is at a disadvantage."

And Mr Haslam M. P. "Why was I not informed before that a campaign of open-air meetings was being arranged in Lincolnshire?" The [party?] truce has to be [ ] at every turn, and ruffled feathers smoothed. And then there was the Southampton [controversy?]. They had had bombs without warning. Something must be done to allay anxiety. A mass meeting of A.R.P. personnel, marching behind the A.R.P. band, and a speaker to explain the difficulties of ~~A.R.P.~~ Air-raid warnings. Could we get anyone from the Air Ministry? No, but we could have Capt. Ricci, so well-known as 'Bartimeus'?. "Yes, says I "that might please the management, but do you think the workers will ever have heard of 'Bartimeus'?" "Oh, yes, the working class often read books." Anyway, would Capt. Ricci talk about air-raid warnings? No, he will talk about the Navy. But that won't do . . . . and so we went on, minueting backwards & forwards. Eventually the Royal Commissioner squashed the whole thing because he said that they had no business to hold a mass meeting in a bombable area. The fact was that he didn't want to go himself.

Anyway – such are my difficulties, and you can, or perhaps you can't, imagine how much I enjoyed reading about Roger & Reality.

I can never get away. I try to meet an intellectual or an artist or even an aristocrat. I am so sick of fat, squat little men at Rotary Clubs and from the City Councils. The working class remain honest or honestly dishonest, silly & simple.

Now I must go to bed. To-morrow I must face the post with its wails from injured committees and howls from outraged members of parliament.

My love to Leonard & yourself

Yours Sebastian Sprott.

Sackville-Stapledon

Walter John Herbert Sprott (1897-1971) was a friend of Maynard Keynes and Lytton Strachey. He was Lecturer in Psychology at Nottingham University at the time, and he published *Psychology for Everyone: An Outline of General Psychology* (1937) and *Social*

Psychology (1956). See Woolf's reply, dated August 15, 1940, *L6* 416 (3629). Woolf uses Sprott's letter in her argument with Ben Nicolson about Roger Fry; see *L6* 419-22.

Sir Lewis Anselm de Casta Ritchie wrote under the name Bartimeus and wrote about the Navy. Henry C. Haslam was Conservative MP for Horncastle in Lincolnshire. I. R. Richards may be I. A. Richards, the critic and linguistics scholar whose studies of meaning, poetry, and the imagination led to close textual analysis and the New Criticism.

See his letter to Leonard Woolf in *A* 137-38.

121
Handwritten
August 19, [1940]

August 19

Macootha
Ruiru
Kenya

Dear Mrs Woolf,

It is a year ago today since you wrote to me – a not-to-be-forgotten anniversary for me, and for you of course, an incident long since forgotten. It was written from Sussex with the filthy war only hovering and to fools like myself, a possibility from which the mind [turned?] back and would not contemplate.

I think of you constantly now; every day we hear of bombs being dropped in Sussex; we have even had two or three nightmare recordings of actual raids, and I wonder whether you are still there.

I have read somewhere that all kinds of precious things 'Old Masters' & the like have been pushed away into vaults for greater safety, but what is happening about the living 'Masters'? How can you think let alone write in the midst of all that infernal horror – but perhaps you have gone away, I hope so.

It is a useless, stupid waste that you should suffer these barbarities; you who have given and should be giving to countless people, the most lasting of pleasures a joy that can be returned to again & again and never fails to leave a deep content.

Apart from one's family and friends, it is the thought that all these things and the makers of them are today living ~~the~~ in the greatest danger which makes life even here (secure for the present) a bleak and depressing affair.

For myself, of little use and no consequence, I would like to be at home, in my own country with my own people, as against being spoon-fed by this wireless machine and waiting week and weeks for letters & papers.

With good wishes for your health and safety

Yours sincerely,
G. Davis

Letters from agents, editors, publishers, etc., Letters about various books

---

In 1936, an H. L. G. Davis was Manager of R. Chamberlain's coffee estate, Macootha, in the Ruiru District of Kenya. An incomplete and undated draft letter to a Mr. Davis, in which Woolf refers to his question about *Orlando* and notes that she has not read it since she wrote it, seems related to this letter's opening paragraph (Mark Hussey, *Major Authors on CD-ROM: Virginia Woolf* [Woodbridge: Primary Source Media, 1997]).

122
Typed; signed
August 31, 1940

TELEPHONE AND TELEGRAMS SURREY GUILDFORD 1053.

FROM DOCTOR WILLIAMSON.

MOUNT MANOR HOUSE,
MOUNT STREET,
GUILDFORD,
August 31st, 1940.

Mrs. Woolf,
c/o The Hogarth Press,
37, Mecklenburg Square,
W.C.1.

Dear Madam,

I have read, with the greatest interest and delight, the very important book that you have written on Roger Fry. I knew him well, from the time when he asked me to come over and see him at Dorking, and during his strange and eventful life. We differed upon almost every important matter, except in one respect. I wrote a little book on Velasquez, which Roger Fry praised in no measured terms, to my great joy. But, though we differed in many other respects, we were none the less friends. I loved the work of Gainsborough, and hated that of Cezanne, and twice I declined to write articles upon Post-Impressionist Exhibitions, because I told him I could say nothing in favour of the work.

You have entered into the details of his life with extraordinary skill, if I may be allowed to say so, and I am greatly obliged to you for having written the book.

I do want, however, to protest against what you have put on page 137. I knew Mr. Morgan intimately, and as a personal friend. He was constantly at my house in London, and I was often at his in America, and I traveled for him all over Europe, gathering up information from archives and documents in various languages. You say that his "ignorance was colossal." He took a very high degree at his university, he was a sound classical scholar, he spoke and read French, and in mathematics he took an especially high position, particularly in the more difficult kind of mathematics – trigonometry, the integral calculus, and so on. There his knowledge was so important that he would have been welcomed as a tutor or professor in any university, and was in fact offered such a position. Moreover, he had a sound knowledge of Italian art and a considerable knowledge of portraiture, and he knew about carved woodwork, jewels and precious stones, so that what you mean by "colossal ignorance" I cannot conceive.

Again, you say that his "vanity was prodigious." On the contrary, he was a very humble man, he kept his own skill and knowledge carefully hidden. He was a religious man, a constant attendant at religious services, and he was always ready to say things in discredit of his own knowledge. Then you say he "required flattery." No man required it less, no man more resented it, no man saw more quickly through it. He did wish to make his museum as good as possible, and I have heard him say again and again that he wished to have as fine things in it as in any of the museums of the old country, and he did everything in his power to carry out this wish.

He did "buy in batches," as you say, because his remark was "I cannot live long enough to make a collection, and therefore I will buy the whole collection of some great collector, and hand it over to my museum." I remember expertising for him a great collection, taking out from it fakes and forgeries, and telling him that what was left was worthy his having, and he there and then, as I later understood, made an offer to the collector for all that I had selected.

I knew Mrs. Douglas, and Fry was not right in the remarks that he made about her. I knew Mrs. Jack Gardner well.

Morgan was anxious to have a fine private collection, but was never anxious to have the "finest in the world." He simply wanted to have a few fine pictures, and in that he succeeded, but he only had about a dozen in his own room, and they were all important ones. What he was most anxious was that his museum should have the very best. Fry misunderstood him again and again, and more-over, Fry had no tact, and therefore it was that he did not get on with Morgan, but there is a great deal in what he said on pages 141-144 that is not accurate. I know Perugia and Siena well; I know what he got and what he bought, and I knew the man thoroughly well. He did get together wonderful things, as you say on p. 144, but it was not to increase his own importance, but to make the museum, which he called his museum, as great as it possibly could be, and to that he spared no pains.

Johnson of Philadelphia I knew perfectly well, he was a man of great independence, he most certainly was never under Mr. Morgan's influence. He bought pictures that he liked, and he never accepted Mr. Morgan's advice or opposed him. His collection was formed entirely separately, it was far larger than Morgan's, it contained a great many things that were comparatively unimportant, together with a great many that were important. Sir George Savage, mentioned on 146, was a great friend of mine.

Your book is a very wonderful one, but I do very much regret that you have looked at a book that was written by a financial opponent of Morgan, instead of looking at the Satterlee biography or getting information from someone who had come into contact with the Maecenas of modern life, as I did myself.

Yours truly,
George Williamson ÀET 83.

Letters from readers, Letters about Roger Fry

George Charles Williamson (1858-1942) published many books about art, miniatures, and collecting, among them *The Amateur Collector* (1924), *Catalogue of the Collection of Miniatures, the Property of J. Pierpont Morgan* (1906-08), and *The Book of Amber* (1932), and he also wrote about Lady Anne Clifford and Angelica Kaufmann. The source he mentions, by a financial opponent, was *Morgan the Magnificent: The Life of J. Pierpont Morgan (1837-1913)* by John Kennedy Winkler (1930), and the source he wishes Woolf had consulted was Herbert Livingston Satterlee's *J. P. Morgan, An Intimate Portrait* (1939).

123
Handwritten
[late August/early September 1940]

BROGYNTYN,
OSWESTRY.

Dear Virginia,

I must write to say how much I admired your life of Roger Fry. Speaking as a fellow-biographer, I can't imagine a harder problem, the writing the life of a friend soon after his death. On the one hand one must know too much: on the other one is allowed to say too little. To compose a portrait definite in outline yet not overweighted with detail would seem nearly impossible. But it is possible: you have done it. Perhaps R. F's ~~fir~~ individuality is a little less vividly realised in boyhood & youth than it is later. But that is inevitable, since you must have made his acquaintance yourself later. As a whole the ~~book~~ portrait is equally consistent & living. I felt I had known him. And I only wished I ~~cou~~ had done so in real life. What a charming character & what an impressive attitude of mind! That mixture of hedonistic philosophy & serious Quaker prejudice is whimsical, but it too has a charm. I don't think I like people to be consistent.

It seems a long time since we met. I have washed up in a sort of backwater of the war in this place, where Rachel the baby & I are spending the long vacation. And I spend my time reading for Oxford Work. It involves deliberately averting one's mind from the war: but I do not know why one should contemplate what one cannot alleviate. Meanwhile I ~~read abt~~ re-read the Victorian poets preliminary to lecturing on them. To my surprise I find that, often Tennyson, Christina Rosetti & Bridges wear much better than anyone else.

Yrs truly
David Cecil

Bosanquet-Cecil

David Cecil (1902-1986) was the son of Robert and Eleanor Cecil and a prolific biographer who wrote about Lord Melbourne, Jane Austen, William Cowper, Walter de la Mare, and Charles Lamb, among others. He also wrote criticism about the early Victorian novelists, edited *Modern Biography*, and compiled anthologies. His teaching and his thinking about the Victorian poets may have contributed to his book on *The English Poets* (1941). See Woolf's reply, dated September 4, 1940, *L*6 426-27 (3642).

124
Handwritten
September 1, [1940]

The Sheffolds
1 Sept. Dorking

Dear Virginia, Bob has just finished reading aloud your Roger Fry to me, and I want so much to tell you what delight it has given me. I think it is a marvelous achievement, and it must often have given you difficulty, just because you were so near to him & all his life & work – the selecting & composing must have been bewildering. There is never too much, never that dreary insistence on formal detail because it is 'biographical' – one is always wanting to know more about this or that, and always one is satisfied. Then I was always conscious of a beautiful rhythm in the book – perhaps in the sense that Roger used the word? – but also more closely in the musical sense, and in a way which I have felt before in yr books. Drawing the analogy too closely is misleading, but the feeling is as of listening to a large scale symphonic movement with a quiet introduction, hinting at later themes – then the gradual statement of those themes & their development & interweaving, and recapitulation & development in other keys – it is all there, and then the quieter coda with remembrance of earlier themes. This may all sound nonsensical to you, and it probably only means that your biography, like all real works of art, convinces one by its own sense of form. I am immensely grateful to you for having written it – this and Morgan's Life of Goldie are to me the two great biographies of our day. I was so very fond of Roger, but always a little shy & afraid of him until the last ten years or so, & then I regret we saw so little of him; he was abroad so much & somehow Bob rather dropped out of his life. I was therefore so glad to read more about those years.

What agony this time of hatred & stupidity would have been to him!

I do hope you & Leonard are keeping well.

yrs affectionately
Elizabeth Trevelyan

Stephen-Turner

Elizabeth (Bessie) Trevelyan (1874-1957) was married to R. C. Trevelyan (1872-1951). Originally from the Netherlands, she translated J. H. van der Hoop's *Character and the Unconscious: A Critical Exposition of the Psychology of Freud and of Jung* (1923) and

Robert Fruin's *The Siege and Relief of Leyden in 1574* (1927) and wrote *The Foreigner in the English Landscape* for the *Abinger Chronicle* in March 1940. See Woolf's reply, dated September 4, 1940, *L6*: 425-26 (3641), along with her letter to Bob Trevelyan, dated August 12, 1940, *L6* 412 (3526).

125
Typed; signed
September 4, 1940

From John Farrelly, Jr.

Published in Melba Cuddy-Keane, "From Fan-Mail to Readers' Letters: Locating John Farrelly," *Woolf Studies Annual* 11(2005): 20-21.

Letters from agents, editors, publishers, etc., Miscellaneous fan mail

---

In "a sort of a love letter," he notes that whenever any conversation turns to books, he asks, "Have you read Virginia Woolf, Emily Dickinson, and Gerard Hopkins?" (20)

126
Handwritten
September 8, 1940

8.IX.40

TELEGRAMS.
SHULBREDE, FERNHURST.

SHULBREDE PRIORY,
LYNCHMERE,
HASLEMERE.

Dear Mrs Woolf,

I rather expect you are bored to distraction at receiving letters about your books. But I am going to take the risk. I am not going to insult you by any patronizing praise. But I knew Roger Fry rather well at one time and subsequently followed all he did and tried to do, with the keenest interest. Reading your Biography in the last few weeks & never missing a line he has been brought alive to me again and it has sharpened my recollections of when I used to see him.

It was in early days about 1903-4 when he was staying with Logan Pearsall Smith that I first met him. We went out sketching together accompanied by Goldie Dickinson. I had been taught by my mother and loved it in a curious way – not for producing pictures but as an opportunity of staring at something I admired for a few hours. He completely converted me to the style of the early English watercolourists and from then onwards I produced funny little drawings in brown ink and drab colours on lovely paper out of 18th Century note books with which he supplied me. Of course they were of no consequence but when he saw them later instead of laughing at them he encouraged me by his comments so that I went on. At the same time he admired quite genuinely a copy of Turner's Crossing the brook which my mother had done in the National Gallery. Generally speaking he must have made allowances for my more conventional type of mind. But never for a moment did he make me feel that he thought me no good in any line. On the contrary in his charming way he entered into everything, we discussed our daughters who were in the same school at Haslemere and he entranced my wife with his humour and originality. He stayed with us here several times later. We were quite at one in our denunciations but not always in our appreciations. Some of his profundities were quite out of my reach as when he talked of "equivoque" and "elusis." His rapture over some figures (I forget who by) which looked like inflated balloons tied with string, I am afraid made us break down into ribald laughter when he declared they were "inaudibly beautiful." He was only twice rather sharp in his reprimand – when I admired some figures by a modern artist which I saw when he explained it to me were only dexterous and slick (like Sargent's satin) and again when I laughed at Gertrude Stein.

Whatever failures and set backs he may have encountered in his life time, he is indeed fortunate to be handed down to posterity after his death by such an intensely sympathetic, understanding and absorbingly interesting portrait as you have drawn.

Just an anecdote as a footnote. Mons. de Beauvoir (page 135). He was a great friend of mine not a "French Aristocrat" at all but an Italian, born in French Canada. His real name was Bosdari. He was a banker with a Greek Partner in Constantinople (where I was for 3 years 1894-7.). We used to go out in a caique at night on the Bosphorus when he would quote Shakespeare by the page and French poetry by the yard. He was most amusing and entertaining and was taken up by the Ambassador & the Edgar Viscounts etc etc. He had an extraordinarily tiresome pretty English wife. Just after I married (1898) I saw him again in

London & was surprised to find he had a flat in Berkely Square and his wife was swathed in beautiful sables. He was a forger on a large scale (either Philips or Pierpont Morgan's signature). He disappeared. First a bric a brac shop in Brusells then America where his knowledge of art procured for him (as M. de Beauvoir) the sub curatorship of the Chicago Gallery. He was a great success. But nearly discovered by Berensen who hearing of him wanted to meet him. But he prevented it, gained confidence decided to return to England. Roger traveled with him. Roger came to see me at Downing Street (where I was CB's private Sec) described him to me. I spotted at once who he was, warned Roger to be careful. Bosdari got a job at Duveen's Gallery – was betrayed and at the age of nearly 70 made to serve his sentence (7 years I think) but friends managed to get his release before he died.*

This is getting too long, but I haven't done yet. Another reason for my being interested in your book is the dexterous way you have managed your material which must have been fairly voluminous.—sometimes quoting only a phrase or a few sentences, sometimes an extract and then a whole letter—. The reason for this is that I am engaged on a "Life" and the carloads, boxes, stacks of letters & papers have almost snowed me under. I have been at it for 3 years & it will take me as long again specially owing to—well you know what. But it has been an invaluable distraction. So I have studied very carefully your admirable method which never breaks the thread, always illuminates and gives little portraits of the other people.

I beg your pardon—But at any rate there is nothing you need answer in this rigmarole

Yours sincerely
Arthur Ponsonby

* I brought him in to a sketch on Criminals in my Casual Observations.

Letters from readers, Letters about Roger Fry

Arthur Ponsonby (1871-1946) was probably working on *Henry Ponsonby, Queen Victoria's Private Secretary; His Life from His Letters*, which he published in 1942. He and his wife had published *Rebels and Reformers. Biographies for Young People* in 1917, which Woolf reviewed in the *TLS*, 20 December 1917 (*E*2: 196-98). He was a pacifist, often writing about peace, and had been the personal secretary to Henry Campbell-Bannerman, the Liberal Prime Minister, from 1905-08. He also published books about English diaries (1923 and 1927) and on English diarists (1930); *Casual Observations* appeared in 1930. Woolf refers to him and this letter in a letter to Ethel Smyth dated September 25, 1940, *L*6 434 (3648). She says she's writing to him on September 26, 1940

(*D5* 324-25); see *A* 57 and 132, n2 about this unpublished letter.

Also see Arthur Ponsonby's letter to Leonard Woolf in *A* 131-32 and Leonard's reply about Woolf's amusement over the forgery.

127
Handwritten
September 23, 1940

ORCHARD HILL
BRENT KNOLL,
HIGHBRIDGE, SOM.
PHONE 77.

23. Sep. 40-

Dear Mrs Woolf. I have had many thoughts of writing to you since, many days ago, I finished the Biography – but in these days it is difficult to bring one's mind to any letter that is not immediate. I have 6 refugees from Poplar – a doctor, wife, sister & 3 children who were roaming about homeless, & 2 boys from Dagenham in the house, so I am domestic only occupied, – tho' I don't mean to imply am cooking or sweeping.

Everyone (one single exception) feels yr. book a great achievement. & I am full of admiration for as much as I can discuss of the craftsmanship. It takes an artist in words to write an artist's life, & here the 2 streams meet & enrich each other. You have woven, or welded, or kneaded yr. material so completely into a new whole, — the real word is composed I suppose, & one just feels the structure enough to admire it. And I admire your omissions – the tedious details & facts wh. a pedestrian writer would have felt bound to give –

I still feel my Parents come out of it badly, but you have shown me much of Roger's life & character that I only dimly recognized before, & made me proud of things I took for granted.

I hope the book is selling, tho' one cannot expect much in these days of horror. — but at least it is there for all time, & it must be a grt. satisfaction to you that you could bring it out this year.

Thank you for all you have done for his memory & reputation.

I am hoping to see Margery here to-morrow & shall try to keep her out of

London's inferno if possible. I suppose you get the fringes of it. even here we know what bombs are.

Yrs. sincerely
Agnes Fry

I expect you will be returning the letters to his father wh. I sent you

Letters from readers, Letters about Roger Fry

Agnes Fry (1868-1958) wrote a memoir of her father, Sir Edward Fry (1921), some poetry, and two books about scientific topics; she also translated Alois Riehl's *Giordano Bruno: In Memoriam of the 17th February 1600* from the German. See Diane Gillespie, "Introduction," *Roger Fry: A Biography* by Virginia Woolf ([Oxford: Shakespeare Head Press, 1995] xi-l) for a discussion of the currents and cross-currents Woolf had to negotiate in writing the biography of Roger Fry.

128
Typed; signed
October 1, 1940

Personal.

23, Great Winchester Street,
London, E.C.2.
1st October 1940.

Dear Mrs Woolf,

Many thanks for your letter of the 24th September, which only reached me this morning. I am sorry to hear your flat has been partly destroyed, and also that you are not going to be in London for some time, because what I wanted to speak to you about could perhaps be more easily described in an interview than in a letter, but I received a cable the other day from my Partner, Jack Pierpont Morgan, and I think the best plan would be to enclose you a copy of this cable. It speaks for itself and if you could do anything to authorize the deletion of the special sentences which have given my Partner so much pain we should all be extremely grateful to you.

Yours sincerely,
Bicester

P.S. As you are in the country and may not have a copy of your book with you I am posting you one to-day by book-post.

Mrs Virginia Woolf,
Monk's House,
Rodmell,
Lewes,
Sussex.

128a
Typed; enclosed cable
September 12, 1940

CABLE FROM J. P. MORGAN & Co., NEW YORK
To MORGAN GRENFELL & CO. LIMITED, LONDON
Received 12th September 1940 10 a.m.

My attention has just been called to a book about Roger Fry by Virginia Wolfe already published in England by the Hogarth Press 37 Mecklenburgh Square and to be published it is said in the United States by Harcourt Brace & Co. (stop) I should be very grateful if you would get a copy of the book and look at the letter quoted on pages 140 to 144 (stop) You will understand the distress this gives me (stop) Naturally I am concerned only with the purely personal references in the sentence near the top of page 141 beginning "I knew the answer beforehand" and the sentence at the middle of page 144 beginning "I always wondered"

I cannot think it would be the wish of Mrs Wolfe or of the Hogarth Press to give unnecessary distress to me and my family and it occurred to me that you might be able to appeal to the author and the English publishers to delete these sentences in future English additions and the forthcoming American edition (stop)

I shall be very grateful if you can secure at any rate the deletion of these special sentences since they are not important to any reader or to anyone else except my family (stop) Of course I might appeal to the American publishers but think it probable they might resent any effort to induce them to change the text of so distinguished an author except upon her own initiative and instructions and also because I think quite frankly your intercession over there would more likely be effective than mine here.

Jack Morgan

Letters from readers, Letters about Roger Fry

Lady Aberconway wrote on September 12, 1940 (Monks House Papers, Aberconway - Blanche) to ask Woolf to see Lord Bicester (1867-1956), Chairman of the Merchant Bankers Morgan, Grenfell & Co. John Pierpont (Jack) Morgan (1867-1943), investment banker and collector of art, rare books, and manuscripts, was the only son of J. Pierpont Morgan (1837-1913), whom Roger Fry had worked with as a buyer for the Metropolitan Museum in Europe. See *D*5 324. The specific deletions are noted in a letter to Donald Brace, dated October 6, 1940, *L*6 438 (3653). See discussion in Gillespie, "Introduction," *Roger Fry: A Biography* by Virginia Woolf ([Oxford: Shakespeare Head Press, 1995], xxxii-xxxiii.

129
Handwritten
October 1, 1940

Temporarily:
Clanmere Nursing Home
Malvern.
Oct. 11. 40.

<u>But after next week:</u>
Church Farm. Buckland.
Aylesbury.

Dear Virginia, (It was to be that I think, wasn't it?) I have been wanting to get a letter written to you for ages to ~~te~~ thank you for Roger's Life. But as I daresay you may have heard – in some roundabout way – I have been wretchedly ill for months, & am only now beginning to be myself again. I read the book when I was still too ill to have any grasp of things & then I have lately gone over it all again. It is impossible I find, even to myself, to criticize something which touches so intimately one's very life-springs, & – indeed – I am sure you don't want my criticism even if I could offer it! But all I want to tell you is that I am impressed by the size of the canvas you have used in portraying him. Everyone reading the book will have to realise the astonishing size & scope of his intellect & sympathies. Further than this I only want to say how happy I am to find how very widely the book is creating new & unexpected admirers. Posthumous appreciation has always in it something tragic, but I can't help knowing that without your work, (in such a world as has followed Roger's death,) the chances were almost dead against his ever being recognised for what he stood for; whereas now you have placed him where he deserves to stand.

I am
Yours sincerely
Isabel Fry.

Letters from readers, Letters about Roger Fry

Isabel Fry (1869-1958) wrote a book about the grammatical analysis of language (*A Key to Language*, 1925) and a couple of novels (1895 and 1901). She is best known for her teaching, as evidenced by Beatrice Curtis Brown's *Isabel Fry, 1869-1958: Portrait of a Great Teacher* (1960); this book includes a memoir by Brown of Isabel Fry, 1-50, a section on educational theory and practice, recollections of students who attended Mayortorne, and several writings by Fry. See letters 4 and 42.

130
Handwritten
October 26, 1940

HOLMGARTH
HENFIELD
SUSSEX
TELEPHONE: 15

Oct. 26th 1940

Mrs Virginia Woolf –
Dear Madam,

Though it is late I want to thank you for your Life of Roger Fry. It makes him come alive to many of us for whom he had been nothing more personal than the author of 'Vision and Design'. Now he is an unique individual. I doubt whether I should have liked him. My bourgeois, philistine, insular outlook would have got in my way. How could he live contentedly with dusty medicine bottles on the mantelpiece, frying pans mixed up with palettes, plates holding salad, and others congealed paint? And then to think Suffolk the only county. What's wrong with Sussex anyhow? We've got lives full of meaning even if our colouring is a bit subdued. My own little mound looks towards Wolstonebury, Saddlescomb, the Dyke and Truleigh Hill on the south, and to the north towards the Horsham line of hills. And every day of every year they are different. If I want them very different I look at them with my head upside-down. I know there isn't really an upside-down to one's eyes; all the same it brings out new aspects. It's like a view seen for the first time. The trees whose height one's mind had exaggerated are seen to be very little above the rest. And the hated electricity poles and wires become almost beautiful in their spacing. Anyhow, certainly we can hold up our heads with Suffolk, even if, being better farmers, we refuse to let our land grow red with poppies.

Sunday Most oddly I feel that Roger Fry would have approved & appreciated your book. There's a lack of compulsion, ~~about it~~ - I don't know how to explain it properly – about your presentation of him which one imagines would have been after his own heart. What a deeply remarkable person he must have been. And it is no small tribute to him that innumerable people who, like me, know nothing of art should have found 'Vision & Design' not merely interesting but absorbing. Thank you for this Life – done as only you could do it. I started reading it because of you. I ended reading it because of him.

There's one thing though that I feel impelled to say, and yet I hate to. That ugly incident on page 33—was it necessary to give it? My own immediate thought on reading it (quite the most unpleasant thing I have read in my life) was "Now I can't give this book to Katharine, (a young niece) and V. W's collected works will forever contain this one (and only) blot." Some friends close by were even more perturbed. One, an elderly kind of art critic, ex-doctor, said he should "never feel quite the same" to you again. And his artist friend, a gentle creature, was quite depressed about it. He always keeps you beside the telephone – A.R.P. early morning duty – (I don't mean he only reads you then). I said it was perhaps a case where people shouldn't just complain behind an author's back but write direct. Because if the public doesn't express itself who's to blame? You see you kind of belong to us, and what you do matters enormously.

But my mind at that moment was half on sorting tomatoes for Covent Garden Market, and what with bombing and one thing and another – well really it was an inhibition about doing it – I've never got down to it till now.

After that brief conversation I went (as soon as I had time: we always work from 7 a.m. till 5 p.m.) and sat on my hill and considered it further. And it seemed to me that you had admitted the offending passage 1) because R. F. had probably intended it's publication – 2) because you felt it <with the rest of his school boy existence> explained things in him that remained throughout life – 3) because your own reaction to it was nearly nil. I mean, just as saints have so little in them of evil that they have no violent revulsion from human ugliness – well, on those lines. It was a bit of each I believe.

But it remains that I can't for years send Katharine the book, and that is so tiresome.

I often wonder how things go in your part of Sussex. Here we are extraordinarily peaceful. On one occasion a poor young girl was killed and on another there was trifling damage to property. Otherwise bombs have fallen harmlessly enough in fields. Hitler has brightened up our village no end, and that's a fact. Our one-time horse-cab driver (a wheel came off once when I was on my way to the station)—his ancient face was shining with joy and pride the morning after his first incendiary bomb fire. He is an auxiliary fireman. And the weather no longer has pride of place with us yokels as a conversational opening. It's the size of your crater versus the other man's. And we are more genial in every way. I wish Hitler could see.

But London . . .

Once more thank you for the book. Please go on writing. We need you more and not less in these times. With every day bringing some fresh debasement of the English language your use of words is like water in a thirsty land.

This expects no reply. I've written because I had to thank you.

Forgive what needs forgiving -
Yours very respectfully and with love
Rachel Dyce Sharp

Letters from readers, Letters about Roger Fry

Rachel Dyce Sharp (fl. 1900-1950) was a nurserywoman and the sister of Cecil Sharp (British folk musicologist), Clifford Sharp (editor), and Evelyn Sharp (feminist journalist). She and Virginia Woolf seem to have had an ongoing correspondence after this letter. Woolf calls Sharp half mad in a letter to Octavia Wilberforce dated January 9, 1941, *L6* 458 (3676). Yet she responds to Sharp's sensitivity to language, writes to her, sets up an acquaintance, and arranges for visits. See *D5* 334 (Oct. 29, 1940) for Woolf's first mention of Sharp's complaint. See letters 134 and 135.

131
Handwritten
November 4, 1940

HAWK WOOD,
CROWBOROUGH,
SUSSEX.

Nov 4, 1940

Dear Mrs Woolf

I have just been reading your biography of Roger Fry – (the "Assault of Modern Ugliness".) His life aims and work make no appeal to me – a man so little aware of himself could not be aware of a great deal else. Your book brings back to me the most painful memories – for in my early twenties I was a very great friend of Helen Coombe.

In your book she is only the pitiful nebulous ghost she had to be, but there was another Helen who does not appear at all – it is as though all trace of her had been lost.

I have to remind myself that that may have been the fact, for as I am in my 80th year perhaps there is no older friend of her now living. I think I was very little older than she was. An aunt of mine discovered her, and her son, my cousin, brought us together. She had just done excellently at the Academy schools, I was a young medical student, my cousin a brilliant "double first" Oxford man of the same age. For some years we met frequently and were a most harmonious trio, all developing the same ideas and ideals. We had of course to separate to go to our separate work. Two of us never married, but to the end we were all friends. My home was not in London but I was invited to Helen's home. They were a large family without a father and all had to work. I remember Mrs Coombe as a lady and a very good mother. I also saw Helen a good deal at the house of her friend and mine Mrs Henry Crompton. Mrs Crompton was always good to her, as long as was possible and I know paid the expenses of the birth of Helen's son, & other expenses. For the years before her marriage I was often abroad and did not see much of her. She had a very hard life and after a starvation year in Paris came home looking very ill and could not have been well when she married. I wished your book could have said something about the courageous charming young Helen of those days, so eager to live and learn, so full of ideas, the most promising open minded of women. I don't use the silly word "unconventional" for she was much more than that. She opened windows—wherever she was—and round her was always clean air.

The last time I saw her she had been in her home for about a year, She wrote and asked me to come to dinner with her at Willows Walk and she had her little son there. Her husband (whom I had never seen) must I think have been in America. My visit horrified me for although she was supposed to be quite well, I considered she was far from it. She was entirely changed, looked battered and dissipated, and was bitter and cynical and unhappy. That she had made the right marriage I shall never believe.

I never saw her again.

I should like to tell you of an occurrence in our younger days. In London I used to play about various men & women, and one of the men thought he was in love with me. He told me all about his life which had included experiences with chorus girls & bought women. The trio had always believed that quite another personal standard than that was a <u>sine qua non</u> for a happy marriage. I told him I did not share his ideas, and turned him down. I was not in any case attracted to him.

Later he was seeing a good deal of Helen, and one day she came to see me and asked me if I cared about him, she had an idea that we had been friends. He had asked her to marry him but she had given him no reply, and of course if I, in any sense, came first, she would not consider it. Of course the young women of today don't do that. I replied that I was not in love with him, and she could do as she wished with a free conscience. She seemed very doubtful, but I said no more. When she had gone, I sent for him and asked him if he intended to marry Helen. He said he did. I said "Helen is my friend. I know what she feels and thinks about the necessary conditions for marriage. You would not suit her. She is free to marry you if she wishes, but you must first tell her what you told me." She would refuse me. "All the more reason why she should know where she stands. I will not interfere in any way – if you will tell her yourself."

I imagine that Helen herself asked the questions, and got some very mitigated replies – but he came back to me and said "She has refused me. How am I ever to marry at this rate?'

"That is no business of mine. You understand perfectly well why you cannot have me, and cannot have Helen."

Helen said when next she saw me – "Mary I have to thank you I believe." We neither of us saw him any more.

We had no conventional outlook, but these things are a question of feelings, insight, attitude, weltauschauung, all good psychological values. This is why I have always thought that Helen would not be, and was not made happy by marriage. Of course her mental condition had introverted her, and in later years, had she recovered, I do not see how a feeling introvert could have lived with the explosive scattered sensational extravert that Roger Fry became with his advancing years.

You tell the story of a man without relationships, without women, without even the one woman – she is obliterated by his shock, and nothing is left in the foreground or the background of his soul. All that is left is a not too sane chase after his own ideas. His other "affairs" and anaemic traces of women are mere mouldy spots on the landscape of his restless unbalanced being. It is even hard on Helen that you claim so little for them. I who had talked with her so often upon the problem of human relationships, cannot help this phantasy of how things may still strike her in the "house not made with hands."

Your book is a story seen through the eyes of the most able of crystal gazes – written with a matchless pen – but it is quite inhuman. The truth probably is that it beats you to tell it as it was.

You must forgive me, who even at my age have the vivid contrasting images before me of the young sane Helen I knew – and then of the heavy inert wreck alone in her dull poor home and about to be drawn again into the abyss of the unconscious as I saw her last.

I need not ask you to keep this letter to yourself. And will you excuse the writing, which I am having to do lying down.

With my best regards

yours sincerely

Mary Gordon.

Letters from readers, Letters about Roger Fry

This correspondent may be Mary Louisa Gordon (b. 1861), who published *Penal Discipline*, about female criminals, in 1922, and *Chase of the Wild Goose: The Story of Lady Eleanor Butler and Miss Sarah Ponsonby, known as the Ladies of Llangollen* with Hogarth Press in 1936. Woolf mentions a Dr. Mary Gordon in a letter to Ethel Smyth dated January 16, 1936, L6 5-6 (3098). See *D5* 270, n16 about Helen Coombe's illness.

132
Handwritten
January 18, 1941

From John Farrelly, Jr.

Published in Melba Cuddy-Keane, "From Fan-Mail to Readers' Letters: Locating John Farrelly," Woolf Studies Annual 11(2005): 21-23.

Letters from agents, editors, publishers, etc., Letters about various books

---

He writes that after reading Woolf's novels, "I feel dizzy – feverish. Your mind is as sensitive as an open wound and you so sensitize your readers" (22).

See also the letter from John Farrelly, Jr. to Leonard Woolf after Woolf's death in Cuddy-Keane, 24-25, and in *A* 155-56.

133
Typed; signed, initialed
January 24, 1941

THE HAY-ADAMS HOUSE
WASHINGTON, D.C. "COMPLETELY AIR-CONDITIONED"
As from
116 East 36th St, New York.

24 Jan. 1941.

Dear Mrs. Woolf,

Just after your Roger Fry came out Geoffrey Garratt wrote telling me to make sure of reading it. I thought it unlikely that the book would be published over here, and so was all the more delighted when the reviews began to appear. I have just read it through at high speed, and with the greatest enjoyment.

I can find no explanation of the fact that I knew so little directly about Roger Fry, notwithstanding the fact that Joan and Isabel are among our friends, my wife being a Quaker, and that Ruth's public work was known for so long to us all. Almost more odd is the fact that I knew nothing of his lecturing, and until I read your account had never heard of his appearances at Queen Hall: for it so happens that my interest in public speech is lifelong, and I thought I knew something about nearly all the men who lectured in London.

It so happened also that my brother was a member of the Camden Town Group, which preceded the London Group (he was associated with Harold Gilman and Spencer Gore), so that I used to hear about Fry in connection with the shows and controversies of those years. Yet I saw him only once, and that was at a Coué meeting in Hampstead, when he was in the chair. Hence I was not surprised to read of his infatuation with Coué and his using the incantation.

It would seem to me that there is one unwritten chapter in your book. Very many readers will be sorry not to have more about the family (I met the old lady near the end of her life, at Joan's little house in the Garden Suburb). They are certain to be curious about his relations with his sisters apart from Margery. If he and his mother became good companions and could talk without restraint, how was it, they will ask, with the positive Isabel, and with Joan who keeps wholly to the old-time religion and speaks in the old simple fashion about the Lord Jesus Christ. I have spoken with her from a League of Nations platform when she did this. You remark that in his later life Fry detested the institution of the family; but would it not be accurate to say that until toward the time of the break he depended to a large extent upon them?

You could never guess which page gave me the funniest jolt. 249.

One Sunday morning, just before, I had been speaking to a New York audience on Hopes and Fears for 1941. One of my auditors attached himself to me as I walked away. He asked me if I knew a certain lawyer of New York, a most brilliant man: the fact that he could speak of him as an acquaintance was evidently something to be immensely proud of; I must have seen his name at the foot of letters to the N.Y. Times. No? Strange. Who was he? Hyacinthe RINGROSE!

191. This manifesto must have been all Wyndham Lewis. He is now in America; came out last winter, and went to Buffalo, where I believe he has a relative. He painted a portrait of the Vice-Chancellor of the University of Buffalo, Dr. Capen; having consented to do a rather conservative job. He behaved anything but well during his long stay in the city. I heard lots of tales about him. He thought he ought to have been identified by any one as a distinguished Englishman: yet he would give his name simply as Mr. Lewis, when calling, for instance, ~~at the~~ on the director of the art gallery. And so forth.

When his job was over and he had left Buffalo he published a satirical short book, America, I Presume? which I think had nothing of a success. It is a hastily-written bad-tempered attack, bringing in many of the people who gave him hospitality. The Capens are nicely treated, and a few others. The rest are touched off meanly. My friends were particularly angry because his worst shots are made at certain members of the group who are ridiculed, with unmistakable traits, for characteristics which they don't possess. He came to New York, and let me know that he was living close by. I did not see him then, and don't know where he has gone to.

The book is extraordinarily discussable: in this respect a most pleasant relief in horrible times. I am led to send you a few notes. In happier days you will be having a new edition.

I get the N.S. & N. and The Spectator. The editorial articles and notes read somewhat strangely just now: as though the whole basis of assumption and expectation were something quite different from the assumptions common to nearly all the men in Washington and New York who are debating, amid endless confusion, the methods and extent of aid to Britain. The event of this week here is Lindbergh's testimony before the House Committee on the Aid Bill and new powers for the President. I seem to be alone among the people I have heard talking about this business in feeling certain that his statement and answers are extremely important and will have great and wide influence on the public.

Sincerely yours,
S. K. Ratcliffe.

{notes}

Picasso, throwing away successive reputations. I think this was shown remarkably ~~a~~ in the exhibition last year, in New York. Moreover, one had the feeling now and again that he had said to himself: those blokes don't know where they are with their own styles. I'll show them. (I remember saying ~~this about~~ something of this kind to L. W. about V. W.'s method when Mrs. Dalloway came out).

202. This I suppose was ~~Mrs. Cr~~ the Cromptons. There could not have been more than one family of six aboard the Lusitania. I wonder what happened to the memorial tablet, which was on a wall in the little Positivist chapel, out of Lamb's Conduit Street?

272. If he had lived, would he have continued to hope for the complete collapse of Anglo-Saxondom?

56. Lady Carlisle, true, preached temperance, or rather prohibition, but not Socialism. She was a Liberal of the straitest sect. Ask Gilbert Murray. Or turn to the fierce old woman in Major Barbara.

118. This should be <u>The</u> Letters <u>of</u> John Chinaman. That was long before the pernicious practice of dropping the article in titles! I believe that I was the first to divulge the authorship, in the old Echo.

<The M.A. articles were those from the East, collected in Appearances. I used to say these things about G. L. D.'s prose but people did not seem to agree!> Bertie. I submit that diminutives such as these should be identified. And that your treatment of Lowes Dickinson's name must be confusing to many readers. You do not give his first name anywhere, so that the unknowing reader would be puzzled by Goldie, and by G. L. It seems to me a curious point that G. L. D. should have had no interest in Fry's life-work. Also, that Forster should have confessed in his Life that he was not interested in G. L. D.'s international concerns, and had never cared much for any one of Goldie's three masters of literature and thought. Imperfect sympathies for a devoted biographer, and a devoted friend?

I have the honour to submit that there was something curiously imperfect, or self-contradictory, in Fry's theory and teaching of Art. E.g., I should argue that point after point in his letter to Bridges could be contested; that, since he held that All Art was one Art (Elgar didn't know how to meet that), he should not have made the strange remark about music and physiological emotion; that his training in science ought to have modified and directed his enthusiasm for some of Cézanne's contemporaries; that his unlimited admiration for Flaubert might have been expected to guide him in other fields. For instance, why should he, with his rigorous attitude toward the modern novel (true, he hadn't read many) have held that view of A Passage to India? It is, of course, a distinguished piece of work; but I would submit that Fry ought not to have thought so. He insisted upon form, and close integration. Forster in this story is indifferent to architecture. Also, he makes both English and Indians contemptible. The two English ~~who are~~ women who are decent, mother and daughter, both go to pieces in the latter part.

Some of Fry's enthusiasms among the painters seem to me just as wrong – that is, as much out of character, as some of Ruskin's. That old boy for instance ought not to have admired either Tintoretto or Turner!

And, in this connection, surely the main point of Clive Bell's recent article on the Roman busts in the N.S. & N. was most disputable. Also in this connection: please note that in the passage quoted for the purpose of illustrating Fry's method of commenting on the excellences of an old master, the points are precisely of the kind that one would expect from an expositor of representational painting.

Again, is it sound to attack Sargent because he made those features so offensive? Portraits such as that of Wertheimer don't support R. F.'s view of his superficiality. And surely he didn't regard McEvoy as an important painter?

New York, Feb. 21 The foregoing, as you see, was written in Washington a month ago. I don't know how it came to be mislaid. Perhaps it is just worth mailing.

The skies are much darker now than they were in January. It is believed that the Aid Bill will go through without much further delay. Hitler will make that certain, for of course he will not hesitate.

I am grateful for L. W. article on Imperialism, and can make use of it.

To-day I met a friend from Boston who had a new story, true, about a small English girl aged twelve. At the well-known, "privileged" Winsor School, Boston, the English mistress told a class to write about the most exciting thing that had happened to them in 1940. The English child said she couldn't do it; nothing had happened to her in the year. It was pointed out that she had left England after the bombings began, had crossed the Atlantic in wartime, had come to a great new country.

"But," she said, "nothing happened to me. The sea was calm all the way, and the British Navy was there"!

S.K.R.

Letters from readers, Letters about Roger Fry

Samuel Kirkham Ratcliffe (1868-1958), journalist and lecturer, wrote for the *Calcutta Statesman*, the *New Statesman* and the *Observer* in London, the *Manchester Guardian*, and many other newspapers as he explained India, the British, and the Americans to each other. He published *The Roots of Violence* with the Hogarth Press in 1934; he also wrote *Sir William Wedderburn and The Indian Reform Movement* (1923) and a history of the South Place Ethical Society (1955).

134
Handwritten
March 9, 1941

HOLMGARTH,
HENFIELD,
SUSSEX.

TELEPHONE.
15 HENFIELD

March 9th 1941.

To Mrs Woolf –
Dear Madam,

In leaving before the end of proceedings yesterday we were guilty of a form of rudeness which I hate, and in this instance not just rudeness but loss. We grudged going away while anything more was forthcoming from Mr Woolf. But we had to go. Our blind friend was due to catch a certain minibus and cannot be hurried down steps and across roads. And I had to visit a Nursing Home in Hove before going home. We should have sat behind & so made less disturbance had we known. But our friend gets hold of the personality of a speaker much better when she is close up.

It was extraordinarily good of Mr Woolf to come & give himself to such an audience. Brighton doesn't know its luck. It is a benighted town.

About common sense. I wanted to say to Mr Woolf, be of good cheer, common sense is on its way. When one finds in oneself, as I do, one prejudice after another breaking down, it's a certainty that the same thing is going on in tens of thousands of people's minds. We are better. Things are moving, in spite of the present eclipse. We seem to go round & round & come to the same place, but it's a spiral circle. Tell him, great historian as he is, it is a spiral circle, and that there's simply no end to the power of an enlightened kindliness such as he was radiating yesterday beyond these walls, beyond the limits of that odd little audience.

After the last war I would have said "hang the Kaiser". After this one I shan't want to hang Hitler – shan't be interested in him. We shall forget our hate in our plans for a better world. And I know lots of stodgy people whose minds are moving away from hate & selfishness towards common sense in the same way. The change is amazing. And it is the thinkers like Mr Woolf who have brought this about. Let him merely sit in a chair and go on with his clear, straight thinking, and millions of ignorant people, (who are yet in tune as it were) will get those firm vibrations of his thought & of those like him, & will act on them. First the individuals, then the State. This is not optimism; it's observation of what is happening. (I beg your pardon for all this!). I came away very happy yesterday. How little I thought years ago that I should ever speak to V . . . .

In case you really meant that you will come & see our garden sometime I want to give a few explanations.

We (my partner Pat Allen and I) trade under the name of Allen – Brown – The Violet Nurseries – Henfield. Mrs Brown died in 1915 after which I became partner. Previously I was a student – pushed out from a happy home by the urge to do something. I couldn't be a monk & illuminate manuscripts and I didn't want to collect rents under Octavia Hill. So it was gardening. It is an intellect-deadening life, in fact we are like cows mentally – which makes me awfully afraid at the very thought of talking to you. But it is a radiantly happy life and I have never regretted it.

Though we are nearly never away from work it would be best if you sent me a post-card about coming. Then I could ring you – (If you rang you would probably only get our book-keeper or a servant).

We are at the corner of Henfield Common. And it is about 6 minutes walk (1/3 mile) from our house to the Nursery. Half of it can be done in a car. (8 minutes from the omnibus).

Once the violets are over (as they soon will be) there isn't a lot to see. We are only commercial growers. I emphasize this because Mr Woolf's hobby being given as Gardening he might if he came hope to learn something, as we always hope to in going round a garden. Actually he wouldn't, as we know little outside our own beaten track – carnations, tomatoes, beans under glass & so on.

How much we should feel honoured I needn't underline. And if you had time for tea – well there it is. I mustn't go on to make a picture of what may never happen.

Would onion plants tempt you? I could give you some if you came before planting out time and they would be earlier than those sown out of doors –

Yours very respectfully
& with love
Rachel Dyce Sharp

Sackville-Stapledon

See letter 130 for biographical information. Leonard gave a talk to the WEA on "Common Sense in History." See *D*5 357 and n1; Woolf mentions being presented with violets by Miss Sharp in the same diary entry (March 8, 1941), *D*5 358 and n3. Woolf evidently replied to this letter with a proposal; see letter 135.

135
Handwritten
March 12, 1941

HOLMGARTH,
HENFIELD,
SUSSEX.

TELEPHONE.
15 HENFIELD

March 12th 1941

Dear Mrs Woolf,

Thank you for your very kind letter with its extremely attractive proposal. I turned it over in my mind today while getting the soil ready for tomatoes and came to the conclusion that it would be stupid to miss the chance of a life-time from fear of having no conversation to contribute. You will talk. You will tell me about Roger Fry, the man and the book, and I shall remember it for Katharine who will one day tell her grandchildren.

Yes, I shall come. But adjustments in our staff, due to the war, which have occurred since I saw you, make me at present rather more tired than usual.

However, a little later on when I can find an afternoon I shall write & ask if I may look in on you.

I didn't know that Mr. Woolf knew Clifford. I hope it was in his earlier years.

Thank you again for this most enviable privilege.

Yours gratefully & respectfully
Rachel Dyce Sharp

Sackville-Stapledon

Clifford Sharp (1883-1935) was the editor of the *New Statesman* from 1913-1931. One of Rachel Dyce Sharp's letters to Woolf is summarized in a letter from Octavia Wilberforce to Elizabeth Robins dated December 23, 1940 (Monks House Papers); see *L6* 458, n2.

See Rachel Dyce Sharp's condolence letter to Leonard Woolf after Virginia Woolf's death in *A* 88-89.

Guide to Library Special Collections

This guide updates the information in volume 11.

Name of Collection: The Beinecke Rare Book and Manuscript Library

Contact: Kevin Repp, Curator of Modern Books and Manuscripts
Patricia Willis, Curator of American Literature

Address: Yale University Library
P.O. Box 208240
New Haven, CT 06520-8240

URL: www.library.yale.edu/beinecke/brblhome.html

Hours: Mon.-Thurs. 8:30AM-8PM
Fri. 8:30AM-5PM

Access Requirements: Register at the circulation desk on each visit.

Holdings Relevant To Woolf: General Collection includes autograph manuscript of "Notes on Oliver Goldsmith." Comments on Edward Gibbon, William Beckford Collection. Letters from Virginia Woolf in the Bryher Papers, the Louise Morgan and Otto Theis Papers, and the Rebecca West Papers. Related material: 41 letters from Vita Sackville-West to Violet Trefusis; files relating to Robert Manson Myers's *From Beowulf to Virginia Woolf* in the Edmond Pauker Papers.

Yale Collection of American Literature includes typewritten manuscripts of "The Art of Walter Sickert," "Augustine Birrell," "Aurora Leigh," "How Should One Read a Book?" "Letter to a Young Poet," "The Novels of Turgenev," "Street Haunting." Dial/Scofield Thayer Papers: manuscripts of "The Lives of the Obscure," "Miss Ormerod," and "Mrs. Dalloway in Bond Street." Letters from Virginia Woolf in the William Rose Benet Papers, the Benet Family Correspondence, the Henry Seidel Canby Papers, the Seward Collins Papers, the Dial/Scofield Thayer Papers, and the *Yale Review* archive. Material relating to translat-ions of Woolf in the Thornton Wilder papers. Related material: Clive Bell, "Virginia Woolf" (Dial/Scofield Thayer Papers); 43 letters from Leonard Woolf to Helen McAfee (*Yale Review*); 11 letters from Leonard Woolf to Gertrude Stein.

Name of Collection: The Henry W. and Albert A. Berg Collection of English and American Literature

Contact: Isaac Gewirtz, Curator

Address: New York Public Library, Room 320
Fifth Avenue & 42nd Street
New York, NY 10018

Telephone: 212-930-0802
Fax: 212-930-0079
E-mail: igewirtz@nypl.org

Hours: Tues./Wed. 11AM -6:00PM
Thurs.-Sat. 10AM-6:00PM
Closed Sun., Mon. and legal holidays

Access Requirements: Apply for card of admission at Office of Special Collections, Room 316. Traceable identification required. Undergraduates working on honors theses need letter from faculty advisor.

Restrictions: Virginia Woolf's MSS are now made available on microfilm. N.B. *All the Berg's Woolf MSS are on microfilm published by Research Publications and available at many research libraries.*

Holdings Relevant To Woolf: Manuscripts of *Between the Acts*, *Flush*, *Jacob's Room*, *Mrs. Dalloway* (notes and fragments), *Night and Day*, *To the Lighthouse*, *The Voyage Out*, *The Waves*, *The Years*; 12 notebooks of articles, essays, fiction and reviews, 1924-1940; 36 volumes of diaries; 26 volumes of reading notes; correspondence with Vanessa Bell, Ethel Smyth, Vita Sackville-West and others. Su Hua Ling Chen's Bloomsbury correspondence.

Name of Collection: The British Library Manuscript Collections

Contact: Manuscripts Enquiries

Address: 96 Euston Road
London NW1 2DB
England

Telephone: 0207-412-7513
Fax: 0207-412-7745
E-mail: mss@bl.uk

Hours: Mon 10:00-5:00PM
Tue-Sat: 9:30-5:00PM

Access Requirements: British Library Reader Pass (signed I.D. required and usually proof of post-graduate academic status, or other demonstrable need to use the collections—see www.bl.uk). In addition, access to most literary autograph material only available with letter of recommendation.

Restrictions: Paper Copies, Microfilms, and Photography of selected items available upon receipt of written authorization for photo duplication from the copyright holder.

Holdings Relevant To Woolf: Diaries 1930-1931 (microfilm); Mrs. Dalloway and other writings (1923-1925) three volumes; letter from Leonard Woolf to H. G. Wells (1941); two letters from Virginia Woolf and three letters from Leonard Woolf to John Lehmann (1941); let-

ter written on behalf of Leonard Woolf to S. S. Koteliansky (1946); notebook in Italian kept by Virginia Woolf; notebook of Virginia Stephen (1906-1909); A sketch of the past revised ts (1940); letters from Virginia Woolf in the correspondence files of Lytton and James Strachey; letter from Virginia Woolf to Mildred Massingberd; letter from Virginia Woolf to Harriet Shaw Weaver (1918); letters from Virginia Woolf to S. S. Koteliansky (1923-27); letter from Virginia Woolf to Frances Cornford (1929); letter from Virginia Woolf to Ernest Rhys (1930); correspondence of Virginia Woolf in the Society of Authors archive (1934-37); letter and postcard from Virginia Woolf to Bernard Shaw (1940); three letters (suicide notes) from Virginia Woolf (1941); two letters from Virginia Woolf and three from Leonard Woolf to John Lehmann (1941).
"Hyde Park Gate News" 1891-92, 1895 (add. MSS 70725, 70726). Letters of Virginia and Leonard Woolf to Lady Aberconway, 1927-1941. Letter from Virginia Woolf to Frances Cornford. Letters from Virginia Woolf to Macmillan Co. 1903, 1908. Collection of RPs ("reserved photo copies"–copies of manuscrips exported, some subject to restrictions).

Name of Collection: Harry Ransom Humanities Research Center

Contact: Research Librarian

Address: The University of Texas at Austin
P.O. Box 7219
Austin, TX 78713-7219

Telephone: 512-471-9119
Fax: 512-471-2899
E-mail: reference@hrc.utexas.edu

Hours: Mon.-Fri. 9AM-5PM
Sat. 9AM-NOON
Closed holidays; intersession Saturdays; one week each in late May and late August.

Access Requirements: Completed manuscript reader's application; current photo identification.

Holdings Relevant To Woolf: The manuscript collection includes the typed manuscript with autograph revisions of *Kew Gardens,* and the typed manuscript and autograph revisions of "Thoughts on Peace in an Air Raid." The Center holds 571 of Woolf's letters, including correspondence to Elizabeth Bowen, Lady Ottoline Morrell, Mary Hutchinson, William Plomer, Hugh Walpole and others. Further mss. relating to Virginia Woolf include letters to her from T. S. Eliot and reviews of her work. A substantial collection of the first British and American editions of Woolf's published works, as well as 130 volumes from Leonard and Virginia Woolf's library and a collection of books published by the Hogarth Press, is also housed. An art collection holds a landscape painting of Virginia's garden and a series of Cockney cartoons in a sketch book, signed "V.W." The center also has extensive holdings of materials related to Leonard Woolf, Ottoline Morrell, Mary Hutchinson, Lytton Strachey, Dora Carrington, E. M. Forster, Clive Bell, Roger Fry, Vanessa Bell, Bertrand Russell, Elizabeth Bowen, William Plomer, Stephen Spender and Hugh Walpole.

Name of Collection: King's College Archive Centre

Contact: Patricia McGuire, Archivist

Address: King's College
Cambridge CB2 1ST

Telephone: 01223-331444
Fax: 01223-331891
E-mail: archivist@kings.cam.ac.uk

Hours: Mon.-Thurs. 9:30AM-12:30PM and 1:30PM-5:15PM. *Closed during public holidays and the College's annual periods of closure.*

Access Requirements: Proof of ID, letter of introduction, appointment in advance.

Holdings Relevant To Woolf: Woolf MSS and letters: Minute book, written up by Clive Bell, of the meetings of a play-reading society, with cast lists and comments on performances by CB. Dec. 1907-Jan. 1909, Oct. 1914-Feb. 1915. Players included variously Clive & Vanessa Bell, Roger & Margery Fry, Duncan Grant, Walter Lamb, Molly MacCarthy, Adrian & Virginia Stephen, Saxon Sydney-Turner. *Freshwater, A Comedy*—photocopy of editorial typescript prepared from the MSS at Sussex University and Monk's House; photcopy of covering letter from the publisher to "Robert Silvers," 1.29.1976. Papers relating to the Virginia Woolf Centenary Conference held at Fitzwilliam College, Cambridge, 9.20-22.1982. TS with corrections of "Nurse Lugton's Curtain." Typed transcript of R. Fry's memoir of his schooldays. Correspon-dence with Clive Bell, Julian Bell, Vanessa Bell, Richard Braithwaite, Rupert Brooke, Mrs. Brooke, Katharine Cox, Julian Fry, Roger Fry, John Davy Hayward, J. M. Keynes, Lydia Keynes, Rosamond Lehmann, Charles Mauron, Raymond Mortimer, G. H. W. Rylands, J. T. Sheppard, W. J. H. Sprott, Thoby Stephen, Madge Vaughan. Woolf-related archival collections held: Charleston Papers; Rupert Brooke Papers; E. M. Forster Papers; Roger Fry Papers; J. M. Keynes Papers; J. T. Sheppard Papers; W. J. H. Sprott Papers. Various works of art by Vanessa Bell, Duncan Grant, and Roger Fry, held in various locations around King's College. Access via Domus Bursar's secretary.

Roger Fry Papers: sketchbooks, 1880s-1920s. The papers of George Humphrey Wolferstan ('Dadie') Rylands (1902-99).

Name of Collection: The Lilly Library

Contact: Breon Mitchell, Director
Saundra Taylor, Curator of Manuscripts

Address: The Lilly Library, Indiana University
1200 East Seventh Street
Bloomington, IN 47405-5500

Telephone: 812-855-3143
Fax: 812-855-3143
E-mail: liblilly@indiana.edu, mitchell@indiana.edu
taylors@indiana.edu

Hours: M-F 9-6; Sat. 9-1;
Closed Sundays and Major Holidays

Access Requirements: Valid photo-identification; brief registration procedure.

Restrictions: Closed stacks; material use confined to reading room; wheelchair accessible reading room and exhibitions (but no wheelchair-accessible restroom)

Holdings Relevant To Woolf: Corrected page proofs for the British edition of *Mrs Dalloway*; letters to Woolf from Desmond and Mary (Molly) MacCarthy; 77 letters (published in *Letters*) from Woolf to correspondents including Donald Clifford Brace, Robert

Gathorne-Hardy, Barbara (Strachey) Halpern, Richard Arthur Warren Hughes, Desmond MacCarthy and Molly MacCarthy; "Preliminary Scheme for the formation of a Partnership between Mr Leonard Sidney Woolf and Mr John Lehmann to take over The Hogarth Press" (includes contract signed by Lehmann, LW, and VW, and receipt for Lehmann's payment to VW to purchase VW's share in the Hogarth Press); photographs of VW, LW, Lytton Strachey, Strachey family, Roger Fry, and Vanessa Bell (Hannah Whitall Smith mss.); (Richard) Kennedy mss. (four hand-colored lithographs of VW: artist's proofs for RK's portfolio, VIRGINIA WOOLF: "AS I KNEW HER"; Sackville-West, V. mss. (10,529 items: includes the correspondence of Vita Sackville-West, and Harold Nicolson); MacCarthy mss. (ca. 10,000 items: papers of Desmond and Molly MacCarthy); correspondence between LW and Mary Gaither regarding publication of *A Checklist of the Hogarth Press* (1976, repr. 1986); Todd Avery, *Close and Affectionate Friends: Desmond and Molly MacCarthy and the Bloomsbury Group* (The Lilly Library / Indiana University Libraries, 1999).

Name of Collection: Archives and Manuscripts, University of Maryland, College Park, Libraries

Contact: Beth Alvarez, Curator of Literary Manuscripts

Address: University of Maryland Libraries
College Park, MD 20742

Telephone: 310-405-9298
Fax: 301-314-2709
E-mail: alvarez@umd.edu

Hours: Mon.-Fri. 10AM-5PM, Sat. Noon-5PM.

Access Requirements: Photo ID.

Holdings Relevant To Woolf: Papers of Hope Mirrlees contain five autograph letters and postcards (1919-28) from Virginia Woolf to Mirrlees. Also in the collection are 113 letters from T. S. Eliot to Mirrlees, and three letters from Lady Ottoline Morrell to Mirrlees.

Name of Collection: Monks House Papers/Leonard Woolf Papers/Charleston Papers/Nicolson Papers

Contact: Dorothy Sheridan, Head of Special Collections

Address: University of Sussex Library
Brighton
Sussex BN1 9QL
England

Telephone: 01273-678157
Fax: 01273-678441
E-mail: Library.Specialcoll@sussex.ac.uk

Hours: By appointment

Access Requirements: Letter, to be received *before* visiting. Photocopying strictly controlled.

Holdings Relevant To Woolf: The University of Sussex holds two large archives relating to Leonard and Virginia Woolf: The Monks House Papers, primarily correspondence and MSS of Virginia Woolf, including the three scrapbooks relating to *Three Guineas*; and The Leonard Woolf Papers, primarily correspondence and other papers of Leonard Woolf. (Monks House Papers are available on microfilm in many research libraries.) The Charleston Papers consist in the main of letters written to or by Clive and Vanessa Bell and Duncan Grant which had accumulated in their home; the library houses Quentin Bell's photocopied set. Also included are c. 900 letters from Maria Jackson to Julia and Leslie Stephen (Charleston Papers Ad. 1); letters from Roger Fry, Maynard Keynes, Lytton Stachey, Virginia Woolf, Vita Sackville-West, E. M. Forster, T. S. Eliot, Frances Partridge and others. The Nicolson Papers complement these three Sussex archives relating to the Bloomsbury Group, and consist of Nigel Nicolson's correspondence relating to his editorial work as principal editor of the six-volume *Letters of Virginia Woolf*, published between 1975 and 1980.

The Bell Papers. A. O. Bell's correspondence relating to her editorial work on Virginia Woolf's Diaries. A parallel collection to Nicolson Papers.

Colection level description may be accessed at www.archiveshub.ac.uk

Name of Collection: Archives & Manuscripts

Contact: Michael Bott, The Archivist

Address: The University of Reading, The Library,
Whiteknights
P.O. Box 223
Reading RG6 6AE
England

Telephone: 0118-931-8776
Fax: 0118-931-6636
E-mail: g.m.c.bott@reading.ac.uk

Access Requirements: Appointment needed to consult material. Permission required to consult or copy material in the Hogarth Press and Chatto & Windus collections from Random House, 20 Vauxhall Bridge Road, London SW1V 2SA, UK.

Holdings Relevant To Woolf: Hogarth Press (MS2750): editorial and production correspondence relating to publications of the Press including Woolf's own titles. Production ledgers 1920s-1950s. Correspondence between Leonard Woolf and Stanley Unwin about progress with his collected edition of the works of Freud.
Chatto & Windus (MS2444): small number of letters 1915-25; 1929-31.
George Bell & Sons (MS1640): 5 letters from Leonard Woolf 1930-66.
Routledge (MS1489): Reader's report by Leonard Woolf on George Padmore's "Britannia rules the blacks" (1935); "How Britain rules Africa."
Megroz (MS1979/68): 2 letters from LW, 1926.
Allen & Unwin (MS3282): Correspondence with LW 1923-24; 1939-40; 1943; 1946; 1950-51, including letters concerning a reprint of *Empire and Commerce in Africa*, and concerning ill-founded rumors about the Hogarth press.

Name of Collection: Frances Hooper Collection of Virginia Woolf Books and Manuscripts/Elizabeth Power Richardson Bloomsbury Iconography Collection.

Contact: Karen V. Kukil, Associate Curator of Rare Books

Address: Mortimer Rare Book Room
William Allan Neilson Library
Smith College
Northampton, MA 01063

Telephone: 413-585-2906
Fax: 413-585-4486
E-mail: e-mail: kkukil@email.smith.edu
URL: www.smith.edu/libraries/libs/rarebooks

Hours: Mon.-Fri. 9AM-5PM

Access Requirements: Appointment to be made with the Curator.

Holdings Relevant To Woolf: The Hooper Collection emphasizes Woolf as an essayist but also includes many Hogarth Press first editions, limited editions of Woolf's works, and translations. The collection includes page proofs of *Orlando*, *To the Lighthouse*, and *The Common Reader*, corrected by Woolf for the first American editions, a proof copy of *The Waves* that Woolf inscribed to Hugh Walpole, and the proof copies of *The Years* and of *Flush*. The Collection also has one of the deluxe editions of *Orlando* that was printed on green paper. Other items include twenty-two pages of reading notes from 1926, three pages of notes on D. H. Lawrence's *Sons and Lovers*, thirty-three pages of notes for *Roger Fry*, a six-page ms. "As to criticism," a five-page ms. of "The Searchlight," and a fourteen-page ms. of "The Patron and The Crocus." The Hooper Collection also owns 140 letters between Woolf and Lytton Strachey as well as other correspondence, including a 13 February [1921] letter to Katherine Mansfield and ten letters to Mela and Robert Spira.

The Richardson Collection is a working collection of books and materials used by Richardson in preparing her *Bloomsbury Iconography*. It includes Leslie Stephen's photograph album, ninety-eight original exhibition catalogs dating back to 1929, clippings and photcopies of such items as reviews of early Woolf works, and Bloomsbury material from British *Vogue* of the 1920s. The Collection also has three preliminary pencil drawings by Vanessa Bell for *Flush*.

The Mortimer Rare Book Room also owns Woolf's 1916 Italian ms. notebook and her corrected typescripts of "Reviewing" and "The Searchlight." In addition, there is a 1923 photograph of Woolf at Garsington. Original cover designs for Hogarth Press publications include *The Common Reader*, *On Being Ill*, and *Duncan Grant*. The Mortimer Rare Book Room also has a Sylvia Plath Collection that includes eight of Woolf's books from Plath's library, several of which are underlined and annotated, as well as Plath's notes from her undergraduate English 211 class at Smith (1951-2) in which she studied *To the Lighthouse*.

Recent Acquisitions: Virginia Woolf's 26 February 1939 letter to Vita Sackville-West, a 1931 bronze bust of Virginia Woolf by Stephen Tomlin, and a 1923 Hogarth Press edition of T.S. Eliot's *The Waste Land.*

Name of Collection: Woolf/Hogarth Press/Bloomsbury

Contact: Robert C. Brandeis

Address: Victoria University Library
71 Queens Park Crescent E.
Toronto M5S 1K7
Ontario
Canada

Hours: Mon.-Fri. 9AM-5PM
URL: http://library.vicu.utoronto.ca/special/bloomsbury.htm
E-mail: vic.library@utoronto.ca

Access Requirements: Prior notification; identification.

Restrictions: Limited photocopying.

Holdings Relevant To Woolf: This collection, the most comprehensive of its kind in Canada, contains all the work of Virginia and Leonard Woolf in various editions, issues, variants and translations; all the books hand printed by Leonard and Virginia Woolf at the Hogarth

Press, including many variant issues and bindings, association copies and page proofs; a nearly comprehensive collection of Hogarth Press machine printed books to 1946 (the year Leonard Woolf and the Press joined Chatto & Windus) including presentation copies, signed limited editions, page proofs, variants as well as substantial amounts of ephemera. The collection is also very strong in Bloomsbury art, especially the decorative arts, and contains important examples of Omega Workshops publications and exhibition catalogues. Vanessa Bell correspondence/MSS; Leonard Woolf correspondence; Ritchie family materials and correspondence re: Anne Thackeray Ritchie/Stephen family. Vanessa Bell dustwrapper designs for Woolf novels; Quentin Bell correspondence; S. P. Rosenbaum mss. 97 additional items: Ephemera Collection.

Bronze bust of Lytton Strachey by Stephen Tomlin (1901-37). A companion piece to Tomlin's bronze of Virginia Woolf. More than 150 additional items including Hogarth Press variant bindings and proof copies; translations of Virginia Woolf and Leonard Woolf; ephemera; including Hogarth Press: Complete Catalogue of Publications to 1939 with annotations by Leonard Woolf; materials relating to Bloomsbury Art and Artists including the catalogue of the second post impressionist exhibition, 1912, and catalogues relating to Vanessa Bell and Duncan Grant exhibitions.

Recent Acquisitions: 228 items, including Hogarth Press proof copies; Hogarth Press publication catalogues; bronze medal of Virginia Woolf by Marta Firlet; oil on canvas portrait of Amaryllis Garnett by Vanessa Bell (c.1958); Duncan Grant and Vanessa Bell designed Clarice Cliff dinner plates.

Name of Collection: Library of Leonard and Virginia Woolf (Washington S U)

Contact: Laila Miletic-Vejzovic, Head
Manuscripts, Archives and Special Collections

E-mail: vejzovic@wsu.edu

Address: Washington State University Libraries
Pullman, WA 99164-5610

URL: www.wsulibs.wsu.edu/holland/masc/masc.htm

Hours: Mon.-Fri. 8:30AM-5PM

Access Requirements: Letter stating nature of research preferred; student or other identification.

Restrictions: Materials must be used in the MASC area under supervision. Photocopying or photographing is permitted only when it will not harm the materials and is permitted by copyright.

Holdings Relevant To Woolf: WSU has the Woolfs' basic working library including many works which belonged to Virginia's father, Sir Leslie Stephen, and other family members. Over 800 titles came from their Sussex home, Monks House, including some works bought at auction soon after Leonard Woolf died in 1969. Later additions include: 1,875 titles from his house in Victoria Square, London; 400 titles from his nephew Cecil Woolf; and over 60 titles from Quentin and Anne Olivier Bell. WSU has been actively collecting: all works in all editions by Virginia; all titles by Leonard; works published by the Woolfs at the Hogarth Press through 1946; books by their friends and associates, especcially those by Bloomsbury authors and about Bloomsbury artists; relevant correspondence and original works of art. Original artwork by Vanessa Bell; scattered letters by Vanessa Bell,

E. M. Forster, Roger Fry, Leslie Stephen, Lytton Strachey, and Leonard Woolf. Original artwork by Richard Kennedy for illustrations in his book *A Boy at the Hogarth Press*; scattered letters by Roger Fry, Leslie Stephen, Ethel Smyth, and Leonard Woolf. Virginia Woolf's initialed copy of *Cornishiana*; Leonard Woolf's annotated copy of *An Anatomy of Poetry* by A. William-Ellis; Leslie Stephen's copy of *Lapsus Calami and Other Verses*, inscribed by James Kenneth Stephen. Several letters from Virginia Woolf, including two written in 1939 to Ronald Heffer, and a letter to Edward McKnight Kauffer. New in the Hogarth Press Collection are a copy of E. M. Forster's *Anonymity, an Enquiry*, bound in cream paper boards, and what Woolmer calls the third label state of Forster's *The Story of the Siren*.

Name of Collection: Yale Center for British Art

Contact: Elisabeth Fairman, Curator of Rare Books and Manuscripts

Address: 1080 Chapel Street
P.O. Box 208280
New Haven, CT 06520-8280

Telephone: 203-432-2814
Fax: 203-432-9613
E-mail: elisabeth.fairman@yale.edu

Hours: Tues.-Fri. 10AM-4:30PM

Access Requirements: Call for e-mail for appointment. Permission needed in order to reproduce.

Holdings Relevant To Woolf: Rare Books & Mss Department: 94 letters from Vanessa Bell and Duncan Grant to Sir Kenneth Clark; Prints & Drawings Department: 4 drawings by Vanessa Bell; 4 drawings by Duncan Grant; 6

drawings by Wyndham Lewis; 1 drawing by Frederick Etchells; Paintings Department: 1 painting by Vanessa Bell, 4 paintings by Duncan Grant (including portrait of Vanessa Bell); 3 paintings by Roger Fry.

Reviews

Modernism and the Architecture of Private Life. Victoria Rosner (New York: Columbia University Press, 2005) xi + 219 pp.

It is a special challenge in offering a review to a journal for Woolf specialists not to fall into a style of "politeness" Woolf (as quoted by Rosner) derided in her own early *Literary Supplement* essays, where, she wrote, "I see myself, not reviewing a book, but handing a plate of buns to shy young men and asking them: do they take cream and sugar?" This is particularly true when the author in question has graciously cited my influence on her thinking. Woolf laid the blame for her juvenile "Victorian manner" on the "tea-table training" (76) she received in her parents' typically Victorian home, with the boundaries of propriety defined by its walls, curtains, and staircases. Casting her study as "a materialist history of modernist literary interiority" (128), Rosner aims to connect conventional uses of interiority as "the representation of consciousness" with the modern "reorganization of home life" (11). From its introduction on "Kitchen Table Modernism" through chapters titled to emphasize the links between "a history of design" and "a history of modernist literary aesthetics" (16), *Modernism and the Architecture of Private Life* offers a rich series of contexts for Woolf's belief in the significance of domestic space. Glancing references include novelists ranging from Jean Rhys and Aldous Huxley to Kazuo Ishiguro. Rosner devotes sustained analysis to the significance of domestic space in Oscar Wilde's *Picture of Dorian Grey*, Lytton Strachey's memoirs, Arthur Conan Doyle's "A Scandal in Bohemia," Radclyffe Hall's *Well of Loneliness*, and E. M. Forster's *Howards End.* Her primary focus and "guiding spirit" (15), however, is Woolf.

A fascinating aspect of Rosner's study is her mapping of fictional against actual interiors, as she guides her readers through the architect's sketches for Wilde's own drawing room, Woolf's childhood house, and other Victorian domestic spaces. Readers of the *Annual* will be most interested in Rosner's analysis of Woolf's prose, however. This begins in the chapter on "Thresholds," which starts from Woolf's and Strachey's strikingly similar memoirs of their childhoods to examine the effects of their shared fascination with borders between public and private in their writing. Ultimately, Rosner argues here, Woolf and Strachey may be less radical than they–or we–like to think. "Woolf's and Strachey's continuity with the Victorian tradition and their reliance on the distinction between public and private life, between propriety and scandal, to give their work meaning" suggests to Rosner that both authors remain "caught up in the logic of the threshold where they love to linger" (90).

The distinction between public and private leads, in the chapter on "Studies," to a focus on secrecy, as Rosner takes up *A Room of One's Own* to argue that "the construction of early-twentieth century female authorship relies on a masculine ability to hide one's secrets from the world's penetrating gaze in the study's interior" (106). As Rosner notes, this assumption "that nothing is more essential for women writers than a traditional masculine study" makes for "a somewhat unsettling conclusion" about *Room*, with its arguments for "a separate female literary tradition" (120) based on thinking back "through our mothers," as Woolf puts it (*AROO* 79). "Rather than debunk the mystique of the study–as she might have used the example of Austen to do–Woolf wishes only to extend its privileges to women," thus breaking "into the closed circle of masculinity, authorship, and privacy," Rosner argues (123).

The final chapter on "Interiors," somewhat paradoxically, breaks out of the house. Here Rosner examines the female *flânerie* of the women in Woolf's *Night and Day* as well as the *plein-air* painting of Lily Briscoe in *To the Lighthouse*. In this chapter Rosner falls back on her assertion of the "double meaning" of the term "interior" as "both one's inner nature or being and the inside of a particular space" (129). She first documents the importance of *flânerie* to *Howards End*, as well as to the women in Woolf's novels and to Woolf herself. In her rush to include these women in the *flânerie* she identifies as "the bedrock of modernist subjectivity" (160), however, Rosner here loses the opportunity to note how these *flâneuses*–who do not always, like the prototypical male *flâneur*, walk alone, but often stroll and converse—extend rituals of domestic conviviality into at least some public spaces. Instead, in order to tie speculation in the street to Lily's painting in *To the Lighthouse*, Rosner adduces a "double meaning of 'abstraction'" as "to think and reflect" or to paint non-illusionistically, which she says "is closely related to the two senses of 'interior' that are crosshatched in Bloomsbury modernism" (160). The chapter offers sensitive readings of the texts in question, and a provocative comparison of *Night and Day* with an Omega Workshops mural Woolf may or may not have known.[1] Nevertheless, the tight

[1] I do not share Rosner's belief that "it is hard to imagine that she was unfamiliar" with these murals, which were created in the Spring of 1916, a point when Woolf was living outside London, by a team of artists she did not know under the direction of Roger Fry, with whom she was not especially close at the time. The murals go unmentioned in her correspondence of the period, despite other references to Fry and the London art world in her letters to Vanessa Bell. My skepticism about Woolf's knowledge of the murals does not, of course, obviate the thematic continuities Rosner brings out between the murals and

focus on domesticity and interiors blurs here amid the several loosely linked double meanings of interiors and abstraction, to the point where a reference to Lily's "artistic view of the interior" obscures that the painting is clearly set outside.

So at this point I will stop passing the metaphorical buns and try to adopt another of Woolf's voices, the one in which, in *A Room of One's Own*, she frankly assesses the strengths and weakness of the young novelist Mary Carmichael. Like Mary Carmichael's (fictional) novel, *Modernism and the Architecture of Private Life* is a first book, written by a colleague (I speculate, in Woolf's words) "without enough of those desirable things, time, money, and idleness." And, like Woolf, I conclude, "she did not do so badly, I thought" (*AROO* 98). Rosner's book has many strengths, primary among them its willingness, evident in some of the quotations above, to challenge the reverential tone often taken in studies of Woolf, and its defiance of conventional disciplinary boundaries that usually separate scholarship in literature and visual culture, and that marginalize scholarly attention to the middle-class home. To pause for a moment on an issue of visual culture, I would also note that this is a very handsome book: fulsome credit is due the designer.

That said, Rosner's laudable interdisciplinary ambition is occasionally greater than her reach. Her characterization of three shutter designs by Duncan Grant as figures that "seem to fly or swim through space" rests on a misunderstanding (reproduced in the way these images are positioned in the book) of these vertical images as horizontal; correctly positioned they are dancing, with one or two feet on the ground. A similar unfamiliarity with the relevant art underlies Rosner's speculations over the prominent hands given Lytton Strachey in a cartoon she reproduces (172-74): the pose is quoted directly from a well known Dora Carrington portrait of Strachey (it appears on the covers of both Jane Hill's *The Art of Dora Carrington* and some editions of Michael Holroyd's Strachey biography). A more surprising misunderstanding of bourgeois British domestic life before mid-century is apparent in Rosner's characterization of Miss Kilman, the expert in modern history, as the "governess" (149) of the nearly adult Elizabeth Dalloway. More important is Rosner's uncritical acceptance of the false contrast—imposed by scholars nervous about the implications of the Aesthetes' sexual radicalism—between Wilde's supposedly "apolitical aesthetic credo" and

---

Night and Day, though I would see these as parallel responses to questions about gender, modernity, and public space.

the "social commitments" of the Arts and Crafts movement (25) as they affected the look of British homes.[2]

My strongest reservations, however, concern the fuzzy definitions of key terms such as "interiority" and "abstraction." I am not sure that the critical term "interiority" is usefully expanded from what Rosner calls "the generally accepted critical view of modernist interiority, which emphasizes the mind's ability to craft an individual reality, to live in a world exclusively populated by personal associations and memories" (11). This is a complex enough idea, without absorbing into it "a cluster of interdependent concepts" that include new ideas of domestic life, including "revised definitions of personal privacy, intimacy, and space; and the new assessments of the sexualized and gendered body" (11). By lumping all this into one term, Rosner spares herself the necessity of analyzing more precisely the relationships among these important ideas, setting the book up for the rather vague generalizations of the concluding chapter.

Modernism and the Architecture of Private Life is, in short, a lively and provocative book by a promising scholar. Its strong points are its specific analyses of texts and particular spaces, which offer surprising new insights into the work of well known authors. I am not content, however, with just passing this commendatory plate of buns. Rather I would encourage us all, in Woolf's mode, to confront the hurdles Rosner has attempted here in setting Woolf's writings into a social context of both texts other than "great literature" and the material culture of domestic life.

— Christopher Reed, *Lake Forest College*

[2] I would here insist on the more complex view of Bloomsbury's relationship to its Victorian forerunners described in my "Making History: The Bloomsbury Group's Construction of Aesthetic and Sexual Identity," in Whitney Davis, ed. *Gay and Lesbian Studies in Art History* (New York: Haworth Press, 1994) [issued simultaneously as a double issue of the *Journal of Homosexuality* (vol. 27, nos. 1-2)], 189-224, see especially 203-206, which discusses Wilde's *Soul of Man under Socialism*, a text Rosner does not engage. The effect of these ideas on the look of some domestic spaces is discussed in my *Bloomsbury Rooms*: *Modernism, Subculture, and Domesticity* (London: Yale University Press, 2004).

On the Horizon: A Poetics of the Sublime in Virginia Woof's The Waves. Ida Klitgård. (Bethesda, MD: Academica Press, 2004) xiv + 237 pp.

In *On the Horizon*, a revised doctoral thesis accepted at the University of Copenhagen in 2001 and now published by Academica Press, Ida Klitgård joins the legions of Woolf commentators who note her concern with the difficulty of representing immediate sensation through writing—what Woolf refers to in *To the Lighthouse* as "that very jar on the nerves, the thing itself before it has been made anything" (qtd. in Klitgård 2). Klitgård focuses on *The Waves* because she sees "the entire novel" as "an attempt to present the unrepresentable moment" (1). She follows J. W. Graham in suggesting that the original such moment behind *The Waves* came in 1926, with Woolf's vision of "a fin passing far out" at sea, and characterizes this vision as "an experience of the primeval, inexplicable zone of significant silence in Woolf's creative imagination" (60-62).

Klitgård opens her book by asserting an analogy between Woolf's "moment of being" and "the sublime as a state of disequilibrium between habitual awareness and elevated consciousness"; she then draws upon a single source, James B. Twitchell's *Romantic Horizons: Aspects of the Sublime in English Poetry and Painting, 1770-1850* (1983), to argue for a "liminal sublime" which finds its expression "in the many images of the horizon" (1). The horizon becomes something of a leitmotif for the book, and is apparently attractive to Klitgård because it allows her to draw a second analogy, this time between "figurative language and the visual horizon," both of which, she argues, "designate a fusion of two dissimilars which form a fictional reality" (1).

Klitgård's characterization of Woolf's sublime forms itself in relation to that of the Romantic poets, which she discusses in only the most vague terms. "Woolf was more conscious of her Romantic heritage than, say, Joyce," Klitgård explains (19), and "the romantic swoon and subsequent self-reflexivity, together with the effect on the reader, form the historical shore from which Woolf embarks" (13). Nor does Klitgård engage very deeply in the pertinent critical discourse "on Woolf and romanticism"—instead, in an odd footnote, she writes that she "wants to refer to" studies by Irma Rantaavaara, James Holt McGavran, and Ellen Tremper, but she never returns to discuss their contributions (13). Instead, Klitgård's argument develops through willful assertion—she writes, for example, that for Woolf, "[u]nlike Wordsworth, sublime transport does not necessarily have to be experienced on a mountain top in rough weather" (24). In this careless summary of Wordsworth's sublime, Klitgård seems to forget his disappointment at Mont Blanc, and to conflate other moments from *The Prelude*—perhaps the epiphanic scene at the peak of Mount Snowdon on "a close, warm, breezeless summer night" (XIV.11) has merged with the scene of the girl "who bore a pitcher on her head," "her garments vexed and tossed/By the strong wind" (XII.251; 260-1)? And although a consideration of the relation between Wordsworth's "spots of time" and Woolf's "moment of being" would certainly be germane to Klitgård's project, she engages neither Wordsworth nor critics like Frank McConnell and Robert Langbaum. The failure to address McConnell's essay on romanticism and phenomenology in *The Waves*, first published in 1968 and recently included in anthologies of Woolf criticism edited by Harold Bloom (1986) and Jane Goldman (1998), is particularly baffling, especially considering that Klitgård twice characterizes *The Waves* as "nearly a phenomenological project" (114 and 130).

Klitgård's turn to Coleridge is nearly as unsatisfying as her treatment of Wordsworth: she cites his famous lines on the sublime twice, but never engages his claim that "I meet, I *find* the Beautiful—but I give, contribute, or rather attribute the Sublime" (34 and 172). Her lack of interest in *interpreting* these lines is surprising, given that one of the strongest points in the book is that Woolf resists "fixed meanings" (81) and strives, not "for a rendering of absolute transcendence..., but for the subsequent sense-making" (87). Woolf, like Coleridge, seems to believe that "[n]o object of sense is sublime in itself; but only as we make it a symbol of some Idea" (Coleridge qtd. in Klitgård 34 and 112).

Klitgård's thesis seems to promise a sustained examination into Woolf's creation of fictional reality through figural language, and the strongest parts of the book—particularly the final sections of chapter two, "A poetics of *The Waves*"—engage in that project. She is right in arguing, for example, that critics who "insist in interpreting the six figures in realist terms" miss the mark (75), and I was fascinated to read her assertion that "[i]n *The Waves* the characters perform or even constitute *figures of speech*" (72), although what Klitgård means by that is much less original and interesting than it first seems—she means simply that "each figure enacts suggestive modes of metaphorical speech" (72-3) which come to operate as "allegorical emblems" (72). I would have liked to see Klitgård explore the implications of her statements further—there seems, for example, to be a strong phenomenological argument lurking in her astute observation that "Woolf stresses the individual's capacity for transgressing identity boundaries, which leads to a dissolution into multiple beings. The reverse would lay stress on the formation of multiple beings into one single, organic identity, one individual" (77). Unfortunately, Klitgård does not stay with the thought long enough to develop a coherent theory.

Indeed, more often than not, Klitgård relies on the figure of the horizon, rather than on an evolving argument, to provide segues between topics. The haphazard organization of the nine chapters—six are broken into subchapters and several are constructed as narratives of particular scenes—reflects this lack of a strong thesis, which is further indicated by the following introductory statement concerning the book's proposed scope. "As regards genre, style and thematics," Klitgård writes,

> *The Waves* goes to the limit of language, to the horizon of elevated consciousness. Genre-wise, by merging figures from the literary genres of prose, poetry and drama with the sister arts, painting and music. Stylistically, by actually describing the visual horizon in a landscape, and by developing an intricate network of image-clusters probing the boundaries between outer and inner perception.... And thematically, by exploring the boundaries between the self and the world, identity and group-consciousness, individual as well as trans-personal integration and disintegration, life and art, formlessness and form. (5)

Although Klitgård repeatedly gestures to "the dialectics of the horizon," her thought-process remains troublingly binary, often expressing itself in nonsensical lists of opposed pairs: she writes, for example, of the "dualisms of general, abstract ideas" of "concentrated states of *being* vs. flickering states of *becoming*" (131). Under "States of *being*" she lists "beauty vs. horror; pain vs. joy; cruelty vs. rapture; local vs. global; microcosmos vs. macrocosmos; solidity vs. the amorphous; light vs. darkness; real vs. unreal; illuminated form vs. dark double; substance vs. shadow" (132). "States of *becoming*," on the other hand, evoke for Klitgård "horizontal progression vs. vertical progression; straight horizontal/vertical lines vs. curves; rise/ascent vs. fall/descent; energy, swiftness vs. slowness; effort vs. deterioration; creation vs. destruction; entanglement vs. development; chaos vs. order; spiritual surging vs. ruthless attack on soft flesh" (132).

Klitgård's chaotic approach may well stem from the resistance to base her critical approach "on any single literary theory" (8). "This study," she explains, "cannot be categorized as belonging to any *one* school," but, she claims, has

> elements of New Criticism in the use of close reading and focus on aesthetics, formalism in the observations of form and defamiliarization, structuralism in the analyses of structures, functions, dualisms, part and whole, phenomenology in the descriptions of the expressiveness of images and things, reader response in the interest in how the text appeals to the reader's sharp memory and pattern-making, and poststructuralism in the concentration on a plurality of significance and on the self-referential aspects of *The Waves*. (9)

In having all these approaches, however, Klitgård essentially has none. Her claims to poststructuralism, for example, are undercut by her intermittent insistence on the importance of deciphering "the meaning of a piece of literature" (70), by her assertion that "words always have to refer to something" (185), and by her misunderstanding of Roland Barthes' argument in "The Death of the Author." For Barthes, "[w]riting is that neutral, composite, oblique space where our subject slips away, the negative where all identity is lost, starting with the very identity of the body writing" (142); Klitgård, however, insists that because "[n]ovels do not write themselves," "the author can never disappear, or 'die' as Roland Barthes suggested" (77).

While Klitgård wants to adopt all critical approaches, she shows very little interest in the work of her colleagues, and she is often unfair when she does address other critics. She attempts, for example, to carve out a space for her work by chiding others for their failures "to be comprehensive," arguing that "a narrow approach may lead to a partial and imperfect understanding of the novel" (7). Klitgård takes one scholar to task for failing to document her assertions and for cementing her argument with a "quick, sweeping reference" to a philosopher "who has not been mentioned before in the piece," thereby committing what Klitgård insists "is characteristic of much Woolf criticism in the 80s" (7). And yet Klitgård is guilty of the same when, in chapter six, she quotes Gaston Bachelard's "major phenomenological study" for his input on "roundness" (173) and "the house" (176), never to mention his work again. Klitgård's desire to be comprehensive often means that her argument becomes incomprehensible, and her haphazard use of secondary material plagues the entire book.

Klitgård's failure to situate *On the Horizon* within the context of Woolf criticism appears to stem from a belief that for her work to be of importance, it has to be new. Because Woolf studies is hardly virgin ground, Klitgård protects herself through ignorance: "To my knowledge," she concludes the book's second introductory paragraph, "this argument has not been made before" (2). She repeats this strategy when she writes, "[s]urprisingly few critics to my knowledge have offered considerable readings of the transgression of literary genres in *The Waves*," but she fails to consult works like Ralph Freedman's 1963 *The Lyrical Novel*, the argument of which much of *On the Horizon* repeats. In fact, *The Waves*' blurring of genres is by now so well-established as to be assumed, and is certainly covered in J. W. Graham and Mark Hussey's excellent overviews of the novel. Indeed, the most frustrating aspect of *On the Horizon* is that it fails to move much beyond such treatments of *The Waves*, and while the summary nature of Graham and Hussey's articles perfectly fits their respective projects, it is not appropriate to Klitgård's monograph.

On the Horizon fails its readers in some further, if minor, ways. It often feels as if Klitgård has in mind a readership for whom English is a second language—for example, she finds it necessary to gloss the meaning of "soluble" as "something which can be dissolved" (83). Finally, Klitgård's prose is littered with nonsequiturs, sentence fragments and misspelled words, which certainly the editors at Academica Press, if not the author herself, should have caught.

—Jessica Fisher, *University of California at Berkeley*

Works Cited

Barthes, Roland. *Image—Music—Text.* New York: Hill and Wang, 1977.

Bloom, Harold, ed. *Virginia Woolf.* New York: Chelsea House Publishers, 1986.

Freedman, Ralph. *The Lyrical Novel.* New Jersey: Princeton UP, 1963.

Goldman, Jane, ed. *Virginia Woolf: To the Lighthouse, The Waves.* New York: Columbia UP, 1998.

Graham, J. W., ed. *The Waves: The Two Holograph Drafts.* Toronto: U of Toronto P, 1976.

Hussey, Mark. *Virginia Woolf A to Z.* New York: Facts on File, 1995.

Langbaum, Robert. "The Epiphanic Mode in Wordsworth and Modern Literature." *New Literary History* XIV/2 (Winter 1983): 335-58.

McConnell, Frank. "'Death Among the Apple Trees': The Waves and the World of Things." *Bucknell Review* 16 (1968): 23-29.

Virginia Woolf: An Inner Life. Julia Briggs. (Orlando: Harcourt, Inc., 2005) xiv + 528 pp.

The illustrations Julia Briggs has chosen for her refreshing new biography of Virginia Woolf entitled *Virginia Woolf: An Inner Life*—draft manuscript pages and book covers (back and front) rather than portraits or photographs of Woolf herself and her social circle—reflect her focus on the work itself and the writing process as what she deems the best measure of the writer's life. Briggs frames different episodes of Woolf's life with a discussion of her works in chronological order, attempting in so doing to bring her art—"the main source of interest for us"—as opposed to her social life, back onto center stage (x).

As her subtitle suggests, Briggs delves into the writer's mind as deeply as possible, privileging "what [Woolf] did when she was alone, walking or sitting at her desk" (x-xi) over her interactions with family and friends. Each chapter closes with an italicized *Aftermath* section which examines the production, distribution and reception of the work dealt with in that chapter. In her introduction Briggs suggests these, along with the endnotes, can be skipped, although they add interesting detail to her discussion of each of the texts.

Briggs looks at the *The Voyage Out* in terms of Woolf's apprenticeship as a writer and her ambiguous early relationship with her brother-in-law Clive Bell, a source, Briggs speculates, for Rachel's ambiguous reaction to Richard Dalloway's advances. *Night and Day* provides the context for a discussion of Woolf's early marriage, her breakdowns, her neurasthenia, her anorexia and her engagement with doctors. While she acknowledges the local causes of Woolf's mental illness, Briggs ties Woolf's mental disorder to "the events of her society and her times"—"as an artist Woolf was committed to telling the truth as she saw it, and the very practice of her art required her to adopt a position as a critic and outsider even as 'mad', if the society she criticized defined its particular prejudice as 'sane'" (47).

A discussion of the short stories of *Monday or Tuesday* is interwoven with a look at the impact on Woolf's writing of the purchase of the hand printing press in 1917 which saw the beginning of the Woolfs' career as publishers and Woolf's much cherished freedom from editors. *Jacob's Room* provides the frame for a focus on the impact of World War One on Woolf's writing and on the Woolfs' family and friends, including Rupert Brooke and Siegfried Sassoon. Briggs highlights in this chapter the self-censorship (particularly in terms of the sexual life of Jacob) in which Woolf engaged in this, the first of her self-published novels. Briggs ties *The Common Reader* to Woolf's apprenticeship as a writer in the field of reviewing and she reads *Orlando* as "a series of variations on the theme of rapture and stillness, sex, time and immortality" (187). The tightly woven biographical and autobiographical contexts of Woolf's sixth novel are ideal for Briggs' emphasis on the work over the life or on the life as revealed by the work (the recreation of life in narrative) and indeed Briggs opens the book's preface with a quote from *Orlando* (ix).

Perhaps acknowledging the contribution to renewed interest in Woolf of Michael Cunningham's novel *The Hours* and Stephen Daldry's film based on the novel (and at the same time speaking to her 'common reader'), Briggs opens her chapter on *Mrs. Dalloway* with a reference to the film and returns to it on several occasions. In this chapter, Briggs covers Woolf's modernist experimentation, the relationship of her work to that of contemporary writers, the evolution of the work from short story to novel and Woolf's engagement with postwar politics. Briggs reads *Flush* and *The Second Common Reader* alongside *The Years* and in terms of a speech Woolf gave alongside Vera Brittain, Winifred Holtby and Ethel Smyth, at a meeting of the National Society for Women's Service. In the context of *Between the Acts*, Briggs revisits the question of Woolf's ambivalent patriotism, her simultaneous desire for and suspicion of a drive towards unity. Using Mitchell Leaska's *Pointz Hall* typescript, Briggs explores the novel's genesis as a play, the relief it offered to the writer engaged in a biography of her friend and colleague Roger Fry, Woolf's unusual use of the typewriter in its composition, and the "foundational" (although eventually excised) role of the poet Edward Thomas.

In her epilogue Briggs steps back from a reading of Woolf's life in terms of her suicide, reminding the reader to balance the "cheerful, lively and creative" Woolf with the "angry, paranoiac or depressed" Woolf, the "warmly sociable, amusing and amused" writer with the "intensely private" writer "absorbed in her imaginary worlds" (394). Rather than tie Woolf's death explicitly to her mental illness, Briggs contextualizes the writer's suicide, placing her in the company of a considerable number of European intellectuals, some of them friends and acquaintances, who, unable to contemplate a second world war, took their own lives.

Largely free of literary critical language, Briggs is successful in providing a work accessible to "'the common reader'" (xi). The book is comprehensive but more strictly focused on the works themselves than Hermione Lee's *Virginia Woolf* (1996), and in this sense an interesting alternative to it. While much of the material is familiar to a reader immersed in Woolf scholarship, Briggs brings new insights to and puts a new twist on the material presented. Briggs leaves little out—she covers Woolf's relationships with friends and family members, her frequently antagonistic relationships with contemporaries such as Mansfield and Joyce, her mental illness, her engagement with the war effort and with the struggle for women's rights, among many other things—despite her avowed effort to play down Woolf's social life. As Briggs' biography demonstrates, Woolf's interactions with others and the events which shaped her life were so central to her work that the two cannot really be set apart. Thus, despite Briggs' stated effort to downplay the life in favor of the work, one is left wondering how possible it really is to distinguish where life ends and writing begins.

—Helen Southworth, *University of Oregon*

Virginia Woolf: The Will to Create as a Woman. Ruth Gruber (New York: Carroll & Graf, 2005) 176 pp.

This book consists of three sections: an introductory personal narrative essay that recounts the author's graduate education, impressions of Nazi Germany in the 1930s, and a face-to-face interview with Woolf in London; facsimiles of "historical documents," including Gruber's brief correspondence with Woolf and Nigel Nicolson; and last and most substantial, her dissertation written in 1931 (originally published by Tauchnitz) at the University of Cologne to obtain a Ph.D. at twenty years old.

While the facsimiles are largely redundant since they reproduce many documents that are quoted in full and analyzed in the introduction, the introduction itself tells an engaging story that taps into an important critical debate in recent Woolf studies concerning Woolf's "genteel" anti-Semitism and its consequences on her effectiveness as an anti-fascist writer. Gruber recounts the course of her critical love affair with Woolf's works. A young Jewish-American from Brooklyn whose graduate studies had taken her to Germany, she was singled out by professors at the University of Cologne as an exceptionally gifted student. There, her academic advisor suggested that she write a study of Woolf to obtain a Ph.D. within one year, and she recounts, "I was soon mesmerized by Virginia Woolf's writing. I hung her picture on my bedroom wall. *A Room of One's Own* became my Bible" (14). Such readerly admiration is not surprising given Gruber's concerns about the intensification of German fascism. (Her copious publications include several memoirs about her work with Jewish refugees in the 1940s as a journalist and activist.)

Germany impressed an incongruent and often surreal combination of experiences on Gruber that year. On one hand, she discovers the continuation of a humanist tradition in the brave political resistance of new friends, and the widespread esteem of humanist artists like Goethe and Beethoven. On the other hand, the Nazi party's brutal degradation of Jews and others, and the direct threat it poses to her, constantly shadow these discoveries. Gruber demonstrates that as a contemporary of Woolf, she shared her political and literary concerns as well as her vexed assessment of inter-war European humanism's capacity to counter twentieth-century methods of political domination. Woolf, after all, similarly pleaded with her readers to consider irreconcilable poles of British culture—its heights and brutalities—side-by-side. When Gruber met with Woolf in London several years later, it was to interview her as part of a book "on women under fascism, communism, and democracy" (2). Although "in rapture" to meet Woolf at last, and to hear her speak about her recent trip to Germany, Gruber quickly jumps ahead to the late 1980s, when her research in the Berg Collection to examine Woolf's diaries and letters temporarily unsettles her veneration. What she finds in those materials will make other readers question Woolf's perceptive and political capacities.

Woolf's repetitive assumptions regarding Gruber begin with a simple mistake of national identity but over time worsen into callous insults. During their meeting, Woolf had said, "We were just in your Germany" (3), presuming that Gruber was a German Jew, a belief confirmed in a 1935 diary entry where she had referred to her as "some good German woman" (26). In escalating levels of misperception, Woolf discloses what Nigel Nicolson refers to in his correspondence with Gruber as her "occasional touch of anti-Semitism" (35). Her words evince a prejudice that was more aggressive than a "touch," however. In view of Woolf's notes about her, Gruber hypothesizes that "Perhaps she decided I was a poor refugee fleeing Hitler, washed up on Britain's shores, importuning her for help" (31). Indeed, Woolf's diaries and letters at times demonstrate an adherence to race and class inequality despite the conscious commitment to democratic principles in almost all of the work published in her lifetime. Gruber poignantly presents the anger and disappointment many readers have experienced in encountering those passages. The introduction is less analytical than it is personal and narrative, however, so that Gruber resolves Woolf's many political contradictions too neatly: "Those two love letters to Leonard, and her three letters to me, helped me work through my own anger and disillusionment, which now seem trifling in comparison to the agony she endured" (36). It seems that in learning of Woolf's manic depression, Gruber has laid those disquieting moments of anti-Semitism to rest for herself. Other Woolf scholars might make more of her presentation of these materials. In particular, the essay contributes significantly to a debate opened up by critics like Phyllis Lassner and Maren Linett who have explored how Woolf's deep ambivalence regarding Jews affected the ways she articulated her commitment to anti-fascism.[1] For this reason, the book is crucial reading for those interested in Woolf in the context of World War II, or in her ambiguous position in discussions of modernism and race.

Gruber's 1931 dissertation was written long before *The Years*, *Three Guineas*, and *Between the Acts*—those works that would have been most relevant for her consideration of Woolf as a political thinker. The focus here is rather on Woolf as a stylist, as evinced by the recurrence of the terms "style consciousness" and "style-conscious" throughout, and the six chapter titles: "The Poet versus the Critic," "The Struggle for a Style," "Literary Influences: The Formation of a Style," "The Style Completed and the Thought Implied," "'*The Waves*'—the Rhythm of Conflicts," and "The Will to Create as a Woman." Woolf's oeuvre is read in terms of its developing inscription of a "feminine" literary voice: "The lyrical cry, echoed throughout her works . . . evinces an ebb and flow of self-confidence, of doubt, of attempted change, and grim resolution" (69). Gruber's analysis is informed by Woolf's own critical writing, especially *A Room of One's Own*. Following suit, she argues for literary experimentation as an important cultural factor in advancing progressive conceptualizations of women. According to the study, Woolf oscillates between the lyrical imagery associated with the feminine writer and the masculine critic's analytical classicism. Along with the growing complexity of her female protagonists, her "heroic defiance" (61) as a feminine poet increasingly pushes aside the analytical voice. In time, she acquires the integrity to be "inflexibly true to herself" (63). The analysis culminates in a reading of *The Waves*, whose characters are "intuitive and more poetic" and where Woolf, "as poet and woman" comes into her own to convey "a philosophy of irrational continuity" (134). Nevertheless, Gruber considers Woolf a "transitional" figure, and concludes that by her own standards, her experiments remain far more conservative than those of the Georgians whom she discusses in "Mr. Bennett and Mrs. Brown" (97).

Unfortunately, her arguments concerning Woolf's stylistic and gender breakthroughs take for granted a metaphysical basis for sexual difference, presuming that women and men diverge stylistically because of fundamental differences in

[1] See Maren Linett's "The Jew in the Bath: Imperiled Imagination in Woolf's *The Years*." *Modern Fiction Studies* 48:2 (Summer 2002): 341-361, and Phyllis Lassner's "'The Milk of Our Mother's Kindness Has Ceased to Flow': Virginia Woolf, Stevie Smith, and the Representation of the Jew" in *Between 'Race' and Culture: Representations of 'the Jew' in English and American Literature*, ed. Bryan Cheyette (Stanford: Stanford UP, 1996): 129-44.

their mental and imaginative capacities. For instance, Gruber claims that *Jacob's Room* "is not intellectual, not philosophic, but ineffably poetic, emotionally feminine" (101). In her explanation of how *Mrs. Dalloway* continues the project to "explore the consciousness of her sex," she writes that the character's "irrelevancies are traces, depicting the mysterious leaps in the mind of a woman from vanity to the most profound experiences in life and back again to the question of dresses and personal beauty" (107). As a woman writer, Woolf thereby "accepts the tradition that women cannot think abstractly, that their scope is smaller than man's. It is this very limitation which she consecrates, availing herself of the smaller scope, of the petty and the concrete" (138). The repetitive assertions that writerly attributes are starkly gendered damages the study's relevance for present-day feminist critique. Despite Gruber's intentions of criticizing the patriarchal bias of traditional academic criticism, her arguments will strike readers as perhaps conceding too much to those very criteria. Furthermore, Gruber conspicuously projects ideological prescriptions for women into Woolf's works. Her discussions of the prevalent theme of maternity in Woolf's oeuvre, for instance, tend to form a normalizing discourse that insists on women's ultimate satisfaction in bearing sons. In her discussion of Lily Briscoe, she writes, "painting and art . . . are suggestive mediums, just as for the normal woman, bearing sons holds a cosmic intimation" (123). Orlando, on the other hand, "marries; she bears a son. She is physically creative, physically complete" (148-9).

Nonetheless, other elements of Gruber's dissertation are quite useful, perhaps especially for young scholars. She proves herself to have been astonishingly prescient in identifying the rich connections between Woolf and writers, philosophers, and visual artists of her time, handling with skill many topics that many critics have subsequently written substantial books or book chapters on (Virginia Woolf and Bergson, Virginia Woolf and impressionism, Virginia Woolf and queer modernism, etc.). Even more than the opportunity to revisit these now familiar themes, the work implies some potential new routes for exploration.

First, Gruber has written not about the place of Woolf in the history of the novel so much as a critical history of prose and Woolf's relationship to both canonized and non-canonized "rhetorical masters" (85). This is a subtle but key difference from currents in Woolf studies that could open up some promising lines of inquiry. The influences of Gibbon, Burke, Lyly, and Thomas Browne suggest a rich yet critically untapped historiographic genealogy in Woolf. Even for the well-trodden terrain of the Woolf/Joyce connection, Gruber suggests a new direction for a comparative study of their divergent methods of "creative criticism" (92), by which she means the self-conscious literary histories embedded in their fiction. Most provocative are the neo-Romantic connections she detects between Woolf and other contemporary female "creative critics" such as

Rebecca West and Dorothy Richardson.

Gruber's own inter-war text might be read along with these others as attempts to stake out literary criticism as an important site for testing the limits of feminist articulation in the present, and to shape the feminist expression to come. The 1930s appears anew from the perspective of Gruber's text, as a moment when the study of women's fiction by women takes on a welcome burden of socio-political significance.

—Judy Suh, *Duquesne University*

Women, Modernism & Performance. Penny Farfan (New York: Cambridge UP, 2004) xi + 173 pp.

Organized as a series of independent yet interconnected essays, Penny Farfan's *Women, Modernism & Performance* examines the diverse strategies employed by an interconnected group of women artists meeting the challenge of finding and creating roles for women that were both theatrical and "acceptable within emerging feminist terms" (11) during the early years of the twentieth century. Though the study is intended, at least in part, to address the insufficient attention paid by theatre historians to the efforts of women artists (as opposed to female characters) to create alternative forms of theatre practice, an interdisciplinary performance studies approach allows Farfan to examine personal and public performative strategies (pageants, lectures, demonstrations) as well as textual and corporeal "performances" in the fields of literature, drama and dance. An elegantly concise yet informative introduction situates the study in light of recent feminist research (Elin Diamond, Rita Felski, Katherine Kelly) regarding the intricate web of activities involved in creating a "feminist-modernist counter-public sphere" (10). The cast of characters entangled in this particular investigative web includes Henrik Ibsen, Elizabeth Robins, Ellen Terry, Virginia Woolf, Djuna Barnes, Edith Craig, Radclyffe Hall and Isadora Duncan. Probably of most interest to Woolf scholars are the essays entitled "Unimagined parts, unlived selves: Virginia Woolf on Ellen Terry and the art of acting" and "Writing/performing: Virginia Woolf between the acts." However, due to the structure of the book, Woolf's voice is heard elsewhere, in relation to the tensions between representation and lived experience and between physical and verbal means of expression that are examined throughout the book.

Farfan begins her chapter on the development of actress/playwright Elizabeth Robins's feminist critique of Ibsen with an image of Hedda Gabler on horseback leading the Actress' Franchise League in the Suffrage Coronation Pageant of 1911. Robins the actress initially found in Ibsen's women "gloriously actable" roles and viewed her performance of Hedda Gabler (and the initiative taken to produce the play herself, with Marion Lea) as the major event in her life and career. Ibsen, "the master," offered not only complex female roles but also a new model for the actor as collaborator and co-creator with the playwright, a model Robins applauds in *Ibsen and the Actress* (part of the Hogarth Press lecture series published by the Woolfs in 1928). An examination of some of Robins's lesser known writing, however, reveals a growing feminist consciousness which Farfan claims is responsible for her abandonment of both "the master" and eventually the theatre itself, though not before she attempted "to redress Ibsen's failings" (12) in her own admittedly didactic dramatic text, *Votes for Women* (1907). The heroine created by Robins the playwright, Vida Levering, seems conventional, attractive and sentimental compared with Ibsen's complex women, which might be read as a step backward. Examining the text as a strategic move in the effort to claim both public and imaginative space for women, however, leads to the conclusion that "Robins's politically expedient dramaturgy communicated her much broader and less topical sense of the need to create—even at the temporary expense of art—conditions conducive to the development of women's potential, the possibility of which is denied in Ibsen's plays, when female characters repeatedly channel their energies though male characters" (32).

Though some tension between artistic expression and political expediency is felt throughout the book, the second chapter introduces the possibility of transcendent idealism in the person of Ellen Terry, a unique transitional figure embracing inherent contradictions in defining the feminine role both onstage and in her own person. She becomes a much more intriguing figure in the third chapter, however, as a figure of imaginative inspiration for Virginia Woolf, both in essay and dramatic form. Farfan lays the groundwork for her reading of Terry as the central figure in *Freshwater* by turning first to Woolf's earlier essays on Sarah Bernhardt and Rachel, exploring Woolf's view of the special privilege of the actress to expand her own being through exploration of imagined lives and her idealization of "the stage as a potential site for expansive and liberating self-expression" (50). The placement of Terry at the core of *Freshwater* allows for a reading of her character as an embodiment of the voice and experience of Woolf herself. When Terry runs away with John Craig (the play's only fictional character), she runs to 46 Gordon Square; she abandons her role as idealized Victorian womanhood ("the Angel in the House"), throws her ring to a porpoise, and develops a desire to swim, which Farfan connects with numerous images of women artists and imagination in Woolf's writing (the fisherwoman, the too-small fish at the end of the line). Reading *Freshwater* and the essays on acting in light of Christine Froula's discussion of Woolf's perception of Shakespeare's writing as autobiography in the sense of anonymous self-expression leads Farfan into an intriguing discussion of the possibility for the woman writer whose body is not present in her art to delineate new and different roles for women in ways that an actress cannot explore due to the very physicality of her presence onstage and the resonances of role expectations that being female implies.

Physicality, and questions of female sexuality, both in art and in life, comprise the subject of the next chaper, "Staging the ob/scene." In it Farfan examines Djuna Barnes' *The Dove* as a parody of *Hedda Gabler*, Edith Craig's portrayal of Rosa Bonheur in *A Pageant of Great Women*, and the trial of Radclyffe Hall. She reads these artistic and public events in light of Brecht's theory of "alienation" as a technique capable of altering the perception of what can and cannot be seen, what can be considered "obscene" and what may be a "proper" subject of a scene, demonstrating how the altering of perception may be construed as a subversive act.

The discussion of subversion through performance continues in what, to this reader, is in many ways the book's most intriguing chapter, "Writing/performing: Virginia Woolf between the acts. " Here Woolf emerges as a feminist artist negotiating the intricate spaces between the acts of writing and performing. Citing the young Virginia Stephen's participation in the *Dreadnought* Hoax as an early indication of interest in the subversive powers of performance, Farfan proceeds with an examination of Woolf's theatre reviews (fascinating for their description of the audience member's journey from the shock of tawdry actuality to eventual engagement in the performance event) and turns finally to the function of performance in *Between the Acts*. The relationship between English patriarchy and war raised in *Three Guineas* is re-examined in Miss La Trobe's pageant, which employs performance and performance text as a means of contesting accepted readings of events and societal structures. Miss La Trobe, perhaps modeled in part on Edith Craig and influenced by the essay on Ellen Terry which Woolf worked on contemporaneously with the novel, is an outsider who invites the audience to see the familiar in a new light, in part through parody. In this she is sometimes aided by the intrusions of nature (the cows, the village idiot), which prove that representations of reality—and hence perhaps that reality itself—are not immutable. Performance thus demonstrates the possibility for subversion of the patriarchal script of heterosexual romance that is the subject of both novel and pageant. Noting Woolf's belief in the intimate connections between life and art as expressed in "A Sketch of the Past," Farfan weaves together the narrative strands of public and private, daily and imaginative to demonstrate how "Woolf suggests that to conceive reconstructed or alternative social realities and to reproduce them onstage is literally to bring them into existence" (99). In this context Woolf's own public appearances, from the *Dreadnought* Hoax through her lectures at Cambridge, can be seen as "putting on the body" which Shakespeare's sister had so often laid down, as a realization of an "unacted part."

The final chapter explores the shaping of the legend of Isadora Duncan, turning her from a woman using her own body as an expressive medium into a tragic figure: the doomed female artist. Duncan's determination to free the female body from male objectification and to claim its own feminine expressive authority led her to declare herself to be more teacher than dancer. Indeed, though her dances seemed spontaneous, they were carefully crafted and often supplemented by program notes and speeches. Her lifelong effort to "embody" the feminine, however, has been undermined by re-writing her life in light of a death that has been made to seem tragically fitting. Reading Duncan's death in light of dramatic criticism (notably Raymond Williams' *Modern Tragedy)*, Farfan demonstrates how co-opting her life and death in this way is dependent on endowing the means of her death with significant destiny and argues that this reading "serves as a means by which the patriarchal sociocultural order that is restored by her destruction can recreate and re-assert itself" (114). She suggests, however, that it is also possible to read Duncan's legacy in "the contemporary female bodies she helped to shape" (115) and thus to see her as one of many "continuing presences" whose varied strategies of artistic and corporeal expressions have transformed gender representations in both art and life.

Though the essays in *Women, Modernism & Performance* do indeed stand on their own, they significantly enrich one another when read in light of one another in the context of this well-annotated interdisciplinary exploration of a kaleidoscope of strategies invoked to create new spaces for women through scripting, performing and embodying feminist roles.

—Kathleen Worley, *Reed College*

Wild Outbursts of Freedom: Reading Virginia Woolf's Short Fiction. Nena Škrbić. (Westport, CT: Praeger, 2004) xxiii + 189 pp.

It has been over twenty years since the publication of Susan Dick's edition, *Virginia Woolf: The Complete Shorter Fiction*, the first scholarly compilation of the numerous published and unpublished short fictions Woolf composed over the course of her writing life. Since the late 1980s, however, when Dean Baldwin published an introductory study of the short fiction, there have been no new books addressing the breadth and variety of Woolf's lifelong engagement with and creative attraction to this genre. While there has been no lack of critical attention to individual stories or groups of stories, there have been no further consolidated attempts to analyze the scope of her contributions to the genre. Woolf tended to turn to writing short fiction during the periods between novels, when she was nudging ideas into new forms, or new "shapes" as she preferred to call them, of expression. Yet these excursions were by no means diversions, or mere marginal scribblings, as much as their disparate critical history, awaiting the imprimatur of the scholarly book, has implied.

2004 changed all that. With near simultaneous publication of Kathryn Benzel's and Ruth Hoberman's edition of critical essays, *Trespassing Boundaries: Virginia Woolf's Short Fiction* (Palgrave 2004) and Nena Škrbić's engaging and energetic monograph, *Wild Outbursts of Freedom: Reading Virginia Woolf's Short Fiction*, the Woolf community can no longer turn a blind eye to Woolf as a short fiction writer, an identification unsubordinated to her roles as novelist, essayist, diarist, and polemicist. In one of those mystical, *zeitgeist*-driven alignments of the publishing sphere, 2004 will come to signify for Woolf's short fiction what 1997 did for her essays: a year that similarly witnessed the production of two significant books, a collection of critical essays, *Virginia Woolf and the Essay*, edited by Beth Carol Rosenberg and Jeanne Dubino (MacMillan), and a book-length study, *Reading Virginia Woolf's Essays and Journalism*, by Leila Brosnan (Edinburgh UP). As ever in Woolf studies, each year brings new ways of excavating previously overlooked aspects of Woolf's oeuvre, offering fresh perspectives and opening up further avenues of inquiry.

Škrbić's book makes an absorbing contribution to debates about Woolf's short fictional accomplishments. It is hard not to read her book from cover-to-cover without coming away with a passionate sense of the injustice done to Woolf by her omission from the modernist pantheon of celebrated short fiction writers, as well as for the variousness and flexibility Woolf discovered in a genre which, perhaps paradoxically, made her hard to pin-down as an innovator of the art. Škrbić makes a persuasive case in her introduction for the personal and narrative liberation story writing represented for Woolf—“[the] sense of freedom is the salient point about Woolf’s short fiction” (1)—and borrows her book’s title from Woolf’s own (retrospectively dismissive) comments about some of her *Monday or Tuesday* (1921) stories in a 1930 letter to Ethyl Smyth: “Green and Blue and the heron were wild outbursts of freedom, inarticulate, ridiculous, unprintable mere outcries” (5). Part of Škrbić’s agenda is not just to challenge Woolf’s tendency to marginalize her own story writing practices in preference for her novels, a preference that in this letter ironically privileges a novel, *Night and Day*, whose merits subsequent critics have themselves pushed to the sidelines. It is also to foreground the pleasures and critical values of intricate and involved close readings whose accumulating force can sometimes serve as playful counterpoint to Škrbić’s assertion that it was precisely the brevity and “contractedness” (xix) of the story form that attracted Woolf’s attentions in the first place. Her detailed study of “Blue and Green” is a case in point. At almost seven pages, it expands our visual, sensory, and even tactile perceptions for a “story” that is no more than two paragraphs. While it takes its lead from a fairly well-known idea that Woolf’s *Monday or Tuesday* stories dialogue with Fry’s post-impressionist conceptions of art, it resituates this approach in light of the writings of key imagist poets, as well as Kandinsky’s art, letting us newly experience this very brief work as the verbal reflection of two types of expressionism, action painting and color-field painting. Such contextualized close analysis certainly makes for a heady and, yes, delightfully vertiginous read.

This kind of perceptive and illuminating close reading dominates Škrbić’s approach throughout, and it models in practice what she argues are the “anti-authorship” and “anti-story” imperatives behind Woolf’s approach to the genre. Woolf’s stories let the reader in, but only if—as with her modernist novels—the reader is willing to make a large contribution to the enterprise. At times, this preference for close reading over a more delineated theoretical approach does lead to long, associational paragraphs that run for more than two pages, compelling in their content, but occasionally iterative in their appeal. Škrbić is conscious, nonetheless, of the difficulty of giving critical structure to the tenuousness and genre-blurring qualities of Woolf’s short fiction, a feature which she suggests is just one part of the reason it has been overlooked: “The reasons behind the disregard of Woolf’s short fiction, about how it should be interpreted, assessed and responded to, stem from critical unease about the short-story genre itself, particularly its ideological distinction from the novel” (xix). She thereby grounds her own readings in several ways: she makes smart connections between Woolf’s own essay commentaries on both former and contemporary short fiction, comparing them to Woolf’s theories of the novel; she often opens chapters with suggestive expository references to autobiographical or diarized sources of origin for particular stories; she highlights thematic or imagistic connections amongst small groupings of stories, resisting the temptation either to cover the entire corpus of Woolf's short fiction (the book only glancingly references the 1930s in its concluding epilogue, and makes selective use of earlier pieces), or to be too wedded to the chronological or genetic contexts of Woolf's writing processes; she broadly situates Woolf's accomplishments amongst those of other modernist writers, such as Mansfield and Joyce, but also earlier forebears, such as Austen, Poe or Irving. Additionally, Škrbić divides her book into two parts, both containing three separate chapters. The emphasis of the chapters in part one tends toward demonstrating how Woolf's theories of fiction writing converged with her writing of short fiction, analyzing how the very brevity of the form contributed to her modernist vision in matters of characterization, consciousness, style and point of view. Part two shifts the focus to "the problematic question of definition" (xix) in methods of grouping the stories into interpretative units; "genre" is here taken as a point of inquiry, not so much between the forms of the novel and the story, but between generic categories which certain groupings of Woolf's short fictions intersect and interrogate, including biography, the ghost story, and the short story cycle.

In the book's opening chapter, Škrbić deploys the evocative idea of a "practitioner criticism" as a flexible approach to interpreting how Woolf's critical comments about the genre—her fascination with the "moment," with emotional intensity, with wordlessness—intersect with her own short fictional experiments. She ranges widely over Woolf's critical writings on the genre in the late teens, when Woolf was beginning to formulate her ideas for "Modern Novels" and "Mr. Bennett and Mrs. Brown." Writers discussed by Woolf (and Škrbić after her) include Percy Lubbock, L. P. Jacks, Joseph Conrad, Henry James, Sherwood Anderson, Ernest Hemingway, Gertrude Stein, and Katherine Mansfield, as well as the Russian writers Woolf famously admired. Škrbić contends that Woolf's aspirations as a short story writer shared particularly strong affinity with American claims to remake the English language—a tantalizing assertion, but one which relies perhaps too insistently on a comparative defense of Woolf as a more innovative practitioner of the art than Mansfield, who also shared a sense of alienation from British culture. Chapter two addresses five of the eight stories in *Monday or Tuesday*, the only collection of short fiction Woolf oversaw during her life. Here, Škrbić's expansive close readings, like those she applies to "Blue and Green," broaden our appreciation for the multiple ways in which Woolf "displace(s) the authorial role onto the reader" (46), and makes us more keenly aware of a muted, often contestatory dialogue between the stories where, for instance, the valorization of language in "Blue and Green" can suddenly appear strategically "squandered" (59) in "Monday or Tuesday." Chapter three rounds out the first part of the book, providing a bridge to part two by linking thematic readings with Woolf's critical manifestos on modernist aesthetics. Translating Woolf's idea of the "semi-transparent envelope" to the trope of the mirror that appears in three later stories, "The New Dress," "The Lady in the Looking Glass," and "The Fascination of the Pool," Škrbić shows how the "nebulous envelope" becomes a metaphor for the short story form, even as it intersects, and undercuts, the "solid integument of the male looking-glass" (64).

The feminist concerns, and origins, of many of Woolf's formative short fictions open the second half of the book. In chapter four, Škrbić studies Woolf's pre-1910 stories, none of which saw publication during her lifetime, for their mediation of traditional narrative formats with experimental feminist themes. Her own tendency to link stories through tropes highlights, for the attentive reader, how some of these themes achieve synchronicity; the metaphor of the "cut," borrowed from the mirrored edges of chapter three, helps explain, in implicitly editorial language, Woolf's struggles to find a narrative form that resists male editorial censorship. Most valuably, this chapter unearths four stories dating from 1906-1908 not included in Dick's edition that still remain unpublished. "The Manchester Zoo," "The Penny Steamer," "Sunday up the River," and "Down the River to Greenwich" are sensitively analyzed, especially for their visually "surrealist" aspects. For anyone interested in the genetic origins of *The Voyage Out*, moreover, these stories make compelling reading. Chapter five moves into the territory of the ghost story genre, arguing through close analysis of "Kew Gardens" and "A Haunted House" that part of Woolf's modernist experimentations with the representation of memory and desire stem from her rewriting of the traditional ghost story; Škrbić's application of Freud's idea of the "uncanny" to these stories is especially inventive and rewarding. Finally, in chapter six, Škrbić reads the series of stories that emerged from *Mrs. Dalloway* as a short story cycle rooted in a "chorus" of voices which exposes "the irony of the party as a collective experience" (145); this is a fruitful idea whose contextual reach is, however, somewhat compromised by a tendency toward tautology–"how we read the collection [depends on] how the cycle's themes are reflected in the cyclical structure"(145)–that might have been avoided with a clearer historical approach both to Woolf's writing practices at this time, and to the merits and distinctions between Stella McNichol's grouping of stories in *Mrs. Dalloway's Party* (1973) and Dick's later editorial work.

It is here at the crossroads of genre, between novel and story, a crossroads Škrbić convincingly defines as that place not of impasse but of liberation, that *Wild Outbursts of Freedom* excites further speculation. It might be argued, of course, that a study whose aim is to foreground a much-neglected part of Woolf's canon need not address that very aspect of her renown that garners the most critical attention. It may be one of the reasons Škrbić's work, while highly adept at situating Woolf within the discipline of short fiction studies in general, and even admirably citing unpublished dissertation work on Woolf's short fiction in particular, positions itself less closely than it might have done with respect to broader developments in Woolf studies that either directly, or indirectly, bear relation to her accomplishments as a short fiction writer. Anna Snaith's work on Woolf's juvenilia in *Virginia Woolf: Public and Private Negotiations*, Panthea Reid Broughton's essay on post-impressionism in *The Multiple Muses of Virginia Woolf*, or Pamela Caughie's *Woolf and Postmodernism* are just some of the broader studies which offer suggestive links to Škrbić's interpretations. Nonetheless, the merits of this first in-depth book on Woolf's short fiction are many, and Škrbić does succeed in convincing us that, without doubt, "[i]t is an exciting time in which to reassess Woolf's stories" (xvi).

—Alice Staveley, *Stanford University*

Matricide in Language: Writing Theory in Kristeva and Woolf. Miglena Nikolchina. (New York: Other Press, 2004) 133 pp.

Over twenty years ago, Toril Moi suggested that Virginia Woolf ought to be read through Julia Kristeva. In *Matricide in Language: Writing Theory in Kristeva and Woolf*, Nikolchina does precisely this to investigate the relentless suppression throughout the ages of women's literary production. Mary Wollstonecraft, Mary Shelley, Elizabeth Barrett Browning, and Virginia Woolf, she writes, experienced a palpable sense of isolation in their literary endeavors, searching for ancestresses and failing to find any. Although Woolf discusses her female predecessors at length in *A Room of One's Own* and in numerous essays, she nevertheless ultimately asks, "Where are the mothers?" Nikolchina employs a psychoanalytic, philosophical, and literary approach in answering Woolf's question.

With an especially riveting section on the female figure of Diotima in Plato's *Symposium*, whom scholars have for centuries tried to disprove, erase, or gender male, so galled are they by the notion of a woman at the center of Western civilization, Nikolchina traces not only the history of male dismissals of women in/and literature, but also those of feminist critics. She locates matricide as "the silent engine behind this vanishing" (2), a necessary act that "dooms the writing woman to be forever the first of her kind" (9), for only in separating fully from the mother—in murdering her—is the human subject launched into language, writing, and individuation. In order for Lily Briscoe in *To the Lighthouse* to achieve her vision, for instance, she requires distance, exile from others, and that her mother and Mrs. Ramsay remain safely dead. Before discussing Woolf, however, Nikolchina focuses, in her first three chapters, on Kristeva's work on the mother, moving swiftly and nonlinearly through Kristeva's individual essays and ideas within the context of her works overall. Solid knowledge of Kristevan theory and the discourse of psychoanalysis will greatly facilitate a reading of *Matricide in Language*.

Nikolchina first highlights Kristeva's work on the mother, which explicates the primeval desire to become a speaking subject as achieved by breaking from, losing, or killing the mother, a phenomenon occurring throughout the history of feminism and women's literature and language. Referencing Joan Scott's observation that "oscillations between phantasies of uniqueness and phantasies of fusion" (8) characterize women's movements, an observation resonating with Kristeva's 1979 essay "Women's Time," Nikolchina turns to Kristeva to expand upon limited visions of female/feminist experience, for such fantasies and oscillation are "largely responsible for the fragility and instability of the feminist discursive field and for its chronically embattled status" (79). In addition, much feminist scholarship cites homogeneity as the benchmark for women and feminism, manifest in Elaine Showalter's "Virginia Woolf and the Flight into Androgyny," an essay that effectively murders Woolf for her failure to fit into preexisting concepts of "female experience."

By focusing on Woolf's body—her "food preferences, sexual relations with Leonard, frigidity, childlessness, molestation by her brother, menstruation, and menopause" (87)—at the expense of her writing, Showalter assumes an abjective stance toward Woolf, Nikochina states, drawing upon Kristeva's theory of the abject—the rejection of the (mother's) body out of horror and reaffirmation of patriarchal ideology. To my understanding, then, Showalter enacts a double-abjection, first by asserting Woolf's rejection of her own body and then rejecting that body herself. In such a manner do we therefore see the "transmutation of texts into punishable bodies," Nikolchina explains, the "massacre [of] the one who dared be singular" (22-3) by those who have internalized paternal authority.

Additionally, Showalter finds Woolf's conscious suppression of anger in *A Room of One's Own* to be a fatal flaw, while Nikolchina questions the assumption that anger is "more authentic than the impulse to win your audience by controlling your anger" (85), an impulse stemming from Woolf's insights into the untapped power of silence and gaps. For Showalter, however, Woolf's childless body retreating to an isolated room of her own provides neither a useful model for androgyny nor for women's literature nor literary history. Conversely, Kristeva's recent work privileges female singularity, eschewing the concept of homogenized masses of women, thereby overcoming the "impasses and dogmatisms of mass movement" (8) adapted by critics to demean women's writing. Only by stepping away from language—the symbolic, the patriarchal social order—and becoming asymbolic can women achieve individuation, Kristeva argues. Nikolchina thus views Woolf as "a restless wanderer" (45), a stranger to language, an exile from whom may descend no lineage. This singular feminine condition dictates the formation and subsequent erasure—matricide—of distinctions.

Singularity nevertheless gives rise to "the potential for renewal and revolt" (81), for within asymbolic/female space, "unique, incommunicable meanings hold sway" (26) until "what cannot be spoken delineates our common horizon" (73). Kristevan abjection again bears relevance, for the "tale/history of maternal loss emerges as the destiny of the speaking being—horrified, persecuted, mournful, and therefore creative. As *abject*, *Thing*, *semiotic*, *chora*, the maternal void shakes and pulverizes meanings, it shatters and produces them" (5). The woman writer comes into being by defeating her silent adversary, the suppressor of speech, the Angel in the House envisioned by Woolf in her 1931 essay "Professions for Women," an Angel dividing woman between the person society says she ought to be and writer she yearns to be. Woolf resolves this feminine split by murdering the Angel: throwing an inkpot at her and killing her. The incident demonstrates that there is no tradition of the mothers, only gaps of silence "separating the solitary female utterances throughout history" and "reproduc[ing] the figure of the missing mother" (84).

While she discusses several of Woolf's essays to explicate her theory, as well as, briefly, *Mrs. Dalloway* and *Three Guineas*, Nikolchina devotes the greatest attention to *A Room of One's Own* and *Between the Acts* for evincing Woolf's life-long fascination with silence and gaps, her struggle to rework patriarchal linguistic and literary convention. *A Room of One's Own* is not without problems, Nikolchina finds, for while early on Woolf concentrates on absent literary mothers, she later turns toward androgyny as a measure of past male literary success and a model for women writers, a move Nikolchina finds disturbing, though for different reasons from those Showalter iterates. The turn toward androgyny "contradicts the discussion it is supposed to close," Nikolchina believes (91):

> Androgyny screens the poignancy of the preceding search for a tradition of the mothers . . . If the first story is a story about the silence of Shakespeare's sister, the second story is about the (androgynous) eloquence of Shakespeare. . . . The first story insists that "it is useless to go to the great men writers for help" (114); the second story affirms that "when I want to stretch my faculties on a book . . . [I] turn back to Shakespeare" (150). (91)

Androgyny nevertheless allows Woolf, or the Woolfian narrator of *A Room of One's Own*, to return to the exclusionary, male-oriented library and enter it masked, seeking fathers and mothers, seeking meaning "on the far side of language" (92)—the spaces, the silences between words that preoccupied Woolf throughout her life. Nikolchina references seminal works on Woolfian silence (e.g., those by Lucio Ruotolo and Patricia Laurence) that posit the intervals between sounds in Woolf's works as significant as the sounds themselves. It is paramount, then, to approach Woolf's writing not only in terms of its language but also in terms of its silence, without losing sight of Woolf's ambivalence toward silence—the silence that suffocates and kills, the Angel suppressing women's speech. Indeed, the problems and pitfalls of silence enlarge upon Woolf's explorations of it.

Ultimately, it is in *Between the Acts* that Woolf locates "a final—and breathtaking—solution to the problem of the murdered mother and the empty spaces through which she returns" (93). Nikolchina prefaces her discussion of the novel by recalling Woolf's late essay, "Sara Coleridge" which discusses the three rows of dots with which Coleridge concluded her brief autobiography. Reflecting on the dots, Woolf tempers her inclination to finish the autobiography—to fill in the dots—with the realization that Coleridge's deliberately open ending stems from her perception of the artificiality of closure in writing. Woolf's comprehension of the purpose of the dots reaches fruition in *Between the Acts*, with its "hieroglyphics of silence rendered as interruption" (121), interruption that paradoxically enables ongoing speech and language. A novel confounding to critics, spawning the belief in Woolf's loss of control over her writing and final capitulation to silence, it is in fact a triumph in which ellipses, gaps, silences, and unfinished and interrupted sentences resist historically male literary conventions and reclaim the silent mother(s).

Having found its way into Woolf's writing, silence in *Between the Acts* presents itself as an "alternative ancestry of anonymity," explaining the absent mothers as silences not to be dismissed—murdered—but as constituting themselves because of their silence, which proffers its own "problematic contribution to talk" (124). *Between the Acts* therefore affirms Kristeva's concept of emptiness as "at the root of the human psyche and at the beginnings of the symbolic function" (126). The novel "claim[s] silence for ancestry" (127) and incorporates series of interruptions that pave the way for further female speech.

An unsettling component of Nikolchina's critique of *Between the Acts* is her musing as to whether the novel "should not be regarded as part of a suicidal teleology behind which we have to read the story of [Woolf's] death" (129). In her final paragraph, she suggests that because *Between the Acts* can never be finished, it "may be precisely in its aspect of a perpetuum mobile" a "prelude to Woolf's suicide" (133). If so, ensuing questions interrupt Nikolchina's claims. Does such a suggestion privilege Woolf's body over her writing, an anti-feminist crime of which Nikolchina finds Showalter guilty? Has Woolf therefore committed matricide against herself, erasing yet again a female ancestry for subsequent women writers to claim? Is the (female) body destroyed so that (male) language may thrive? Has Woolf's singularity precipitated her death/murder? Eliciting such questions, Nikolchina's provocative book enacts that which it argues. With its own resistance to closure, *Matricide in Language* leaves voices at liberty to carry on with the story.

—Kristin Czarnecki, *University of Louisville*

Death, Men, and Modernism: Trauma and Narrative in British Fiction from Hardy to Woolf. Ariela Freedman (New York: Routledge, 2003) 155 pp.

Ritual Unbound: Reading Sacrifice in Modernist Fiction. Thomas J. Cousineau (Newark: University of Delaware Press, 2004) 187 pp.

In general, two examples of that stodgy old genre, the monograph, may not have much to say to each other. Narrow in scope and stuffed with esoteric detail, the monograph has traditionally exhibited relevance incommensurate with the effort required to produce it. Today's standards of scholarship and market forces often preclude such tomes. Even so, Thomas J. Cousineau's *Ritual Unbound* and Ariela Freedman's *Death, Men, and Modernism* are good examples of scholarly works that use the monograph form to propose solidly articulated theses that, while closely focused on the texts they take as their objects, gesture toward larger contexts and applications. Indeed, their conjunction is fortuitous, for Cousineau mounts an indirect response to Freedman's account of sacrificial death. For neither is Woolf a central focus (Freedman's analysis of *Mrs. Dalloway* occupies only six and a half pages, while Cousineau devotes a chapter to *To the Lighthouse*), yet their work is useful for the way it situates Woolf in the broader modernist landscape.

Freedman's book, which is part of the Routledge series Literary Criticism and Cultural Theory: Outstanding Dissertations (ed. William E. Cain), proceeds in a literary historical vein, charting a shift from Victorian plots set in motion by dead mothers to modernist plots consummated by dead young men. (Of course, one need only think of Dickens's Sydney Carton to realize that such plots are not entirely restricted to modernism.) Freedman is concerned to correct the perception that World War I was directly and primarily responsible for the thematic content of modernist texts; thus, even as she traces an evolutionary line from Hardy through Forster, Lawrence, and Ford to Woolf, Mansfield, and H.D., she stresses that the war served to intensify the preoccupations of pre-war fiction rather than to shift paradigms of form and theme altogether. Psychoanalysis serves as an agent of continuity in this sense: relocating Freud in his historical context of the early twentieth century, Freedman reads his evolving theories of the death drive alongside fictional texts that contemporaneously work out death narratives parallel to Freud's own.

The proposed trajectory begins with works by Hardy and Forster that are marked by a "death economy," in which male protagonists owe the debt of death to the narrative, whose substance is the story of their inability to pay that debt. Transitional authors Lawrence and Ford begin to challenge the economy by creating narrators who "reject a spectatorial relationship to the death of the other" (14), while Mansfield and Woolf shift into a "gift economy," in which narrative repetition is no longer the subject's drive toward the inanimate state of death, but a system of exchange which is self-perpetuating, "a continuous cycle of giving, having, and receiving" (24). This shift is not merely coincident with these novels' increased emphasis on female subjectivity: Mansfield and Woolf's protagonists appropriate male death through their acts of witnessing; the indirection of second-hand experience is therefore a necessary component of female subjectivity in these texts. This receives its fullest expression in H.D.'s *Tribute to Freud*, in which "[t]he story of male death in the twentieth century becomes the story of female subjectivity built 'over his dead body'" (23). Throughout the book, Freedman's prose is clear, straightforward, and even economically lyrical in her felicitous turns of phrase.

In her penultimate chapter, titled "After the Party: Woolf, Mansfield, and World War I," Freedman forgoes biographical debates about the relationship between the two authors, focusing instead on an elemental structural equivalence between "The Garden Party" and *Mrs. Dalloway*: they are "remarkably similar narrative[s] in [their] plot, character, approach to sexuality and emphasis on revelation" (96). Both are war narratives though they are displaced from the scene of the warmaking—in fact, Freedman claims that they can be classified as war narratives *because* of this distance, since "the mediation of the second-hand spectator" is the prerequisite for this modernist aesthetic, which eschews direct experience (82). Such distance is also concomitant with the pacifism that the gift economy promotes. Freedman emphasizes Clarissa's difference from Septimus in class, mental state, narratological importance, and especially gender; Clarissa lives on through the sacrifice of Septimus's life, but their incommensurability ensures that his suicide is a gift that can neither be fully accepted nor reciprocated. Clarissa assumes the position of witness to trauma, and she responds to Septimus's sacrifice by reminiscing about the idyllic days at Bourton. Thus what Freedman calls "emotional memory" is born from this moment as the repayment of the gift of death (101).

In equating the activation of this emotional memory with Clarissa's accession to female subjectivity, Freedman runs the risk of regilding tired clichés about feminized affect. Even if "[t]his sense of self, found in nostalgic evocation of the past, is the antidote to her moment of vicarious emotion" experienced upon hearing of Septimus's suicide, we learn nothing about how the content of that past lends itself to turning "golden in the light of memory" (102). What is more, Freedman is never quite clear about the direction of the gift economy. In her introduction, she tells us that "[t]he effect of the gift plot on narrative is not to provoke a retroactive reading but to provoke the desire for a sequel" (24), yet later we learn that "[f[or Mansfield and Woolf the desire to memorialize the past is presented as a deflection of the trauma of the present. The role of the artist becomes to remember everything but the moment of disaster" (102). This would imply a retroaction that, while conserving narrative momentum, takes us back to a prequel rather than forward to a sequel. Freedman's reading of the last pages of *Mrs. Dalloway* also elides certain key features: it is not strictly true that "Clarissa's first response...is [the] bodily, involuntary one" of imagining herself in Septimus's place (102). Clarissa's first response is surprise and indignation, expressed with an exclamatory "Oh!" The old woman in the building across, with whom Clarissa locks eyes and who serves as another, female surrogate, also goes unmentioned.

These weaknesses are specific to Freedman's reading of *Mrs. Dalloway*, and are not representative of the strength of her argument as a whole. Nevertheless, however insightful and original Freedman's other readings are, they remain somewhat limited given her partial engagement with trauma and gift theories. Her command of psychoanalytic theory is impressive, though she cites few psychoanalytic readings of *Mrs. Dalloway* and engages with none of the work done in trauma theory since the publication of Cathy Caruth's *Unclaimed Experience* in 1996. Marcel Mauss suffices for her thinking on gift theory, though it would have been more than appropriate to consider inheritors of Mauss such as Baudrillard. It would also have been interesting for comparative purposes to hear her thoughts on the dead young men of American modernism, such as Faulkner's Quentin Compson, Hemingway's Robert Jordan, and Cather's Emil Bergson. In the end, however, none of these omissions is serious enough to detract from the overall quality of her work.

Thomas J. Cousineau's book is the work of a senior scholar, not a revised dissertation, but Cousineau too considers Woolf to be the keystone of the pattern he observes in modernism. His account of modernism is inimical to Freedman's however, because he is writing against the critical tradition in which female subjectivity comes at the expense of others. Like Freedman, Cousineau exhibits a laudable commitment to structural analysis, but Cousineau's critique also encompasses an ethics of reading: *Ritual Unbound* owes its genesis to more than a little irritation at the persistent gullibility of readers and critics who have, in his opinion, been seduced by the first person narrators of the first four novels he takes on: *The Turn of the Screw, Heart of Darkness, The Good Soldier,* and *The Great Gatsby*. Cousineau contends that these narrators, while explicitly condemning certain scapegoating practices, redirect their blame toward other characters, undermining the force of their moralistic judgments with subtle hypocrisy. Cousineau draws on the work of René Girard while couching this ambivalence toward scapegoating in psychoanalytic terms, as the return of the repressed, the result of an "atavistic inheritance whose hold...proves to be remarkably tenacious" (27).

Nevertheless, Cousineau states, the form of the novels under consideration, if read carefully and correctly, ultimately resists the narrators' scapegoating impulses by presenting evidence that fails to jibe with the narrators' accusations, judgments, and conclusions. The dissonant intersection of the novels' form with the content of the narration is therefore the primary didactic tool through which the alert reader is instructed about the dangers of scapegoating. Thus, in *The Turn of the Screw*, James expects us to understand that his governess exculpates Miles but blames Quint and Jessel because she is locked in a rivalry for the children's affection that requires her to proclaim her superiority over others, a rivalry she cannot consciously acknowledge but which readers can infer. Cousineau essentially argues that the texts' dramatic irony should result in more ethical communities of readers that no longer engage in exclusionary practices because the novels ultimately work to demystify scapegoating as cruel and unwarranted. Psychological interpretation has been oversympathetic to the narrators, thus endorsing them or even scapegoating them for "our own susceptibility to delusive constructions of reality" (82), but the "genuinely moral dimension" of modernist fiction lies in the space in which we *dis*identify with narrators and thus learn to resist the scapegoating they commit (137).

An example of this from the strong, nuanced chapter on *Heart of Darkness* (which also presents a thoughtful response to Chinua Achebe's critique of the novel) begins with the way that Marlow successively excuses and convicts Kurtz of wrongdoing in the process of deriding the female characters and excluding all but white males in his subsequent recounting of the story. By maintaining Kurtz as an outsider to all conceivable human communities, Marlow reinscribes him in the place of the scapegoat. But this belies his narrative's insistence on Kurtz's similarity to, not difference from, others. The whites' torture and abjection form the same set of "unspeakable rites" as the blacks' cannibalism, contesting Marlow's version of mutual exclusivity. Cousineau identifies the same pattern of unreliability in each of the novels he reads, the least compelling of which is the chapter on *The Great Gatsby*. Cousineau assumes that Nick Carraway displaces his own desires onto the other characters, through whom he lives vicariously, maintaining the ability to critique them without implicating himself. This ignores the possibility Gatsby is not the channel for Nick's desires but their object.

The chapter on *To the Lighthouse* is the strongest in the book, however, and the most polemical, as Cousineau writes against Woolf critics such as Tina Barr, Val Gough, Joan Lidoff, Jane Lilienfeld, and Diana Swanson, whom he sees as participating in scapegoating practices by placing unwarranted blame on male characters. Although the novel is continuous with the others chosen for this study in its "recognition of the contradiction inherent in a social practice that is both necessary and unjust" (141), Cousineau claims that the third-person narrator functions in a more straightforwardly ethical manner by refusing to scapegoat any character, even that favorite scapegoat of critics, Mr. Ramsay. As evidence that men and the history made by men have not been excluded from the artistic community into which Lily Briscoe inserts herself, Cousineau cites Augustus Carmichael's presence in the closing paragraphs of the novel, as well as Lily's ineluctable position in an art historical tradition dominated by men.

Although *To the Lighthouse* displays a consciousness that communities are constituted around excluded members, its "commitment to inclusion" (146) ultimately prevails in the form of people and things crossing boundaries, for example the French Boeuf en Daube served by servants to an English family who consume it together. As he did in his chapter on *Heart of Darkness*, Cousineau rejects more explicitly gendered critiques of the novel in favor of a reading that has *To the Lighthouse* dramatizing "the disappearance of firmly maintained distinctions," be they of gender, race, class, or sexuality (152). This disappearance of boundaries threatens the group in the "Time Passes" section, but coherence returns in "The Lighthouse," coming first in the form of James, Cam, and Lily's desire for the violent expulsion of Mr. and Mrs. Ramsay. Cousineau argues that James and Cam's "caricature" of their father, expressed aggressively in their urges to kill or harm him, is moderated with tenderness or at least a softening of accusation against him late in the novel. And Lily, who had earlier scapegoated Mrs. Ramsay as an obstacle to her aesthetic consummation, now attempts to recuperate her memory, even repenting of her animosity toward Charles Tansley, another excluded member. These examples form the basis for Cousineau's argument that "'The Lighthouse' begins, then, with a threat of chaos that is warded off by successive exclusionary acts that are, in their turn, repudiated by the three chief perpetrators of this atavistic ritual: Cam, James, and Lily Briscoe" (161).

Cousineau hedges a bit when, in his penultimate paragraph, he allows for the possibility that "the exclusion that made [Lily's painting] possible was only a temporizing strategy to which [Woolf] attaches no permanent significance" (162). As weak a statement as this is, it points to an implicit consequence of Cousineau's reading: if the position of the scapegoat is highly variable, to the degree that an individual may occupy the position of the excluder or the excluded serially or even simultaneously, then a rotating scapegoat position may be the most ethical configuration, by which communities are still able to constellate around outsiders without consigning them permanently to outsider status. Cousineau's analysis also leads us to the conclusion that a narrative voice able to shift perspectives and portray these multiple dimensions is more ethically effective than one which asks readers to disidentify with it. This amounts to a near-admission that, atavistic though it may be, scapegoating is yet a necessary process in modernity, though its objects are plural and impermanent. Cousineau's disavowal of scapegoating as an unethical practice unseemly in modernity is therefore not as strong as it may appear to be at earlier points in the text; perhaps this is the function of a sometimes too-easy equivalence between the terms "exclusion," "scapegoating," and "sacrifice." However, Cousineau's prose is equally as clear as Freedman's, at the slight cost of occasional repetitiousness. He tends to hang his readings on just a few words ("trials of witchcraft," "unspeakable rites," "holocaust") from each of the novels he reads, resulting in admirably spun close readings that sometimes seem slightly constrained.

Together, these two volumes show that monographs continue to make vital contributions to literary scholarship. One difference between them, however, will likely mean that Cousineau's work will reach a wider audience than Freedman's. The University of Delaware Press has priced *Ritual Unbound* at $37.50, which, while not entirely affordable for such a slender volume, is at least within reach of graduate student, adjunct, and professorial budgets. Routledge has not found a way to price *Death, Men, and Modernism* below its absurd $75.00, however, which will relegate it to the library market. This is a shame both for the author and her potential readers, who will find much to think about—or, like Cousineau, think against—in her work.

—Mia L. McIver, *University of California, Irvine*

Memory in Literature: From Rousseau to Neuroscience. Suzanne Nalbantian (New York: Palgrave Macmillan, 2003) x + 185 pp.

Interdisciplinary research on the relations among literature, science, technology, and medicine has exploded in recent years, posing important questions about the cultural meaning of scientific data and theories, the impact of medical practices on identity, the aesthetic strategies available for representing our experience of technology, and more. Neurobiology and physiological brain research, with all their current claims on public attention (from *Newsweek* stories about your baby's brain to debates over Prozac), provide rich material for literary scholars interested in representations of the psychic operations that make up subjectivity. The importance of such research lies in the fact that we have brains as well as minds, and that these physical organs are a determining condition of our being. What knowledge about the brain offers literary studies is a complex, even delicate matter—debates about the brain are contentious enough without the politics of literary studies—but we would be foolish to ignore the insights of neuroscience just because we already have psychoanalysis, philosophy, and political theory to explain how minds work. Turning to the brain to understand minds does not imply that literature (let alone personality) is a simple mechanical function of brain chemistry and structure, but it does imply that literature has at least as much to do with the brain as it does with the rest of the body, which has achieved its own prominence in theory and criticism. And even if we are not interested in explaining certain features of literature with neuroscience, we might be interested in tracing how literary writers have harnessed, responded to, and refashioned the scientific imagination.

In *Memory and Literature: From Rousseau to Neuroscience*, Suzanne Nalbantian reports that the scientific imagination has been hard at work on memory. After "immersing [her]self" in the field of brain research "for over a decade and engaging in some dialogue with leading figures in brain research abroad," she has staked out ambitious terrain for a wide-ranging study: the correlations between "the intuitive and experiential expression of memory by literary subjects and theories in neuroscience about the encoding, storage, and retrieval of memory" (2, 1-2). This efficient, fast-paced exploration takes her through two centuries, about nineteen poets and novelists, and three painters in 158 pages, mapping out broad comparisons of memory in different literary periods. It is definitely a macro-approach at the expense of micro-analysis; while Nalbantian is no doubt intimate with a wide range of literature, this intimacy gives way somewhat quickly to broad generalizations about how a given literary historical period correlates to a specific, scientifically-intelligible memory process. The comparison breaks down as follows: Rousseau and the Romantics need no external memory trigger, but remember voluntarily through intentional, "self-induced emotional states of longing for the past" which they then project on the external world (41); Baudelaire and the Symbolists physicalize memory, locating its drug-like effects in the senses and the brain, instead of emotional or spiritual yearnings; Proust, influenced by Bergson, dramatizes the work of the senses (as opposed to emotions) in involuntarily recuperating long-term memories; Anglo-American modernism (including Woolf) makes long-term memory retrieval dependent on environmental cues (more on this below); Apollinaire and the Surrealists create an aleatory memory without causality, rationality, or linear temporality; and Latin-American modernists (Nin, of Cuban descent, is grouped with Borges and Paz) use mythically-inflected metaphor and metonymy to transform memory into art.

This descriptive schema, the essence of the book, shows that neuroscience can help us break down memory into discernible elements and operations. These elements and operations–the initial creation of a memory in the brain, its storage there, and its later retrieval and experience by a subject—are a very different focus than the usual thematics of memory in literary criticism. Nalbantian's work has something important to offer such approaches, so it is unfortunate that she barely mentions, for example, trauma, nostalgia, or the politics of memory in a historicist culture. In other words, Nalbantian's study has little in common with books like Fussell's *The Great War and Modern Memory* or James Olney's *Memory & Narrative* (she briefly mentions the latter). This turn from cultural, political, or other non-scientific contexts is not a problem, in principle, but it coincides with a turn away from its own critical context; the study barely acknowledges a wider conversation about memory in literature, or how neuro-scientific understandings of it enhance or problematize other understandings. Because Nalbantian does not articulate the larger significance of her descriptions—why, for example, it is important that Romantics represent memory as an intentional exercise of spiritual yearning while Anglo-American modernists make memory a response to environmental cues—the study feels like a first take on issues that need further exploration. If different literary periods and movements treat memory creation, storage, and retrieval so differently, we surely have to wonder what this means.

Early on, Nalbantian misses the opportunity for an important debate about her critical context by not elaborating her polemical assertion that neuroscience provides a "more precise and objective criteria for evaluating mental phenomena in literary works than the vagaries and imprecisions of standard psychological criticism" (3). This assertion about mental phenomena "in" literature suggests that representations of memory work like a real person's memory, and that a novel's fictional character and poem's lyrical voice are what a scientist could analyze as a "remembering human subject" (1). This suggestion becomes explicit and is fundamental to the book: Nalbantian writes that the "literature of memory can provide a rich and complex array of data that is tantamount to field studies for capturing episodes of memory" (2-3). Set aside for the moment that we don't know what, exactly, a "literature of memory" is—what literature does not have something to do with memory? More important, the idea of equating literature to scientific data (or "case histories" [3]), a claim for the epistemological equivalence of art and lived experience, is a complicated one for both scientists doing empirical research and literary scholars doing criticism, and requires a great deal of explanation. Unfortunately, Nalbantian does not provide a serious reflection on this idea that literature is a discourse in which "the memory process" is "divulged" (23) instead of imagined and re-invented, a discourse that counts as something like data or evidence for a scientific discipline that proves and disproves hypotheses about the natural world. Her approach is a collapsing of text and world that lies, I suspect, at the logical extreme of biographical criticism that reads the author's life as or through her literary texts. To go along with this, we need more than the peremptory claim that "so much of the literary material [included in this study] is overtly and emphatically autobiographical" (3). This literary material is also literary.

Nalbantian's lack of discussion about her interdisciplinary position and methods leads to a further confusion: when she cites the influence of, for example, Bergson on Proust or Pierre Janet on Breton, she compromises literature's status as raw data or evidence about how memory works. Responding to philosophers of memory and experimental psychologists, these writers are doing a different kind of work, not providing raw data about the memory process but their own interpretations of it. This question of intellectual exchange among writers, experimental psychologists, and philosophers of memory is very important, but Nalbantian does not explain how it is compatible with reading literature as a neuroscientist's case study. Nor, given the large scope of her study, does she satisfactorily develop the details of any specific intellectual exchange. We have seen how dense and exhaustive studies of such interdisciplinary exchanges can be–in, say, Ann Banfield's work on Woolf and the Cambridge philosophers–but this is not a project that Nalbantian seriously undertakes.

Despite its problems, there are very worthwhile parts in this unique book. In chapter five, "Woolf, Joyce and Faulkner: Associative Memory," Nalbantian provides some interesting, if abbreviated, readings of *To the Lighthouse* and *Mrs. Dalloway*. She calls the former "the quintessential memory novel" and describes its three parts in terms of the three memory-functions of encoding, storage, and retrieval (80). She argues that Woolf makes memory an especially visual phenomenon, reading Lily's painterly perspective as the one most burdened with the problems of memory. Vision triggers memory in association with place: "it is the physical place which is the source for the retrieval of memory" (82). Nalbantian claims that such memory processes demonstrate, in neuroscientific terms, "the classic memory phenomenon of 'cued retrieval'" in which "the encoding [of a memory], which originally introduces the links of association, [is] the basis for the retrieval in a similar environment" (82). This claim helps us think about Woolf's exploration of the dependence of interiority on the exterior world (a dependence that Nalbantian claims is ultimately avoided by the Romantics), the way subjectivity is bound to its exteriority. With this memory process in mind, Nalbantian provides an original reading of a familiar image of Lily from "The Lighthouse":

> She rammed a little hole in the sand and covered it up, by way of burying in it the perfection of the moment. It was like a drop of silver in which one dipped and illumined the darkness of the past. (Woolf 172; qtd. in Nalbantian, 82)

Nalbantian sees this as a metaphor for memory-encoding, imagistically associated "with a drop of silver that the painter dips her brush into to illuminate the past. The digging and the dipping suggest the encoding and the retrieval respectively" (82). Thinking of the connection between Lily and Mrs. Ramsay in terms of the science of memory function is an especially striking twist on psychoanalytic readings of this relationship, even if Nalbantian does not ramify this twist.

Nalbantian suggestively applies this focus on visual memory associated with environment to *Mrs. Dalloway* in her reading of Septimus Smith. He is pathological because he remembers incorrectly, not by the associations of the external world but by the voices and visions "ingrained" in his own mind (84). Nalbantian asks, "[c]ould the Septimus figure be a symbol for a type of secondary memory, which lurks beneath the primary memory of Mrs. Dalloway?" (85) Comparing *how* each character remembers shifts focus from the easier question of *what* they remember, and begins to get at demanding questions about how subjectivity is involved in the mechanics and chemistry of cognition.

Nalbantian also provides useful surveys of debates in experimental psychology and neuroscience. Chapter One, on the "web of interconnections" among 19th century students of dynamic psychology, animates questions about memory's role in the obscure relationship between the brain and mind (8). Nalbantian helps us appreciate William James's relevance to French psychology, and the common attempt by James, Bergson, and Janet to discern the "psychic element" of memory beyond its purely biological, mechanical dimension that was often privileged by researchers. Nalbantian ends the book with a chapter dedicated to more recent neuroscientific work. Focusing on the different memory functions of the brain's amygdala and hippocampus, she makes a complex body of scientific literature surprisingly accessible. She shows how scientific debates about memory eventually encounter metaphysical problems, and are forced to deal with consciousness and subjectivity as well as its enabling hardware. While science can describe the physical processes involved in memory, it must also, as Nalbantian quotes neuroscientist Alain Berthoz as saying, "'pass from the brain to thought'" (145). This is a passage that literary studies, like neuroscience, has not considered enough. We have taken the neurological work of the brain for granted just as some scientists have bracketed off the lived, phenomenological experience of having one. This book moves us toward overcoming these limitations, even if a great deal of work remains to be done.

—David R. Sherman, *New York University*

Fiction, Intuition, & Creativity: Studies in Brontë, James, Woolf, & Lessing. Angela Hague (Catholic U of America P, 2003) 310 pp.

This relatively unorthodox work offers a largely admirable contribution to the understanding of literary composition. D. H. Lawrence once averred, "Never trust the teller, trust the tale," but in recent decades trusting the tale has often blurred into strictly trusting the interpreter of the tale, which isn't quite the same. What is slightly radical in *Fiction, Intuition, & Creativity* is Hague's willingness to "to trust the tellers rather than the theorists" (6) and her conviction that the unconscious, intuitive origins of fiction are relevant to literary study. Implicit in this argument is a criticism of the absolute severing of texts from their authors that was so very essential for New Criticism and deconstruction. In so doing, Hague rescues the aesthetic legitimacy of many dismissed literary legacies—all by the bold step of considering that these writers just might have been sincere in their treatment of intuitional consciousness, how we sometimes spontaneously realize truths without the intervention of rationality or strict, physical evidence.

Fiction, Intuition, & Creativity commences with a sextet of thinkers on intuition, partitioned off into three disciplines: Henri Bergson and William James (philosophy); Carl Jung and Robert Ornstein (psychology); and Benedetto Croce and Jacques Maritain (aesthetics). This literature survey is conscientiously thorough but almost too ponderous. The ideas seem repetitive, and the disciplinary partitions sometimes seem arbitrary—categorizing William James strictly as philosophy, when he too is psychology, or Carl Jung as strictly psychology, when he is, well, Jung, or classifying aesthetics as separable from philosophy, with so much diaphanous overlap at every turn (although to her credit Hague does often cross-reference these thinkers). Such an attempt at orderly classification is, paradoxically, itself counterintuitive, although perhaps rhetorically necessary for *Fiction, Intuition, & Creativity* to be an academic tome. I do not believe there is a superior way to craft such a theoretical framework on intuition than the way Hague has done, except perhaps to be more succinct. This chapter culminates with a section devoted to "A Definition of Intuition" (63-68); the definition is largely a summary of the theories that have already been discussed rather than anything compact enough to appear as a single sentence, or even two sentences.

Chapter two consists of a topical survey of creative writers on the subject of intuition, the unconscious, and creativity. In many respects, the testimony of this chapter duplicates the first chapter from a less analytical perspective, but it is effective in conveying how *central* intuition is in the origins of literary work. From Samuel Richardson to Derek Walcott, writers tell how they passively yield to the nonrational flux and emotional pyrotechnics of the unconscious, abandon the ego, allow the boundaries between self and other, between past, present, and future, to dissolve. As an academic who happens to be a fiction writer myself, I can only concur. These are matters that literary theorists have long ignored as irrelevant, the text either being considered complete in itself or else culturally determined in meaning; as Hague demonstrates, however, an understanding of the impulsive, subconscious nature of literary origins is necessary in some circumstances of reading.

A slightly unnerving problem in this overview of authors occurs in the procrustean attitude Hague adopts towards Anthony Trollope, for while there is some degree of intuitional discourse in his *Autobiography*, she strains too far, I think, to make him seem *exemplary* of intuitive consciousness. If Trollope does speak of interpenetrating with his characters, this is not precisely tantamount to a loss of ego, considering how proprietary his discourse about characters tends to be. This novelist, after all, kills off Mrs. Proudie, one of his most formidable recurring characters, after overhearing two men complaining about her at his club. To J. Hillis Miller's meticulous, if harsh, judgment of Trollope's *Autobiography*, Hague offers only a generalization as rebuttal: "In fact, Trollope's discussion of his creative process, particularly his relationship with his characters, is very similar to that of many other writers" (111 n). Only in some aspects, however. Surely Hague could have shown Trollope's intuitive side without simply ignoring what would problematize such a view of him. This unnuanced misreading is a minor flaw, but I dwell on it at length because it is indicative of a sort of mistake Hague makes a few times (248 n., 298-99, 299 n.).

Overwhelmingly, however, this prodigious procession of authorial confessions is effective, and is essential for the rest of the book, where four novelists are placed in the context of their aesthetic heritage. An understanding of intuitive consciousnesses in the early stages of literary creation helps us to understand the literal ways in which intuition can be sensibly interpreted *in these texts*. This is not intentional fallacy, I think, but rather offers a seldom-considered context for regarding such emphasis given to unconscious experience, and argues that such a view is at least possible for both writers and readers of these texts.

The next two chapters explore the fictions of Charlotte Brontë and Henry James. Hague does remarkable work about the former in arguing that the intuitional and outright paranormal events in *Jane Eyre* should not be theorized, psychologized, or otherwise explained away, but read as sincere expressions of intuitional thought. The much-maligned "mysterious summons" from Rochester that Jane Eyre manages, in all material improbability, to hear is shown in a context that makes compelling sense, despite many contemporary responses that make that portion of the narrative seem inexplicable. With a disarming simplicity, Hague tells us, "it is what it is" (141). As for James, Hague surveys his abundant prefaces and essays on writing, tracing how the themes of these early, indistinct, unconscious impulses that arrive at the beginning of the creative process span all his plots, becoming increasingly important over time, especially in the almost inconceivable cerebrations of his late fictions, which, according to her reading, struggle between the language of the traditional novel and the undiscovered language necessary to express nonrational consciousness accurately, and fully.

Virginia Woolf, she argues, found that language. Hague's excellent chapter on Woolf begins with a methodical defense of her dependence on the nonrationality and dissolution of ego associated with intuitive modes of creativity. If we have read Hague's second chapter, then what Woolf says about the yielding of her ego, of rejecting the reductiveness of rationality, of dissolving mental boundaries between herself and her characters, all sounds very familiar, and not especially extreme. Yet this almost common discourse about her creativity, present in her diaries, letters, and personal essays, has too often been used as if it were extraordinary evidence for theorists in pathologizing Woolf and her writing, thus denigrating her artistic genius as, among other things, a death-wish. (Because T. S. Eliot did not take his own life, his own famous discussion of the need to "escape from personality" [58] generally escapes academic condescension or psychic foreboding.) Similarly, Woolf's ceding of conscious control over her creative output has also been sometimes interpreted by feminists as revelatory of either Woolf's victimization as a woman, or else as evidence of the essentially intuitive nature of womanhood itself—both of which seem, again, to place a narrow, particular emphasis on the generalities of her understanding of her own gifts that are consistent with that of the wide array of authors of both genders that appear in chapter two. After establishing Woolf's own testimony about the origins of her writing, Hague argues that Woolf, in an evolution of the novel form as altered by Henry James, not only makes intuition central to the commencement of literary endeavor, but throughout her career, "embeds the creative process in the content and structure of her novels with increasing skill, making intuitive thought processes an integral part of her modernist experiments with fictional form" (229).

These experiments consist of the use of only partly understood symbols for the levels of consciousness, such as the lighthouse in *To the Lighthouse*, or the fin in *The Waves*, and an emphasis on the permeability between consciousnesses, described in *The Voyage Out* as a sort of dreaming out into a collective unconscious, but becoming more and more important to how Woolf's characters relate to one another as her career as a novelist progresses. Thus Hague traces a sort of lineage from Rachel Vinrace to Clarissa Dalloway to Mrs. Ramsay. Of particular merit is the illumination she provides for the latter, in remarkable readings of the "wedge-shaped core of darkness" passage (244-45) and the interior dialogues of the dinner scene, in which Mrs. Ramsay serves as a sort of psychic medium facilitating unspoken communication (248-53). Hague demonstrates that as Woolf translates nonverbal communication as if it was dialogue, and almost confusingly alters the thoughts of one sentence from one character to another character, "the reader becomes comfortably submerged in silent exchanges of thoughts and the relegation of spoken language to irrelevant asides" (251). *The Waves*, in Hague's view, represents a profound amplification of this intuitive mode of fiction, as the novel consists almost entirely of interior dialogues. With this radical experiment, in which "narrative" itself is utterly marginalized, Woolf was realizing what she had been attempting as early as *The Voyage Out*: to avoid the necessary, arbitrary falsifications and oversimplifications of the world necessary to express anything resembling the common form of a story.

By strictly focusing on the internal relationship between her characters, Woolf seemed at least in part to face the interconnectedness of her mental illness and her creativity. Hague cites a diary entry in which Woolf speculates about the metaphorical "screens" that people erect between one another, a maneuver that limits our sympathy, but also, in Woolf's words, "probably ... preserves our sanity" (264). *The Waves*, by its very "form," shows characters in a screenless existence, a psychically-exposed situation that causes varying reactions from the six characters, including—besides the emotional resistance of Neville and Louis, the fearless physicality of Jinny, the maternal selflessness of Susan—the painful, psychological vulnerability of Rhoda and the aesthetic elation of Bernard. In discussing Woolf's illness, Hague is more aesthetic than clinical in arguing that Woolf identifies with both Rhoda and Bernard, but more so with Bernard—the character whose sense of aesthetics can appreciate the loss of self that constantly occurs in the novel. This portraiture depicts Woolf the writer as someone who knew her illness, and was conscious enough to use that understanding to enhance her aesthetics and epistemology rather than devalue everything she experienced during her bouts of illness.

While Hague is an especially insightful reader of Brontë, James, and Woolf, she is less persuasive, at least, with Doris Lessing. The emphasis in this chapter is on Lessing's speculative fiction, especially the Canopean saga—a series about an ideal, intuitionally-attuned race whose ontological purpose is to encourage the inferior remainder of the universe's creatures to become less wretched. Against a veritable host of detractors of this fiction, Hague (again) levels a vague defense of Lessing, and seems genuinely unaware of the moral and mental condescension implicit in the idea that the imaginary ideal race of Canopeans is in exclusive and permanent possession of intuitive consciousness.

If in her enthusiasm to "trust the tellers" Hague seems a tad too credulous to converse with those hostile to Lessing's later work, nevertheless *Fiction, Intuition, & Creativity* generally offers a surprisingly substantial contribution to the understanding of the role intuition plays in the genesis of literary composition, and in understanding the role that intuition plays in literary texts themselves.

—John King, *Florida Atlantic University*

Works Cited

Eliot, T. S. "Tradition and the Individual Talent." *The Sacred Wood.* London: Routledge, 1989: 47-59.

Trespassing Boundaries: Virginia Woolf's Short Fiction. Eds. Kathryn N. Benzel and Ruth Hoberman (NY: Palgrave Macmillan, 2004) 223pp.

Writing to Ethel Smyth in 1930 Woolf describes the stories collected in *Monday or Tuesday* as "mere tangles of words," "little pieces ... written by way of diversion ... treats," written in "all in a flash," "wild outbursts of freedom, inarticulate, ridiculous, unprintable mere outcries" (*L*4 231). It seems that earlier critics of her writing have taken these flippant assessments as a cue for how to respond to these short works. However, Woolf's response to the rejection of her first short story, "Memoirs of a Novelist," in 1909 by the editor of the *Cornhill* magazine is perhaps a better indication of the importance she attached to her short fictions: as Susan Dick notes in her Foreword to *Trespassing Boundaries*, Woolf immediately stopped reviewing for *Cornhill* (xv). As critical work on Woolf's short fiction develops, it is clear that not only did she take this writing seriously, but also that it was crucial to the development of her career. The fact that Woolf wrote, revised, reviewed and discussed short stories throughout her life demonstrates further the importance of this genre to her writing life both creatively and materially. It was, of course, the publication of her story "The Mark on the Wall" with Leonard Woolf's "Three Jews" that formed the first publication from the Hogarth Press, *Two Stories* (1917). The commercial success of this not only ensured the Press could develop and go on to provide Woolf with the security of an avenue for publication, but also helped consolidate her professional identity by leading to other commissions.[1] As Kathryn Benzel and Ruth Hoberman suggest in their introduction to this collection, the Hogarth Press "with its laboriously handset type, encouraged the writing not only of experimental, but also of *short* fiction by Woolf herself and by her friends" (3).

Further, writing "The Mark on the Wall" was both a "treat" whilst writing the longer fiction *Night and Day*, and a radical departure from the more conventional form of her first two novels. This story is now perceived as a work in its own right, a landmark of formal and aesthetic innovation vital to Woolf's literary and professional development. However, such recognition of the importance of Woolf's experiments and innovations in this genre, and the consideration of the centrality of Woolf's short fictions to her development as a modernist writer, form a relatively new critical perspective. In the past, critical evaluations of her *oeuvre* have sidelined and overlooked her short works (in keeping with a sense of the short story as a marginal genre more generally). *Trespassing Boundaries* is the first collection of essays devoted to Woolf's short fiction and marks a major step in this process of re-evaluation and appreciation of the diversity and complexity of Woolf's short fiction.

Avrom Fleishman's essay "Forms of the Woolfian Short Story" (1980) was perhaps the first to view Woolf's short fictions as works in their own right, to begin to identify their formal qualities and developments over time, and to locate them in a specific moment of change and experiment in the short story genre. Importantly, he criticized approaches to Woolf's short fictions which treated them simply as reference points, drafts and prototypes for her longer, supposedly more important works. Since then several critics have taken up the challenge of reading Woolf's short fictions as works in their own right, with their own formal experiments and thematic concerns. This process of re-evaluation has been made possible by the development of a new critical and theoretical interest in the short story genre over the last twenty years or so and, crucially, by the watershed publication of Susan Dick's *Virginia Woolf: The Complete Shorter Fiction* (1985). Collecting together the relatively small number of stories Woolf published in her lifetime, along with posthumously published and previously unpublished stories, sketches and drafts with details of writing and publication,

[1] These were "An Unwritten Novel" published in *London Mercury* in July 1920, and "Solid Objects" published in *Athenaeum* in October 1920 (as Dick notes, xvi).

Dick's collection opened up exciting possibilities for exploring the processes of creation and for tracing interconnections and thematic concerns across the stories.

Trespassing Boundaries is the first collection of essays fully to capitalize on the possibilities Dick's work has opened up, and the editors acknowledge the essays as "an attempt to come to terms with Dick's edition" (2). The essays in this collection more than adequately "come to terms" with the diversity of Woolf's short fictions. Although the tendency to see the short stories as limbering exercises for the challenges of the longer works lingers very occasionally even here, this in no way detracts from the main objective of this collection. Ranging across the whole of Woolf's short fiction *oeuvre*, contributors offer fresh insights on those stories already given critical attention, and original readings of the many under-explored stories. Woolf's description of the differences between men's and women's writing in her essay "Women Novelists" in terms of the "infinite differences in selection, method and style" usefully sums up not only her own short fictions as explored here, but also the wide range of critical and theoretical approaches taken by the contributors to this collection (71). Their essays provide a rich context for new readings of Woolf's work, drawing on her diaries, letters, essays, biographies, longer fictions, and on the contemporary literary, social, political and cultural contexts in which she produced her works.

Taking as a starting point Woolf's advice in her essay "The Leaning Tower" to "trespass freely and fearlessly" throughout literature (qtd. 1), the essays explore the various trespasses and transgressions Woolf's stories make. They focus on the ways Woolf's stories question any single, simplifying definition of the short story as they cross generic boundaries, resist formal expectations, and "rouse the reader to participate in the making of textual meaning" so that each reading produces a different text (6). The book is organized broadly into two parts. The first, "The Modernist Context," locates Woolf's short fictions in the context of the "wave of experimentation in British short fiction" at the turn of the century (3), and in relation to broader cultural, economic and technological changes of this period. The second part, "Crossing Generic Boundaries," explores more fully the interconnections and intersections of Woolf's short fiction with other genres, media and visual art forms, questioning and subverting established notions of the short story.

Ruth Hoberman's essay locates four of Woolf's stories in the context of a burgeoning commodity culture about which Woolf felt so ambivalent. Perceiving in Woolf's writing two contrasting attitudes to Modernist art (encapsulated in the role of the collector seeking to own objects and fix value and the shopper at ease with shifting spectacle and negotiated values), her essay persuasively argues for a position which trespasses the literary "great divide" by revealing Woolf's valuing of her writing as both Art and a commodity to be marketed. The emphasis on the role of the reader is a thread running throughout the collection and here Hoberman argues that Woolf "redefines the act of reading as a kind of shopping" (81). Others similarly suggest several ways in which this important role seems to be reconceptualized in Woolf's short stories (Benzel and Colburn for instance). For Nena Škrbić Woolf's emphasis on the reader's role in interpretation is part of the Russian influence on the development of Woolf's aesthetic and intellectual concerns.

Across the collection there is a focus on the many ways in which Woolf adapts, manipulates and transforms the short story, a genre already very much in transition. Nena Škrbić's essay carefully traces the formal and aesthetic influence of Russian writers, especially Chekhov, on the changing conceptions and formal developments of the modernist short story in Britain. Through detailed intertextual readings of three stories by Woolf, Chekhov, and Brussof, her essay successfully demonstrates the values and techniques they share. The qualities that distinguish Chekhov's stories as outlined and explored in Škrbić's essay—extreme brevity, compression, omission, ambiguity and ephemeral moments, and the attempt to articulate the unspeakable—inform critical perspectives in other readings in this collection. For instance, as a lesbian reader, Krystyna Colburn explores these qualities in relation to the suggestion of unspoken, or barely articulated lesbian eroticism across the breadth of Woolf's short fiction. Her essay identifies numerous strategies employed to suggest lesbian desire, but considers also the masking of lesbian passion as drafts get closer to publication.

One or two of the essays here tend to be a little over-descriptive at times, and despite the argument Levy puts forward for the inclusion of *Flush*, I feel this might be pushing the definition of "short fiction" a little too far—even given Woolf's transformations of the genre! One of the major strengths of this collection, however, is the way that these essays speak to and debate with one another, generating multiple, distinctive and sometimes overlapping interpretations. For instance, Colburn's reading of the natural world of "Kew Gardens" as replete with sensual lesbian imagery differs radically from Michelle Levy's reading in the second part of this collection, which focuses on the ways Woolf's story decenters human experience and explores the sometimes blurred relationship between the human and non-human world. Both of these readings also differ from that offered by Alice Staveley for whom "Kew Gardens" is an articulation of domestic and public oppressions in relation to class, gender and sexuality. Staveley's feminist narratological reading focuses attention on the conversations, which tend to be overlooked in critical assessments of this story, and argues that these encode Woolf's criticism of the interconnected oppressions of marriage, class, and war in a patriarchal society.

As she explores the publication history of "Kew Gardens" and its critical reception, Staveley also demonstrates the specific connections to be made between Woolf's experimental fiction and her first experimental novel, *Jacob's Room*, as well as with later works, *To the Lighthouse* and *Three Guineas*. These kinds of interconnections are what Beth Rigel Daugherty explores in more detail as she reveals an interactive, two-way process, Woolf's idea of a "corridor," of creative generation between the stories Woolf wrote after *Mrs. Dalloway* and *To the Lighthouse*. Not only does this reading offer further insights into Woolf's highly innovative genre-bending practices, inviting us to "question the nature of 'genre,'" but crucially shows how her fictions function simultaneously as product and process, generating creativity "on a continuum of fiction making" (120). Both Staveley and Daugherty specifically read Woolf's literary innovations and the erosion of generic boundaries and hierarchies as synonymous with Woolf's political challenges to class and gender hierarchies, and it is this perspective from which Anna Snaith also reads Woolf's earliest stories. She stresses the importance of these critically under-explored stories for Woolf's development of what she called in a 1927 review, "new biography" (Woolf, cited 128). Paying attention to the personal, professional and broader cultural influences on Woolf's writing, Snaith argues that the hybridity of form that Woolf develops in these early stories is crucial to her rethinking of ways to represent women's experience, lives and history.

Kathryn Benzel extends this idea of generic hybridity and trespass across boundaries to focus on the interaction and interrelation of the verbal and visual arts in the only collection of Woolf's stories published in her lifetime, *Monday or Tuesday*. Woolf's close connections with Vanessa Bell, Roger Fry, Clive Bell, and Duncan Grant and her lifelong interest in the visual arts and the interdisciplinary possibilities of art and writing provide the context for Benzel's engaging exploration of Woolf's lyrical strategies for representing human consciousness. Employing metaphors and concepts drawn from the visual arts, Benzel argues that Woolf creates a new intensity of relationship between reader and narrator in which "the act of reading" is reconceived as "a visionary moment" (164). Julia Briggs is also interested in Woolf's sense of the "sudden intensities" of writing short fiction (qtd. 175) and her interaction with the visual arts. Briggs considers the stories Woolf wrote from 1929 onwards in relation to Woolf's novels of this period and to the specific context of writing, and in particular to Woolf's more general preoccupations with the "conceptual problems" of "the relation of experience to imagination, and the crystallization of meaning, both in the mind and in a work of art" (176).

It is indeed these concerns—"as much philosophical as political or psychological"—and the importance of the imagination for knowing and feeling which

Joanne Trautmann Banks's 1985 essay highlights at the beginning of this collection. Banks's essay begins with a reading of "The Searchlight" and this seems an apt starting point for her study which spotlights some of the thematic, generic and political issues which this impressive new collection more fully illuminates. In sum, this collection successfully "light[s] a torch" in the relatively unexplored "chamber" of a woman's writing that we thought we knew so well (*AROO* 80). With insight, creativity, imagination and pleasure these essays have "lighted on small things and showed that perhaps they [are] not small after all" (*AROO* 88).

—Kathryn Simpson, *University of Birmingham, UK.*

Works Cited

Woolf, Virginia. "Women Novelists." In Michèle Barrett, ed. *Women and Writing.* London: The Women's Press, 1979.

—. *A Room of One's Own.* London: Grafton, 1979.

—. *The Letters of Virginia Woolf. Volume 4: 1929 - 1931.* Ed. Nigel Nicolson and Joanne Trautmann Banks. London: Hogarth Press, 1978.

Virginia Woolf. Michael Whitworth (Oxford: Oxford University Press, 2005). xvii + 268 pp.

Mr. Ramsay, Virginia Woolf's philosopher-patriarch in *To the Lighthouse*, famously devotes his life to understanding "subject and object and the nature of reality." These three concerns, suggests Michael Whitworth in this fine study, lie at the heart of Woolf's own literary and critical *oeuvre*. Whitworth's book—a new addition to Oxford's Authors in Context series—balances historical narrative with philosophical concepts to situate Virginia Woolf amidst the political, scientific, medical, and literary dialogues of her lifetime. As Whitworth guides readers through several decades of cultural change, he describes Woolf principally as a novelist of ideas; his commendable emphasis on intellectual development rather than private experiences produces a fresh portrait of Woolf and her multi-faceted contributions to English letters. Whitworth maintains that

Woolf's explorations of "subject and object and the nature of reality" arise from a complex interleaving of cultural discourses, and his book's accessible treatment of those discourses makes it a valuable resource for the study of Woolf, modernist literature, and British history.

Virginia Woolf begins with the historical-biographical claim that "The 'Britain' in which Virginia Woolf died was not the same nation in which Virginia Stephen had been born" (31), and Whitworth's seven-chapter analysis of Woolf's artistry takes its shape from the complex cultural transitions that rocked Britain between the fin-de-siècle and the Second World War. The opening chapter, a concise biographical narrative of Woolf's life, describes Woolf's departure from the world of Victorian propriety and her subsequent work as an influential maker of experimental modernism. Whitworth explores the privileges and problems of Woolf's lineage, calls attention to her independence and intelligence, and offers miniature portraits of the 'Bloomsburyites' and public figures who surrounded her until her death. Biographical evidence anchors the history of each of Woolf's novels; Whitworth covers familiar territory as he explains that Woolf memorialized her parents in *To the Lighthouse*, that Vita Sackville-West inspired *Orlando*, and that the ghost of Thoby Stephen haunts *Jacob's Room* and *The Waves*. Although Woolf scholars will find few surprises here (except, perhaps, for Whitworth's refusal to believe that Gerald Duckworth abused the young Virginia Stephen, or his claim that Woolf intended Septimus Smith to be Clarissa Dalloway's illegitimate son), this chapter's summation of key moments in Woolf's career is notable for its refusal to sensationalize or sentimentalize Woolf's madness, sexuality, or suicide. Whitworth's engaging, pithy opening chapter leads into a history of early 20th-century Britain that explains imperial politics, labor politics, industrial production, women's suffrage, the English educational system, and the Great War. This wealth of clear, well-organized information will be especially welcome for American students unfamiliar with the larger social world into which Woolf delivered her writings.

Following his broad-based overview of British society, Whitworth trains his focus on the dynamic literary *milieux* in which Woolf emerged as an author and publisher. "The Literary Scene," this study's most intellectually satisfying chapter, describes the Hogarth Press's simultaneously anti-institutional and institutional influence over the world of modern literature. Whitworth investigates the shifting terrain of literary production between the fin-de-siècle and the early 20th century, drawing on Woolf's 1924 essay "The Patron and the Crocus" to explain how modern writers reacted against a late-19th-century readership whose tastes had been shaped by serialized fiction and Mudie's Select Library. The challenge that confronted Woolf and other modernists, Whitworth argues, was to avoid writing literature for mass audiences but to nevertheless safeguard literature's relevance for the world that those audiences inhabited. Modernist writers met this challenge through formal experimentation: the new modes and genres pioneered by Woolf, Eliot, and Pound "could engage with the world while maintaining a critical distance from it and from mere literary entertainments" (75). Whitworth traces Woolf's hallmark revisions to the *Bildungsroman*, the marriage-plot, the novel of adultery, and the biography—forms popularized for middle-class readers in the second half of the 19th century—and argues that modernism's radical new genres demanded the autonomy supplied by independent or avant-garde publishers. The Hogarth Press, founded at a moment when Woolf and her contemporaries sought alternatives to popular realism, substantially altered both the aesthetics and the market economics of English literary tradition. This chapter's elegant blend of factual information (e.g., the sales of Woolf's novels; changes in copyright law; censorship cases) and textual analysis (especially of *Orlando* and its critique of the publishing industry) illuminates the ways in which Woolf re-made the "subject and object" of modern literature and, simultaneously, altered "the nature of reality" for literary production.

Whitworth suggests that Woolf's re-invention of subjects, objects and reality "borrows eclectically from various disciplines" (182). The foundational questions of her fiction reflect an awareness of similarly foundational questions in modern-era philosophy, sociology, medicine, and science. Whitworth's sophisticated explanation of the Bergsonian distinction between *temps* and *durée*–that is, between clock—time and psychological time—leads into an analysis of the tension between fragment and flow that characterizes Woolf's writing. This tension (which pervades not only Woolf's depictions of time but also of politics, history, art, and intimacy) stems from an obsession with the profound differences between group identity and individual identity. In a volatile historical epoch when the relationship between the imperial nation-state and its citizens was repeatedly thrown into question, Woolf devised methods for portraying reality that resisted British cultural conventions of hierarchy and linearity. Whitworth argues that Woolf found meaning in the French doctrine of unanimism, which offered a language to describe "group consciousness"—that is, a conflict-free collective social identity not prescribed by the rules of religion, nation, or family. Unanimism is the philosophy behind the social merging that occurs in Mrs. Dalloway's party and Mrs. Ramsay's dinner; it is the concept that explains the simultaneous connectedness and separateness of the six characters in *The Waves*. Whitworth also ties Woolf's investigations of connection and separation to fast-proliferating developments in 20th-century physics, evolutionary theory, eugenics, and astronomy. Concrete developments in the worlds of science and technology, he reveals, imprint themselves in the abstract "innumerable shower of atoms" through which Woolf transcribed lived experience.

This book's presentation of modern British literary and cultural history makes it a rich resource for Woolf scholars and an illuminating introduction for students. Whitworth supplements his wide-ranging arguments with numerous illustrations, a seven-page chronological chart of Woolf's life, and a well-selected bibliography; the book's historical breadth promises that it will hold its own next to other recent studies of Woolf. To be sure, Whitworth's *Virginia Woolf* is less exquisitely detailed than Hermione Lee's 1997 biography, and Whitworth does not offer the sustained readings of individual novels that one finds in recent work by Christine Froula and Julia Briggs. Nevertheless, this volume's delineation of Woolf's intellectual priorities provides an excellent entry-point into the formal accomplishments of her writings. Whitworth distinguishes himself from many Woolf scholars by refusing to pathologize Woolf's artistic goals and political convictions, demonstrating that her ideas developed as much through active engagement with the world around her as they did in reaction to domestic, familial, or social experiences. What is surprisingly absent from this study, however, is a discussion of Woolf and developments in the modernist arts. Whitworth provides a history of the modern British novel, but he does not address innovations in poetry, the performing arts, visual arts, or music. A full understanding of the "author in context," as the OUP series would have it, should include an account of the cultural spheres that swirled around Woolf: the rise of Imagism, Vorticism, and Futurism; Roger Fry's Omega Workshops; and the spectacular and influential performances of Diaghilev's Ballets Russes. Whitworth privileges social history to the near-exclusion of artistic history, a striking omission in an otherwise comprehensive study of Woolf.

This omission is somewhat compensated for by the book's final chapter, "Recontextualizing Virginia Woolf," which turns to Woolf's legacy in contemporary popular culture. Whitworth covers three cinematic adaptations of Woolf novels (Colin Gregg's BBC film *To the Lighthouse* [1983], Sally Potter's *Orlando* [1992], and Marleen Gorris's *Mrs. Dalloway* [1998]), as well as Eileen Atkins's stage performance in Patrick Garland's *A Room of One's Own* (1990) and Robin Lippincott's novel *Mr. Dalloway* (1999). His discussion of these texts leads, of course, to the two works through which readers and movie-goers have most recently encountered Virginia Woolf: Michael Cunningham's *The Hours* (1998) and Stephen Daldry's Oscar-winning 2002 cinematic adaptation of Cunningham's novel. Whitworth steers clear of indicting these two works–admirably, to my mind, as so many Woolf scholars have dismissed Cunningham and Daldry outright–and instead explores the simultaneously liberating and constraining process of literary adaptation. Channeling Woolf's own declarations in "Modern Fiction," Whitworth argues that today's artists may need to "break and bully" Woolf's literary principles to extend the creativity she so highly valued. *Virginia Woolf* concludes with these respectful words: "The creative interpreter may find him- or herself in Lily Briscoe's position towards Mrs Ramsay, wanting to remain faithful to the much-loved, much-admired forebear, while retaining his or her own personal and artistic independence; wanting to pay tribute to the power of Woolf's work, but also acknowledging her historical limitations, and, where necessary, overriding her wishes."

—Urmila Seshagiri, *University of Tennessee, Knoxville*

A Desire for Women: Relational Psychoanalysis, Writing, and Relationships between Women. Suzanne Juhasz (New Brunswick and London: Rutgers UP, 2003) 219pp.

Suzanne Juhasz's book focuses on writing and reading as a woman–that is, in her terms, as either a family member or a lover: mother, daughter, grandmother, lesbian. Juhasz's framework is derived from the British tradition of object relations theory inaugurated by Klein and Winnicott and probably most famously represented in this country by Jessica Benjamin (*The Bonds of Love*, *Like Subjects, Love Objects*). After the first chapter, in which Juhasz gives a useful and lucid exposition of relational psychoanalysis, albeit a gynocentric one, Juhasz's chapters are organized around writing that reflects the roles that women play in their families and erotic lives: daughter writing (Vivan Gornick, Dorothy Allison, Susannah Moore, and Woolf in chapters 2 and 3); mother writing (Mary Gordon, Toni Morrison, Liza Nelson in chapters 4 and 5); lesbian writing (Merle Woo, Thérèse Murdza, Judy Grahn and a number of other poets, Audre Lorde in chapters 6 & 7; women readers and women's memoir (Joan Gould in chapter 8). As this list of names makes clear, writing by well-recognized women writers such as Woolf and Morrison is linked to writing by contemporary writers who have not yet attained canonical status: Woo, Murdza, Gould. Juhasz's focus is not so much a newly definitive reading of any of her writers as an account of their work that grounds them in women's experience. Like Roberta Rubenstein's *Home Matters*, this is not a book about Woolf, but one that reads Woolf as one among many women writers.

In prefacing her book with her childhood memories of her mother in a section entitled "Memoirs of Mommy"—even in her use of the word mommy—Juhasz underlines her belief that the relation to the mother is "the formative relationship in our lives: powerfully important both in its own right and as it establishes a template for all of the loving relationships to come." Juhasz calls the mother-infant bond the "first romance" and quotes Jo March from *Little Women*: "Mothers are the best lovers in the world" (15). She then describes the inscription of a variety of mother/daughter relations in writing: writing by daughters for mothers, by mothers for daughters, by lesbians for their lovers and companions, by lesbian daughters for their mothers, and by women readers for women writers. All of these relations can be reimagined and reinvented in writing; all are modeled on that first crucial relationship of the infant to its mother.

Juhasz's argument aligns the psychic space of writing with the "transitional space" of object-relations psychoanalysis. This space is marked by the child's desire: she wishes to love and be loved, that is, to be recognized. Juhasz believes that recognition, analytic therapy, writing and reading function in analogous ways: all are fueled by desire and by language. Writing parallels the therapeutic encounter in that it rehearses and rehashes the central relation of child for mother and mother for child: desire and writing both involve the imaginative acknowledgment of an other by a speaking subject. For Juhasz the work of development that happens in the mother/infant pairing is the model for all later relationships, a belief she illustrates by beginning and ending her book with an account of the cards and letters she made as a child for her mother. (She reproduces some of these cards, which are quite wonderfully funny and affectionate.) Although she delineates different family roles for women, for Juhasz every woman writes about her mother as she herself does: the cards with which she begins her book reappear at the end, by which time she has "worked through" to a different appreciation of her own maternal dynamic.

Juhasz's reading of *To the Lighthouse* models her method. She focuses on Lily Briscoe's painting as a double for Woolf's relation to writing to the exclusion of any other thread in the novel. Where Elizabeth Abel's well known reading suggests that the novel enacts two competing versions of psychoanalysis by contrasting the Cam/James story to Lily Briscoe's, Juhasz reads the novel as entirely centered on Lily's painting: the search for the "wedge-shaped core of darkness" that represents Mrs. Ramsay. Using Benjamin's concept of attunement, a congruent joy in the moment shared by two separate consciousnesses (usually mother and child), Juhasz sees Lily's ability to finish her painting as directly related to her ability to "attune" rather than to possess. Lily's initial failure stems from her desire to locate Mrs. Ramsay in the same way that the child greedily wishes to possess the fantasmatic Mother. But Lily can only paint Mrs. Ramsay when she moves from the desire to be and to have the Mother to a nuanced understanding of Mrs. Ramsay as a person in and for herself. Lily's final achievement is possible because she is able to slip at the end of the novel into Mrs. Ramsay's role by having sympathy for Mr. Ramsay and his new boots. In that moment of attunement Lily comes to recognize Mr. Ramsay and through him finally to perceive Mrs. Ramsay. Lily's final achievement, "her vision," results from her ability to accept Mrs. Ramsay as an independent consciousness: reconceiving the maternal allows Lily finally to place Mrs. Ramsay in her long-delayed painting.

For Juhasz, Lily's moment of vision stands for Woolf's re-writing of her relation to her mother: "Art is what reproduces a pattern that is really there. Reality and art thus become versions of each other" (67). Illustrating her thesis by quotes from Woolf's "A Sketch of the Past" in which she describes her mother—"there she was, in the very centre of that great Cathedral space which was childhood; there she was from the first" (66)—Juhasz aligns Woolf's complicated relation to her mother to her character's complicated relation to Mrs. Ramsay. For Juhasz, Woolf's novel allows her to rewrite–to reimagine–herself as Lily, and in doing so to find an emotional distance that allows her, at least momentarily, to understand her mother: "Woolf's tale of how a woman could be an artist and a daughter . . . represents an attempt to change her lifelong obsession with her mother into a relationship (albeit in her art) which is more life giving" (69). In this account, only in recognizing and valuing the mother—"albeit in art"—can Woolf/Lily succeed in becoming an artist.

Juhasz's reading of Woolf is emblematic of her method. In each writer she discusses, art allows the writer to reconfigure the primary relationship of child to mother. Even the chapters on "mother" writing—that is, writing from the point of view of the mother (as opposed to Woolf/Lily, who look at the mother from the point of view of the child)—end up being chapters on the relation of child to mother because, for Juhasz, any mother must look to her relation to her mother in order to understand her relation to her child. This is writing as therapeutic intervention: "the space of writing can be seen . . . as a transitional or potential space. Here language's paradoxical ability to create a new kind of distance and a new kind of intimacy becomes of value for instituting change, or transformation" (26). In her final chapter the therapeutic effect of art is repeated for herself as a reader: Juhasz rehearses her own relation to Joan Gould's memoir, *Spirals*. Reading Gould becomes a method of working through for Juhasz: she creates a transferential relationship to Gould that allows her finally to return to the cards she wrote to her mother and create for herself a newer, more loving version of her mother.

In Juhasz's work, writing and reading are essentially therapeutic encounters in which the artist or reader returns to the initial relation to the mother in order to rehearse it, reimagine it, reinscribe it: she sees reading as an attempt to "mak[e] inroads in the world beyond the book" (218) at least in her own life. The effect of this move is to identify the situation of the woman writer with that of her creation: to cite only one instance, in her discussion of Morrison's *Beloved* Juhasz writes, "Sethe and her creator enable the repressed to be re-created and transcended" (118). The complete identification of the author and her work (fostered by the fact that many of the novels Juhasz discusses are first-person narratives) and the emphasis on the dynamics of the therapeutic situation lead to a peculiar flattening: differences are glossed over as novels and novelists are discussed purely in the language of personal growth and reconciliation. Lesbians, ex-slaves, grandmothers, run-away daughters, abused children—all are working through a primal relationship to maternity.

In tracing the importance of the mother in fiction Juhasz has ended with something approaching a highly literary self-help book. The personal "space of transition" becomes the be-all and end-all of writing: questions of art are subordinated to a problem in "relating." There is an almost medicinal element to her relation to literature: read this, think about it, and you'll feel better about your Mom and yourself. The assumption that what really matters in life is the acquisition of personal autonomy and self-satisfaction becomes, by the end, an exercise in narcissism. The cards to her mother that she reproduces are charming but also, finally, a little creepy. One can applaud a focus on maternity as an answer to, and perhaps antidote for, the years of focus on paternity without wishing for a mode of reading so closely focused on familial patterns. Perhaps, after all, it's time to leave home?

—Margaret Bruzelius, *Smith College*

The Intersecting Realities and Fictions of Virginia Woolf and Colette. Helen Southworth (Columbus: The Ohio State University Press, 2004) xii + 240 pp.

Virginia Woolf had strong affinities with France and French writers and her work was quickly translated and appreciated in France. Woolf was Francophile with a keen interest in and enjoyment of artistic and literary developments across the channel; thus, her works, letters, and diaries provide fertile ground for numerous comparative studies within a variety of broader contexts too–feminist, lesbian/gay studies, modernist women's writing and more. Helen Southworth's study develops these comparative possibilities through her consideration of social, personal and textual connections between Woolf and her French contemporary, Colette. Parallels between the two writers have been recognized but not explored for a number of reasons Southworth lists but then refutes. This forms the main thrust of her thesis, that the apparent differences between the two writers, "social and educational, geographic and linguistic [,]... provide the foundation of a study of the two writers and their work" (9). Difference is in fact key to the analysis:

> It is at those moments where the two bodies of work, the two agendas, the two writing styles come momentarily together and then veer off in different directions that provide the most fruitful insights. It is in those places where the work of the one bridges the gaps in the work of the other that connections might be made. Such an approach enables a redrawing of the map on which the literary and biographical voyages of Woolf and Colette have been traced. Rather than locate each writer simply within her particular national, cultural, and geographical setting, this study resituates the writer and in so doing raises questions about style, themes, and influence that have yet to be explored. (9)

Pinpointing and tracking these moments of intersection, Southworth creates a broad literary, historical, biographical and cultural canvas on which to redraw this map, and the presence of quotations from Colette in the original as well as in translation (often by the author), adds to the richness of the material. At the same time, reading Colette and Woolf through these momentary intersections makes for a study that is at once diverse, (from outlining the web of friendships and literary connections that link the two writers to a discussion images of food and sex in their writing), but also at times fragmented.

The iconic portraits and photographs of Woolf and Colette by Jacques-Emile Blanche and Gisele Freund, respectively, that Southworth includes at the outset of her study, establish quite clearly many of the connections she goes on to examine in the first two chapters of the book. The network of friends and mutual acquaintances the two writers shared is shown to be extensive, crossing national, social and sexual boundaries through travel, letters and the visual arts. The relationships between this diverse collection of mainly Anglo-American writers, some self-exiled to the more bohemian and liberal Paris, form a network "that informs the relationship between contemporary French and English literary cultures" (29). Ethel Smyth, Vita Sackville West, Violet Trefusis, Winnie de Polignac, Anna de Noailles, Radclyffe Hall, Una Troubridge, Sylvia Beach and Adrienne Monnier are all shown to be part of what is described as "a paper trail, in French and in English, that leads from Woolf to Colette and from Colette to Woolf" (11). The connection traced between Woolf and Colette is never direct–it is likely that they never met, although Woolf certainly read Colette and she writes about her in numerous letters to friends. Sending messages to each other through friends rather than meeting or writing, the relationship is characterized by coyness and evasiveness, an unspoken dialogue that once listened to, opens up multiple possibilities for a comparative reading.

The discussion of Woolf's *A Room of One's Own* and Colette's *Le Pur* that follows this carefully worked out web that is textual and social, reveals most clearly some of the problems that can arise in comparative studies. Apart from having to summarize both texts in perhaps more detail than is necessary because there are two different audiences that need to be catered to, this chapter is also the most speculative about the connections between the two writers, creating analytical gaps and tensions. For example, Southworth begins the chapter pointing out the lack of evidence as to whether Colette read Woolf's work, but argues that an analysis of *Le Pur* will show it to be a possible response to *A Room.* The intertextual and interpersonal connections between these texts are meticulously worked out, however, as they are elsewhere in this book – *Le Pur* includes an account of the Ladies of Llangollen, "two English women of wealthy families who eloped together and set up home in rural Wales in the eighteenth century" (36), a story that Woolf was also familiar with and referred to in her writing. Radclyffe Hall and Una Troubridge, friends of Colette's who introduced her to the story of the Ladies of Llangollen, may also have given her a copy of Woolf's *A Room.* From here the speculation ceases and *A Room* is discussed as if Colette definitely had read it. "Colette 'translates' Lady Eleanor's diaries quite liberally into her native language as she translates Woolf's *A Room*" (938-39) and "what draws Colette to *A Room* is the unsaid, the gaps, ellipses, and prohibitions in the text" (40). This slippage is unfortunate, since the comparative discussion of the two texts that follows would be just as interesting in the more speculative mode, perhaps more so.

Comparisons of the two texts are more successful when, in Chapter Three, Southworth examines Woolf and Colette's treatment of space and writing. Like

Woolf, "Colette uses the concept of space, both physical and textual, in her novels to raise questions about where a woman stands in relation to the literary tradition in which she writes" (74). Most usefully, Southworth chooses to read Colette's writing through the lens of Woolf's treatment of space, raising a set of specific questions about Colette's work, most importantly for this study, "in what sense does Colette's work provide a response to Woolf's call for a woman's sentence?" (75). Woolf's response to Colette is more easy to trace, her letters recording her enthusiasm for her French contemporary, describing her writing in special terms: "a shape I haven't grasped" and "a new combination" (75). As Southworth suggests earlier, Woolf was never threatened by Colette's writing (as she was arguably by the work of both James Joyce and Katherine Mansfield), finding her achievements invigorating, her differences and similarities safely enticing.

Reading Woolf and Colette's earliest novels together in Chapter Four makes for a revealing discussion of connecting intersections that also link them to other first novels by women writers of this period—semi-autobiographical works, absent mothers and an erratic education through books and surrogate parents. Of particular interest to Woolfian readers is the analysis of *The Voyage Out* in this chapter, where the significance of father figures in Woolf's first novel and four of Colette's *Claudine* novels is considered. Here "the father as an at least temporarily constructive figure" is argued for, "one who provides the daughter with access to a tradition otherwise closed to her" (96), in opposition to most feminist treatments of Woolf's novel. Southworth's discussion about the variety of father figures and consideration of difficult parent-child relations in the novel provides a unique critical perspective and much persuasive material. More controversially, she argues that "it is the realization of the permanence of the father's absence, because she will marry Hewett and live away from the father, that results in Rachel's illness" (109).

The final two chapters, one on literary reception and one comparing recurring preoccupations and connections between sex, food and writing in their work, diverge somewhat from the textual comparisons of the earlier chapters. That French women writers have consistently appreciated Woolf more than the British and that Colette has been admired more thoroughly across the channel is revealed in an outline of contemporary and later French and English writers who have written against them, in response to these two national icons. For scholars interested particularly in literary reception, intertextuality and "the anxiety of influence," the ways in which a diversity of women writers, some of whom knew Colette and Woolf personally, have responded to their work, are usefully outlined. Dorothy Richardson, Rebecca West, Muriel Spark, Doris Lessing and Angela Carter are discussed and shown to have "turned away from their predecessor, characterizing her work as detached, elitist, and inaccessible" (119). Likewise, "In the 1930s and on, French writers like Marguerite Yourcenar, Nathalie Sarraute, Simone de Beauvoir, and Marguerite Duras rejected their maternal foremother as representing and perpetuating the image of a certain France to which they felt they did not belong" (120-121). At the same time, writers' responses to literary predecessors cannot be so clear cut, and Southworth touches on the some of the complexities of these literary responses to Woolf and Colette. Rebecca West, for example, who wrote some of the first admiring reviews of Woolf's *A Room* and *Orlando*, is much more critical of her writing and of Bloomsbury itself, fifty years later. West's admiration for Colette is less ambivalent. Angela Carter was clearly influenced by Virginia Woolf, but she is the most forthright among more recent writers in her criticism. Despite Julia Kristeva's recent efforts to celebrate Colette and Jeanette Winterson's overt identification with Woolf, declaring herself "Woolf's natural heir" (143), Southworth concedes that both Colette's French successors and Woolf's English successors "celebrate the foreign voice. Geographically, socially, and politically freer, the foreign writer is less clearly defined as one thing or another, less predictable, and more mysterious than one's own foremother" (143).

The chapter on food, sex and writing in Colette and Woolf is a particularly suggestive one, introducing again the idea of an unspoken dialogue between the two writers, Colette filling the gap left by Woolf by not writing about the body in *A Room*. The exploration of connections between food and seduction in Woolf's texts raises more comparative and intertextual possibilities too. Curiously, the concluding proposal here that "reading Woolf's work alongside Colette's makes Woolf's work more palatable, more accessible" (147) seems to reinforce in the end some of the stereotypes about Woolf (effete, blue stocking, ethereal) that this study sets out to question.

But reading together two apparently very different writers—different because of their social background, culture and language—foregrounds the web of cross channel connections that form the unspoken dialogue between these two writers, as well as reinforcing, separately and together, the rich literary legacy of Woolf and Colette. This careful and very informative study of intersecting realities and fictions will also encourage Woolf scholars to read more Colette, and Colette scholars to search out more Woolf.

— Kathryn Laing, *National University of Ireland, Galway*

The Artist, Society & Sexuality in Virginia Woolf's Novels. Ann Ronchetti (New York & London: Routledge, 2004) 230 pp.

After reading Ann Ronchetti's monograph, I couldn't help but think of "Blue & Green," the prose-poem in which Woolf meditates on the many shapes those colors take in nature, dissolving form into form, sea monster to fish scale to bluebell. Ronchetti's subject is not color, but the artist, a figure that likewise appears and recedes, shifts shape, and diffuses across multiple characters in any one novel of Woolf's oeuvre. In other words, the artist in Woolf's works is a challenging figure to delineate, especially within the confines of academic exposition, but Ronchetti's *The Artist, Society & Sexuality* admirably rises to that challenge. Indeed, as labile and shifty as Woolf's artist-figures are, Ronchetti offers a central thesis to guide us in these waters: that Woolf's novels search out an "optimal relationship" between artists and the world (11), and that over time her artist-figures move away from "living and working in isolation" to "plying one's art while living among them," positions which Ronchetti terms "the Ivory Tower" and "the Sacred Fount," respectively (131). This thesis is not without its qualifications: though Woolf's artist-figures are increasingly enmeshed with the social world, they are also increasingly "outsider" figures. Yet, as Ronchetti explains, this is no paradox: even as outsiders, Woolf's artist-figures are not withdrawn into the exile of the "Ivory Tower," but rather engaged in the position of the anonymous observer (15).

The book is organized into eleven chapters, each covering one of Woolf's major novels from *The Voyage Out* to *Between the Acts*. The virtue of this organization is that most every chapter offers a discrete and well-managed reading which situates the artist-figure amidst a novel's more general themes. You could send a student or colleague to Ronchetti's book if they wished to quickly orient themselves on what any one novel means; and because the artist-figure is entwined with so many important motifs of Woolf's novels, Ronchetti's more topic-limited readings are still useful to the general reader. Ronchetti is very aware of the scholarship already produced on the topic of Woolf and creativity, and her footnotes are generous, quoting extensively from secondary sources and carefully noting her indebtedness to and difference from others; the bibliography likewise is an asset to the scholar who plans to take up the topic. Each chapter ponders just which of a novel's characters qualify as artist-figures, and how far they succeed in living this vocation: what routs these characters are social pressures (to be mothers, to serve the Empire) and sexual pressures (to be wives, lovers, companions). As one might suspect from this description, for Ronchetti the social and the sexual are on the same continuum; at times I wondered if it was "sociability" (rather than "society & sexuality") that would have better served the monograph's interests, as the term encompasses both the acceptance and exclusion of others (a faculty essential to Ronchetti's artist-figure), and reaches across the realms of the public, private, and intimate. Whatever terms we choose, it is clear that Woolf's novels are preoccupied with the stymied creativity that pervades "this late age of the world's experience" and especially with that of women.

Ronchetti meditates fully on how each of Woolf's major novels explore the constraints put upon sensitive, creative, and crafty persons. Even *Jacob's Room*, which has no meaningful artist-figure in it (as Ronchetti notes, 42), tells us much about Woolf's vexed attempt to find an "optimal relationship" between the artist and society: in that chapter, Ronchetti implicitly reads Woolf herself as the artist-figure who aims to capture the perfect youth Jacob represents, as artists like Keats have before her, and at the same time, to lament the death which ironically preserves that perfection. This is hard work for the artist, made harder by the pressing need to criticize the warring society that killed Jacob; fittingly, the novel is strewn with (other) unfulfilled women. In *Mrs. Dalloway*, by contrast, nearly every major and minor character qualifies as an artist-figure. Clarissa, Peter, and Septimus all struggle to be artists against the demands put upon them by family, nation, and empire; the woman here manages better because her creativity has been channeled in socially appropriate ways. The most sustained of Ronchetti's interpretations center on *To the Lighthouse* and *Between the Acts*, as each novels' primary artist-figure (Lily Briscoe and Miss LaTrobe) are women who physically, emotionally, intellectually succeed at bringing her vision before the world. And yet, it was in the *To the Lighthouse* chapter that the monograph's broad definition of the artist-figure turned into a troubling polymorphism. Although Ronchetti is very sensitive and nuanced in her readings of character and point of view, it seemed to me that Lily Briscoe's status is somehow impoverished by also viewing Mrs. Ramsay's "visual pleasure in Rose's arrangement of fruit" as a form of artistry (68). However, I was fascinated by Ronchetti's discussion of how Lily's formalist approach in particular allowed her to thwart the demands of emotional life aroused and made by the Ramsays. The same chapter also showcases what is a secondary interest of Ronchetti's: how the popular image of the late Victorian aesthete finds its way into Woolf's work, often (as with the drug-addled Augustus Carmichael) to be offered up for disapproval.

The aesthete is indeed an extreme version of the type of artist Ronchetti identifies with "the Ivory Tower," sensitive and yet fastidiously removed from the stream of ordinary life. An achievement of *The Artist, Society & Sexuality* is its careful differentiation between this popular image of the aesthete and the actual philosophy of aestheticism at the fin de siècle. (Ronchetti gives much credit in this particular strain of argument to Perry Meisel's 1980 *The Absent Father*.) By focusing on Walter Pater, and especially his novel *Marius the Epicurean*,

Ronchetti argues that aestheticism in its "pure" form does persist in Woolf's writings as a viable philosophy through her latest works, and is manifest in the "outsider"-observer role of the "Sacred Fount" artist described above. I found the linkages between Pater and Woolf to be especially compelling in her *Night and Day* chapter: it contains a fine and close comparison of flame imagery in *Marius* and *Night and Day*, so revealing the promise of innovative creativity in the novel's decidedly conventional ending. This Paterian twist is all the more refreshing as the marriage and "heterosexual coupling" (138) with which *Night and Day* ends prove the most persistent obstacle to women's development as artists throughout Woolf's novels. While *Orlando* would thus seem exceptional, as it portrays a woman who has integrated marriage, children, and art, in Ronchetti's view this integration is rather suspect: the husband and children disappear, and it might only be the fortunate model of Vita Sackville-West that makes this integration imaginable.

Ronchetti does take care to consider how practicing artists Woolf knew served as models for her artist-figures, and it is in such moments that other members of Bloomsbury enter the frame. However, Ronchetti's interest in "real" artists is for the most part focused on Pater and the influence of his ideas and texts; indeed, the monograph ultimately suggests that our familiarity with any one artist is not all that helpful in understanding Woolf, as her artist-figures are, increasingly, figures of anonymity. *The Waves* serves as the exemplary case for this argument, and Ronchetti details how we can read it as an enactment of self-transcendence, a move toward anonymity that the purest creativity and receptivity requires. There were times when the book's organization–discrete analyses of each novel rather than chapters developing a particular line of argument–frustrated me. Connections to related ideas in other novels had to be made quickly, and were at times distracting, and at others tantalizingly brief. Sometimes, however, this organization led to pleasant surprises, as it allowed Ronchetti to read her artist-figures against other, seemingly incomparable characters in a given novel. *The Waves* chapter concludes with one such plum, in which Percival is analyzed as the charismatic authority of the novel, a figure (like political leaders of pre-Second World War Europe) who compels us with the sheer force of personality, and who thereby threatens to eclipse the very existence of artists of anonymity.

— Andrea P. Zemgulys, *University of Michigan*

Note on Contributor

Beth Rigel Daugherty is Professor of English at Otterbein College. She is the co-editor, with Mary Beth Pringle, of *Approaches to Teaching Woolf's* To the Lighthouse (MLA 2001), and with Eileen Barrett, of *Texts and Contexts: Selected Papers from the Fifth Annual Conference on Virginia Woolf* (Pace UP 1996). Her edition of the holograph draft of "How Should One Read a Book?" appears in *WSA* 4 (1998), and "Teaching Woolf/Woolf Teaching" appears in *WSA* 10 (2004). She has articles about Woolf's essays and short stories in various edited collections, and she is working on a book titled *The Education of a Woman Writer: Virginia Woolf's Apprenticeship*.

Policy

Woolf Studies Annual invites articles on the work and life of Virginia Woolf and her milieu. The Annual intends to represent the breadth and eclecticism of critical approaches to Woolf, and particularly welcomes new perspectives and contexts of inquiry. Articles discussing relations between Woolf and other writers and artists are also welcome.

Articles are sent for review anonymously to a member of the Editorial Board and at least one other reader. Manuscripts should not be under consideration elsewhere or have been previously published. Final decisions are made by the Editorial Board.

Preparation of Copy

1. Articles are typically between 25 and 30 pages, and do not exceed 8000 words.

2. A separate page should include the article's title, author's name, address, telephone & fax numbers, and e-mail address. The author's name and identifying references should not appear on the manuscript.

3. A photocopy of any illustrations should accompany the manuscript. (Black-and-white photographs will be required for accepted work.)

4. Manuscripts should be prepared according to most recent MLA style.

5. Three copies of the manuscript and an abstract of up to 150 words should be sent to: Mark Hussey, English Dept., Pace University, One Pace Plaza, New York NY 10038-1598. Only materials accompanied by a self-addressed, stamped envelope (or international reply coupon) will be returned.

6. Authors of accepted manuscripts will be asked to submit two hard copies and an electronic version. Authors are responsible for all necessary permissions fees.

Please address inquiries to: Mark Hussey, English Department, 41 Park Row Rm. 1510, New York, NY 10038. Email: mhussey@pace.edu
Fax: (212) 346-1754.

www.ingramcontent.com/pod-product-compliance
Lightning Source LLC
Chambersburg PA
CBHW031939110726
47902CB00001B/235

* 9 7 8 0 9 4 4 4 7 3 7 5 7 *